Proverb Stories

by

Louisa M. Alcott

Double 9
BOOKS

Proverb Stories
by Louisa M. Alcott

Copyright © 2024

All Rights reserved.

ISBN: 978-93-65784-28-2

Published by

DOUBLE 9 BOOKS

2/13-B, Ansari Road
Daryaganj, New Delhi – 110002
info@double9books.com
www.double9books.com
Tel. 011-40042856

ABOUT THE AUTHOR

Louisa May Alcott, an American novelist and poet, was born in 1832 in Germantown, Pennsylvania. Alcott was the daughter of the famous visionary Bronson Alcott and was friend of Emerson and Thoreau. Her education was under the direction of her father, for a time at his old Temple School in Boston and, later, at home. She turned to writing in order to increase the family income and had many short stories printed in magazines and newspapers. In addition to writing, she worked as a teacher, governess, and Civil War nurse, as well as being an advocate of abolition, women's rights, and prohibition. After her experiences she wrote Hospital Sketches (1864) which won wide praise, followed by an adult novel, Moods. She is best known as the author of the novel Little Women and its sequels Little Men and Jo's Boys. Little Women is generally based on Alcott's childhood experiences with her three sisters. Alcott was writing of her own incense experiences with fame. She expired in 1888 and is buried in Sleepy Hollow cemetery in Concord Massachusetts.

CONTENTS

PREFACE

Being forbidden to write anything at present I have collected various waifs and strays to appease the young people who clamor for more, forgetting that mortal brains need rest.

As many girls have asked to see what sort of tales Jo March wrote at the beginning of her career, I have added "The Baron's Gloves," as a sample of the romantic rubbish which paid so well once upon a time. If it shows them what *not* to write it will not have been rescued from oblivion in vain.

L. M. ALCOTT.

KITTY'S CLASS DAY

"A stitch in time saves nine."

"OPRIS, Pris, I'm really going! Here's the invitation—rough paper—Chapel—spreads—Lyceum Hall—everything splendid; and Jack to take care of me!"

As Kitty burst into the room and performed a rapturous *pas seul*, waving the cards over her head, sister Priscilla looked up from her work with a smile of satisfaction on her quiet face.

"Who invites you, dear?"

"Why, Jack, of course,—dear old cousin Jack. Nobody else ever thinks of me, or cares whether I have a bit of pleasure now and then. Isn't he kind? Mayn't I go? and, O Pris, what *shall* I wear?"

Kitty paused suddenly, as if the last all-important question had a solemnizing effect upon both mind and body.

"Why, your white muslin, silk sacque, and new hat, of course," began Pris with an air of surprise. But Kitty broke in impetuously,—

"I'll never wear that old muslin again; it's full of darns, up to my knees, and all out of fashion. So is my sacque; and as for my hat, though it does well enough here, it would be absurd for Class Day."

"You don't expect an entirely new suit for this occasion,—do you?" asked Pris, anxiously.

"Yes, I do, and I'll tell you how I mean to get it. I've planned everything; for, though I hardly dreamed of going, I amused myself by thinking how I could manage if I *did* get invited."

"Let us hear." And Pris took up her work with an air of resignation.

"First, my dress," began Kitty, perching herself on the arm of the sofa, and entering into the subject with enthusiasm. "I've got the ten dollars grandpa sent me, and with eight of it I'm going to buy Lizzie King's organdie muslin. She got it in Paris; but her aunt providentially—no, unfortunately—died; so she can't wear it, and wants to get rid of it. She is bigger than I am, you know; so there is enough for a little mantle or sacque, for it isn't made up. The skirt is cut off and gored, with a splendid train—"

"My dear, you don't mean you are going to wear one of those absurd, new-fashioned dresses?" exclaimed Pris, lifting hands and eyes.

"I do! Nothing would induce me to go to Class Day without a train. It's been the desire of my heart to have one, and now I *will*, if I never have another gown to my back!" returned Kitty, with immense decision.

Pris shook her head, and said, "Go on!" as if prepared for any extravagance after that.

"We can make it ourselves," continued Kitty, "and trim it with the same. It's white with blue stripes and daisies in the stripes; the loveliest thing you ever saw, and can't be got here. So simple, yet distingué, I know you'll like it. Next, my bonnet,"—here the solemnity of Kitty's face and manner was charming to behold. "I shall make it out of one of my new illusion undersleeves. I've never worn them; and the puffed part will be a plenty for a little fly-away bonnet of the latest style. I've got blue ribbons to tie it with, and have only to look up some daisies for the inside. With my extra two dollars I shall buy my gloves, and pay my fares,—and there I am, all complete."

She looked so happy, so pretty, and full of girlish satisfaction, that sister Pris couldn't bear to disturb the little plan, much as she disapproved of it. They were poor, and every penny had to be counted. There were plenty of neighbors to gossip and criticize, and plenty of friends to make disagreeable remarks on any unusual extravagance. Pris saw things with the prudent eyes of thirty, but Kitty with the romantic eyes of seventeen; and the elder sister, in the kindness of her heart, had no wish to sadden life to those bright young eyes, or deny the child a harmless pleasure. She sewed thoughtfully for a minute, then looked up, saying, with the smile that always assured Kitty the day was won,—

"Get your things together, and we will see what can be done. But remember, dear, that it is both bad taste and bad economy for poor people to try to ape the rich."

"You're a perfect angel, Pris; so don't moralize. I'll run and get the dress, and we'll begin at once, for there is much to do, and only two days to do it in." And Kitty skipped away, singing "Lauriger Horatius," at the top of her voice. Priscilla soon found that the girl's head was completely turned by the advice and example of certain fashionable young neighbors. It was in vain for Pris to remonstrate and warn.

"Just this once let me do as others do, and thoroughly enjoy myself," pleaded Kitty; and Pris yielded, saying to herself, "She shall have her wish, and if she learns a lesson, neither time nor money will be lost."

So they snipped and sewed, and planned and pieced, going through all the alternations of despair and triumph, worry and satisfaction, which women undergo when a new suit is under way. Company kept coming, for news of Kitty's expedition had flown abroad, and her young friends must just run in to hear about it, and ask what she was going to wear; while Kitty was so glad and proud to tell, and show, and enjoy her little triumph that many half hours were wasted, and the second day found much still to do.

The lovely muslin didn't hold out, and Kitty sacrificed the waist to the train, for a train she must have or the whole thing would be an utter failure. A little sacque was eked out, however, and when the frills were on, it was "ravishing," as Kitty said, with a sigh of mingled delight and fatigue. The gored skirt was a fearful job, as any one who has ever plunged into the mysteries will testify; and before the facing, even experienced Pris quailed.

The bonnet also was a trial, for when the lace was on, it was discovered that the ribbons didn't match the dress. Here was a catastrophe! Kitty frantically rummaged the house, the shops, the stores of her friends, and rummaged in vain. There was no time to send to the city, and despair was about to fall on Kitty, when Pris rescued her by quietly making one of the small sacrifices which were easy to her because her life was spent for others. Some one suggested a strip of blue illusion,—and that could be got; but, alas! Kitty had no money, for the gloves were already bought. Pris heard the lamentations, and giving up fresh ribbons for herself, pulled her sister out of a slough of despond with two yards of "heavenly tulle."

"Now the daisies; and oh, dear me, not one can I find in this poverty-stricken town," sighed Kitty, prinking at the glass, and fervently hoping that nothing would happen to her complexion over night.

"I see plenty just like those on your dress," answered Pris, nodding toward the meadow full of young white-weed.

"Pris, you're a treasure! I'll wear real ones; they keep well, I know, and are so common I can refresh my bonnet anywhere. It's a splendid idea."

Away rushed Kitty to return with an apron full of American daisies. A pretty cluster was soon fastened just over the left-hand frizzle of bright hair, and the little bonnet was complete.

"Now, Pris, tell me how I look," cried Kitty, as she swept into the room late that afternoon in full gala costume.

It would have been impossible for the primmest, the sourest, or the most sensible creature in the world to say that it wasn't a pretty sight. The long train, the big chignon, the apology for a bonnet, were all ridiculous,—no one could deny that,—but youth, beauty, and a happy heart made even those absurdities charming. The erect young figure gave an air to the crisp folds of the delicate dress; the bright eyes and fresh cheeks under the lace rosette made one forget its size; and the rippling brown hair won admiration in spite of the ugly bunch which disfigured the girl's head. The little jacket set "divinely," the new gloves were as immaculate as white kids could be, and to crown all, Lizzie King, in a burst of generosity, lent Kitty the blue and white Paris sunshade which she couldn't use herself.

"Now I could die content; I'm perfect in all respects, and I know Jack won't be ashamed of me. I really owe it to him to look my best, you know, and that's why I'm so particular," said Kitty, in an apologetic tone, as she began to lay away her finery.

"I hope you will enjoy every minute of the time, deary. Don't forget to finish running up the facing; I've basted it carefully, and would do it if my head didn't ache so, I really can't hold it up any longer," answered Pris, who had worked like a disinterested bee, while Kitty had flown about like a distracted butterfly.

"Go and lie down, you dear, kind soul, and don't think of my nonsense again," said Kitty, feeling remorseful, till Pris was comfortably asleep, when she went to her room and revelled in her finery till bedtime. So absorbed was she in learning to manage her train gracefully, that she forgot the facing till very late. Then, being worn out with work and worry, she did, what girls are too apt to do, stuck a pin here and there, and, trusting to Priscilla's careful bastings, left it as it was, retiring to dream of a certain Horace Fletcher, whose aristocratic elegance had made a deep impression upon her during the few evenings she had seen him.

Nothing could have been lovelier than the morning, and few hearts happier than Kitty's, as she arrayed herself with the utmost care, and waited in solemn state for the carriage; for muslin trains and dewy roads were incompatible, and one luxury brought another.

"My goodness, where did she get that stylish suit?" whispered Miss Smith to Miss Jones, as Kitty floated into the station with all sail set, finding it impossible to resist the temptation to astonish certain young ladies who had snubbed her in times past, which snubs had rankled, and were now avenged.

"I looked everywhere for a muslin for to-day and couldn't find any I liked, so I was forced to wear my mauve silk," observed Miss Smith, complacently settling the silvery folds of her dress.

"It's very pretty, but one ruins a silk at Class Day, you know. I thought this organdie would be more comfortable and appropriate this warm day.

A friend brought it from Paris, and it's like one the Princess of Wales wore at the great flower-show this year," returned Kitty, with the air of a young lady who had all her dresses from Paris, and was intimately acquainted with the royal family.

"Those girls" were entirely extinguished by this stroke, and hadn't a word to say for themselves, while Kitty casually mentioned Horace Fletcher, Lyceum Hall, and Cousin Jack, for *they* had only a little Freshman brother to boast of, and were *not* going to Lyceum Hall.

As she stepped out of the cars at Cambridge, Jack opened his honest blue eyes and indulged in a low whistle of astonishment; for if there was anything he especially hated, it was the trains, chignons and tiny bonnets then in fashion. He was very fond of Kitty, and prided himself on being able to show his friends a girl who was charming, and yet not over-dressed.

"She has made a regular guy of herself; I won't tell her so, and the dear little soul shall have a jolly time in spite of her fuss and feathers. But I do wish she had let her hair alone and worn that pretty hat of hers."

As this thought passed through Jack's mind he smiled and bowed and made his way among the crowd, whispering as he drew his cousin's arm through his own, —

"Why, Kitty, you're got up regardless of expense, aren't you? I'm so glad you came, we'll have a rousing good time, and you shall see all the fun."

"Oh, thank you, Jack! Do I look nice, really? I tried to be a credit to you and Pris, and I did have such a job of it. I'll make you laugh over it some time. A carriage for me? Bless us, how fine we are!" and Kitty stepped in, feeling that only one thing more was needed to make her cup overflow. That one thing was speedily vouchsafed, for before her skirts were smoothly settled, Jack called out, in his hearty way, —

"How are you, Fletcher? If you are bound for Chapel I'll take you up."

"Thanks; good-morning, Miss Heath."

It was all done in an instant, and the next thing Kitty knew she was rolling away with the elegant Horace sitting opposite. How little it takes to make a young girl happy! A pretty dress, sunshine, and somebody opposite, and they are blest. Kitty's face glowed and dimpled with pleasure as she glanced about her, especially when *she*, sitting in state with two gentlemen all to herself, passed "those girls" walking in the dust with a beardless boy; she felt that she could forgive past slights, and did so with a magnanimous smile and bow.

Both Jack and Fletcher had graduated the year before, but still took an interest in their old haunts, and patronized the fellows who were not yet through the mill, at least the Seniors and Juniors; of Sophs and Freshs they were sublimely unconscious. Greeted by frequent slaps on the shoulder, and hearty "How are you, old fellows," they piloted Kitty to a seat in the chapel. An excellent place, but the girl's satisfaction was marred by Fletcher's desertion, and she could not see anything attractive about the dashing young lady in the pink bonnet to whom he devoted himself, "because she was a stranger," Kitty said.

Everybody knows what goes on in the Chapel, after the fight and scramble are over. The rustle and buzz, the music, the oratory and the poem, during which the men cheer and the girls simper; the professors yawn, and the poet's friends pronounce him a second Longfellow. Then the closing flourishes, the grand crush, and general scattering.

Then the fun really begins, as far as the young folks are concerned. *They* don't mind swarming up and down stairs in a solid phalanx; they can enjoy half a dozen courses of salad, ice and strawberries, with stout gentlemen crushing their feet, anxious mammas sticking sharp elbows into their sides, and absent-minded tutors walking over them. They can flirt vigorously in a torrid atmosphere of dinner, dust, and din; can smile with hot coffee running down their backs, small avalanches of ice-cream descending upon their best bonnets, and sandwiches, butter-side down, reposing on their delicate silks. They know that it is a costly rapture, but they carefully refrain from thinking of the morrow, and energetically illustrate the Yankee maxim which bids us enjoy ourselves in our early bloom.

Kitty did have "a rousing good time;" for Jack was devoted, taking her everywhere, showing her everything, feeding and fanning her, and festooning her train with untiring patience. How many forcible expressions he mentally indulged in as he walked on that unlucky train we will not record; he smiled and skipped and talked of treading on flowers in a way that would have charmed Kitty, if some one else had not been hovering about "The Daisy," as Fletcher called her.

After he returned, she neglected Jack, who took it coolly, and was never in the way unless she wanted him. For the first time in her life, Kitty deliberately flirted. The little coquetries, which are as natural to a gay young girl as her laughter, were all in full play, and had she gone no further no harm would have been done. But, excited by the example of those about her, Kitty tried to enact the fashionable young lady, and, like most novices, she overdid the part. Quite forgetting her cousin, she tossed her head, twirled her fan, gave affected little shrieks at college jokes, and talked college slang in a way that convulsed Fletcher, who enjoyed the fun immensely.

Jack saw it all, shook his head and said nothing; but his face grew rather sober as he watched Kitty, flushed, dishevelled, and breathless, whirling round Lyceum Hall, on the arm of Fletcher, who danced divinely, as all the girls agreed. Jack had proposed going, but Kitty had frowned, so he fell back, leaving her to listen and laugh, blush and shrink a little at her partner's flowery compliments and admiring glances.

"If she stands that long she's not the girl I took her for," thought Jack, beginning to lose patience. "She doesn't look like my little Kitty, and somehow I don't feel half so fond and proud of her as usual. I know one thing, *my* daughters shall never be seen knocking about in that style."

As if the thought suggested the act, Jack suddenly assumed an air of paternal authority, and, arresting his cousin as she was about to begin again, he said, in a tone she had never heard before, —

"I promised Pris to take care of you, so I shall carry you off to rest, and put yourself to rights after this game of romps. I advise you to do the same, Fletcher, or give your friend in the pink bonnet a turn."

Kitty took Jack's arm pettishly, but glanced over her shoulder with such an inviting smile that Fletcher followed, feeling very much like a top, in danger of tumbling down the instant he stopped spinning. As she came out Kitty's face cleared, and, assuming her sprightliest air, she spread her plumage and prepared to descend with effect, for a party of uninvited *peris* stood at the gate of this Paradise casting longing glances at the forbidden splendors within. Slowly, that all might see her, Kitty sailed down, with Horace, the debonair, in her wake, and was just thinking to herself, "Those girls won't get over this very soon, I fancy," when all in one moment she heard Fletcher exclaim, wrathfully, "Hang the flounces!" she saw a very glossy black hat come skipping down the steps, felt a violent twitch backward, and, to save herself from a fall, sat down on the lower step with most undignified haste.

It was impossible for the bystanders to help laughing, for there was Fletcher hopping wildly about, with one foot nicely caught in a muslin loop, and there sat Kitty longing to run away and hide herself, yet perfectly helpless, while every one tittered. Miss Jones and Miss Smith laughed shrilly, and the despised little Freshman completed her mortification, by a feeble joke about Kitty Heath's new man-trap. It was only an instant, but it seemed an hour before Fletcher freed her, and snatching up the dusty beaver, left her with a flushed countenance and an abrupt bow.

If it hadn't been for Jack, Kitty would have burst into tears then and there, so terrible was the sense of humiliation which oppressed her. For his sake she controlled herself, and, bundling up her torn train, set her teeth, stared straight before her, and let him lead her in dead silence to a friend's room near by. There he locked the door, and began to comfort her by making light of the little mishap. But Kitty cried so tragically, that he was at his wit's end, till the ludicrous side of the affair struck her, and she began to laugh hysterically. With a vague idea that vigorous treatment was best for that feminine ailment, Jack was about to empty the contents of an ice-pitcher over her, when she arrested him, by exclaiming, incoherently,—

"Oh, don't!—it was so funny!—how can you laugh, you cruel boy?—I'm disgraced, forever—take me home to Pris, oh, take me home to Pris!"

"I will, my dear, I will; but first let me right you up a bit; you look as if you had been hazed, upon my life you do;" and Jack laughed in spite of himself at the wretched little object before him, for dust, dancing, and the downfall produced a ruinous spectacle.

That broke Kitty's heart; and, spreading her hands before her face, she was about to cry again, when the sad sight which met her eyes dispelled the gathering tears. The new gloves were both split up the middle and very dirty with clutching at the steps as she went down.

"Never mind, you can wash them," said Jack, soothingly.

"I paid a dollar and a half for them, and they can't be washed," groaned Kitty.

"Oh, hang the gloves! I meant your hands," cried Jack, trying to keep sober.

"No matter for my hands, I mourn my gloves. But I won't cry any more, for my head aches now so I can hardly see." And Kitty threw off her bonnet, as if even that airy trifle hurt her.

Seeing how pale she looked, Jack tenderly suggested a rest on the old sofa, and a wet handkerchief on her hot forehead, while he got the good landlady to send her up a cup of tea. As Kitty rose to comply she glanced at her dress, and, clasping her hands, exclaimed, tragically,—

"The facing, the fatal facing! That made all the mischief, for if I'd sewed it last night it wouldn't have ripped to-day; if it hadn't ripped Fletcher wouldn't have got his foot in it, I shouldn't have made an object of myself, he wouldn't have gone off in a rage, and—who knows what might have happened?"

"Bless the what's-its-name if it has settled him," cried Jack. "He is a contemptible fellow not to stay and help you out of the scrape he got you into. Follow his lead and don't trouble yourself about him."

"Well, he *was* rather absurd to-day, I allow; but he *has* got handsome eyes and hands, and he *does* dance like an angel," sighed Kitty, as she pinned up the treacherous loop which had brought destruction to her little castle in the air.

"Handsome eyes, white hands, and angelic feet don't make a man. Wait till you can do better, Kit."

With an odd, grave look, that rather startled Kitty, Jack vanished, to return presently with a comfortable cup of tea and a motherly old lady to help repair damages and soothe her by the foolish little purrings and pattings so grateful to female nerves after a flurry.

"I'll come back and take you out to see the dance round the tree when you've had a bit of a rest," said Jack, vibrating between door and sofa as if it wasn't easy to get away.

"Oh, I couldn't," cried Kitty, with a shudder at the bare idea of meeting any one. "I can't be seen again to-night; let me stay here till my train goes."

"I thought it had gone, already," said Jack, with an irrepressible twinkle of the eye that glanced at the draggled dress sweeping the floor.

"How *can* you joke about it!" and the girl's reproachful eyes filled with tears of shame. "I know I've been very silly, Jack, but I've had my punishment, and I don't need any more. To feel that you despise me is worse than all the rest."

She ended with a little sob, and turned her face away to hide the trembling of her lips. At that, Jack flushed up, his eyes shone, and he stooped suddenly as if to make some impetuous reply. But, remembering the old lady (who, by the by, was discreetly looking out of window), he put his hands in his pockets and strolled out of the room.

"I've lost them both by this day's folly," thought Kitty, as Mrs. Brown departed with the teacup. "I don't care for Fletcher, for I dare say he didn't mean half he said, and I was only flattered because he is rich and handsome and the girls glorify him. But I shall miss Jack, for I've known and loved him all my life. How good he's been to me to-day! so patient, careful, and kind, though he must have been ashamed of me. I know he didn't like my dress; but he never said a word and stood by me through everything. Oh, I wish I'd minded Pris! then he would have respected me, at least; I wonder if he ever will, again?"

Following a sudden impulse, Kitty sprang up, locked the door, and then proceeded to destroy all her little vanities as far as possible. She smoothed out her crimps with a wet and ruthless hand; fastened up her pretty hair in the simple way Jack liked; gave her once cherished bonnet a spiteful shake, as she put it on, and utterly extinguished it with a big blue veil. She looped up her dress, leaving no vestige of the now hateful train, and did herself up uncompromisingly in the Quakerish gray shawl Pris had insisted on her taking for the evening. Then she surveyed herself with pensive satisfaction, saying, in the tone of one bent on resolutely mortifying the flesh, —

"Neat but not gaudy; I'm a fright, but I deserve it, and it's better than being a peacock."

Kitty had time to feel a little friendless and forlorn, sitting there alone as twilight fell, and amused herself by wondering if Fletcher would come to inquire about her, or show any further interest in her; yet when the sound of a manly tramp approached, she trembled lest it should be the victim of the fatal facing. The door opened, and with a sigh of relief she saw Jack come in, bearing a pair of new gloves in one hand and a great bouquet of June roses in the other.

"How good of you to bring me these! They are more refreshing than oceans of tea. You know what I like, Jack; thank you very much," cried Kitty, sniffing at her roses with grateful rapture.

"And you know what I like," returned Jack, with an approving glance at the altered figure before him.

"I'll never do so any more," murmured Kitty, wondering why she felt bashful all of a sudden, when it was only cousin Jack.

"Now put on your gloves, dear, and come out and hear the music; your train doesn't go for two hours yet, and you mustn't mope here all that time," said Jack, offering his second gift.

"How did you know my size?" asked Kitty, putting on the gloves in a hurry; for though Jack had called her "dear" for years, the little word had a new sound to-night.

"I guessed, — no, I didn't, I had the old ones with me; they are no good now, are they?" and too honest to lie, Jack tried to speak carelessly, though he turned red in the dusk, well knowing that the dirty little gloves were folded away in his left breast-pocket at that identical moment.

"Oh, dear, no! these fit nicely. I'm ready, if you don't mind going with such a fright," said Kitty, forgetting her dread of seeing people in her desire to get away from that room, because for the first time in her life she wasn't at ease with Jack.

"I think I like the little gray moth better than the fine butterfly," returned Jack, who, in spite of his invitation, seemed to find "moping" rather pleasant.

"You are a rainy-day friend, and he isn't," said Kitty, softly, as she drew him away.

Jack's only answer was to lay his hand on the little white glove resting so confidingly on his arm, and, keeping it there, they roamed away into the summer twilight.

Something had happened to the evening and the place, for both seemed suddenly endowed with uncommon beauty and interest. The dingy old houses might have been fairy palaces, for anything they saw to the contrary; the dusty walks, the trampled grass, were regular Elysian fields to them, and the music was the music of the spheres, though they found themselves "Right in the middle of the boom, jing, jing." For both had made a little discovery,—no, not a little one, the greatest and sweetest man and woman can make. In the sharp twinge of jealousy which the sight of Kitty's flirtation with Fletcher gave him, and the delight he found in her after conduct, Jack discovered how much he loved her. In the shame, gratitude, and half sweet, half bitter emotion that filled her heart, Kitty felt that to her Jack would never be "only cousin Jack" any more. All the vanity, coquetry, selfishness, and ill-temper of the day seemed magnified to heinous sins, for now her only thought was, "seeing these faults, he *can't* care for me. Oh, I wish I was a better girl!"

She did not say "for his sake," but in the new humility, the ardent wish to be all that a woman should be, little Kitty proved how true her love was, and might have said with Portia,—

"For myself alone, I would not be

Ambitious in my wish; but, for you,

I would be trebled twenty times myself;

A thousand times more fair,

Ten thousand times more rich."

All about them other pairs were wandering under the patriarchal elms, enjoying music, starlight, balmy winds, and all the luxuries of the season. If the band had played

"Oh, there's nothing half so sweet in life

As love's young dream—"

it is my private opinion that it would have suited the audience to a T. Being principally composed of elderly gentlemen with large families, they had not that fine sense of the fitness of things so charming to see, and tooted and banged away with waltzes and marches, quite regardless of the flocks of Romeos and Juliets philandering all about them.

Under cover of a popular medley, Kitty overheard Fletcher quizzing her for the amusement of Miss Pink-bonnet, who was evidently making up for lost time. It was feeble wit, but it put the finishing stroke to Kitty's vanity, and she dropped a tear in her blue tissue retreat, and clung to Jack, feeling that she had never valued him half enough. She hoped he didn't hear the gossip going on at the other side of the tree near which they stood; but he did, for his hand involuntarily doubled itself up into a very dangerous-looking fist, and he darted such fiery glances at the speaker, that, if the thing had been possible, Fletcher's ambrosial curls would have been scorched off his head.

"Never mind, and don't get angry, Jack. They are right about one thing,—the daisies in my bonnet *were* real, and I *couldn't* afford any others. I don't care much, only Pris worked so hard to get me ready I hate to have my things made fun of."

"He isn't worth a thrashing, so we'll let it pass this time," said Jack, irefully, yet privately resolving to have it out with Fletcher by and by.

"Why, Kitty, I thought the real daisies the prettiest things about your dress. Don't throw them away. I'll wear them just to show that noodle that I prefer nature to art;" and Jack gallantly stuck the faded posy in his button-hole, while Kitty treasured up the hint so kindly given for future use.

If a clock with great want of tact hadn't insisted on telling them that it was getting late, Kitty never would have got home, for both the young people felt inclined to loiter about arm in arm through the sweet summer night forever. Jack had meant to say something before she went, and was immensely surprised to find the chance lost for the present. He wanted to go home with her and free his mind; but a neighborly old gentleman having been engaged as escort, there would have been very little satisfaction in a travelling trio; so he gave it up. He was very silent as they walked to the station with Dr. Dodd trudging behind them. Kitty thought he was tired, perhaps glad to be rid of her, and meekly accepted her fate. But as the train approached, she gave his hand an impulsive squeeze, and said very gratefully,—

"Jack, I can't thank you enough for your kindness to your silly little cousin; but I never shall forget it, and if I ever can return it in any way, I will with all my heart."

Jack looked down at the young face almost pathetic now with weariness, humility, and pain, yet very sweet, with that new shyness in the loving eyes, and, stooping suddenly, he kissed it, whispering in a tone that made the girl's heart flutter, —

"I'll tell you how you may return it 'with all your heart,' by and by. Good-night, my Kitty."

"Have you had a good time, dear?" asked Pris, as her sister appeared an hour later.

"Don't I look as if I had?" and, throwing off her wraps, Kitty revolved slowly before her that she might behold every portion of the wreck. "My gown is all dust, crumple, and rags, my bonnet perfectly limp and flat, and my gloves are ruined; I've broken Lizzie's parasol, made a spectacle of myself, and wasted money, time, and temper; yet my Class Day isn't a failure, for Jack is the dearest boy in the world, and I'm very, very happy!"

Pris looked at her a minute, then opened her arms without a word, and Kitty forgot all her little troubles in one great joy.

When Miss Smith and Miss Jones called a few days after to tell her that Mr. Fletcher was going abroad, the amiable creatures were entirely routed by finding Jack there in a most unmistakable situation. He blandly wished Horace "bon voyage," and regretted that he wouldn't be there to the wedding in October. Kitty devoted herself to blushing beautifully, and darning many rents in a short daisy muslin skirt, "which I intend to wear a great deal, because Jack likes it, and so do I," she said, with a demure look at her lover, who laughed as if that was the best joke of the season.

AUNT KIPP

"Children and fools speak the truth."

I

"WHAT'S that sigh for, Polly dear?"

"I'm tired, mother, tired of working and waiting. If I'm ever going to have any fun, I want it *now* while I can enjoy it."

"You shouldn't wait another hour if I could have my way; but you know how helpless I am;" and poor Mrs. Snow sighed dolefully, as she glanced about the dingy room and pretty Mary turning her faded gown for the second time.

"If Aunt Kipp would give us the money she is always talking about, instead of waiting till she dies, we should be *so* comfortable. She is a dreadful bore, for she lives in such terror of dropping dead with her heart-complaint that she doesn't take any pleasure in life herself or let any one else; so the sooner she goes the better for all of us," said Polly, in a desperate tone; for things looked very black to her just then.

"My dear, don't say that," began her mother, mildly shocked; but a bluff little voice broke in with the forcible remark,—

"She's everlastingly telling me never to put off till to-morrow what can be done to-day; next time she comes I'll remind her of that, and ask her, if she is going to die, why she doesn't do it?"

"Toady! you're a wicked, disrespectful boy; never let me hear you say such a thing again about your dear Aunt Kipp."

"She isn't dear! You know we all hate her, and you are more afraid of her than you are of spiders,—so now."

The young personage whose proper name had been corrupted into Toady, was a small boy of ten or eleven, apple-cheeked, round-eyed, and curly-headed; arrayed in well-worn, gray knickerbockers, profusely adorned with paint, glue, and shreds of cotton. Perched on a high stool, at an isolated table in a state of chaos, he was absorbed in making a boat, entirely oblivious of the racking tooth-ache which had been his excuse for staying from school. As cool, saucy, hard-handed, and soft-hearted a little specimen of young America was Toady as you would care to see; a tyrant at home, a rebel at school, a sworn foe to law, order, and Aunt Kipp. This young person was regarded as a reprobate by all but his mother, sister, and sister's sweetheart, Van Bahr Lamb. Having been, through much anguish of flesh and spirit, taught that lying was a deadly sin, Toady rushed to the other extreme, and bolted out the truth, the whole truth and nothing but the truth, at all times and places, with a startling abruptness that brought wrath and dismay upon his friends and relatives.

"It's wicked to fib; you've whipped that into me and you can't rub it out," he was wont to say, with vivid recollection of the past tingling in the chubby portions of his frame.

"Mind your chips, Toady, and take care what you say to Aunt Kipp, or you'll be as poor as a little rat all the days of your life," said Polly, warningly.

"I don't want her old money, and I'll tell her so if she bothers me about it. I shall go into business with Van and take care of the whole lot; so don't you preach, Polly," returned Toady, with as much dignity as was compatible with a great dab of glue on the end of his snub nose.

"Mother, did aunt say anything about coming this week?" asked Polly, after a pause of intense thought over a breadth with three darns, two spots, and a burn.

"Yes; she wrote that she was too feeble to come at present, as she had such dreadful palpitations she didn't dare stir from her room. So we are quite safe for the next week at least, and—bless my soul, there she is now!"

Mrs. Snow clasped her hands with a gesture of dismay, and sat as if transfixed by the spectacle of a ponderous lady, in an awe-inspiring bonnet, who came walking slowly down the street. Polly gave a groan, and pulled a bright ribbon from her hair. Toady muttered, "Oh, bother!" and vainly attempted to polish up his countenance with a fragmentary pocket-handkerchief.

"Nothing but salt fish for dinner," wailed Mrs. Snow, as the shadow of the coming event fell upon her.

"Van will make a fool of himself, and ruin everything," sighed Polly, glancing at the ring on her finger.

"I know she'll kiss me; she never *will* let a fellow alone," growled Toady, scowling darkly.

The garden gate clashed, dust flew from the door-mat, a heavy step echoed in the hall, an imperious voice called "Sophy!" and Aunt Kipp entered with a flourish of trumpets, for Toady blew a blast through his fingers which made the bows totter on her bonnet.

"My dear aunt, I'm very glad to see you," murmured Mrs. Snow, advancing with a smile of welcome; for though as weak as water gruel, she was as kind-hearted a little woman as ever lived.

"What a fib that was!" said Toady, *sotto voce*.

"We were just saying we were afraid you wouldn't"—began Mary, when a warning, "Mind now, Polly," caused her to stop short and busy herself with the newcomer's bag and umbrella.

"I changed my mind. Theodore, come and kiss me," answered Aunt Kipp, briefly.

"Yes'm," was the plaintive reply, and, closing his eyes, Toady awaited his fate with fortitude.

But the dreaded salute did not come, for Aunt Kipp exclaimed in alarm,—

"Mercy on us! has the boy got the plague?"

"No'm, it's paint, and dirt, and glue, and it *won't* come off," said Toady, stroking his variegated countenance with grateful admiration for the stains that saved him.

"Go and wash this moment, sir. Thank Heaven, *I've* got no boys," cried Aunt Kipp, as if boys were some virulent disease which she had narrowly escaped.

With a hasty peck at the lips of her two elder relatives, the old lady seated herself, and slowly removed the awful bonnet, which in shape and hue much resembled a hearse hung with black crape.

"I'm glad you are better," said Mary, reverently receiving the funereal head-gear.

"I'm *not* better," cut in Aunt Kipp. "I'm worse, much worse; my days are numbered; I stand on the brink of the tomb, and may drop at any moment."

Toady's face was a study, as he glanced up at the old lady's florid countenance, down at the floor, as if in search of the above-mentioned "brink," and looked unaffectedly anxious to see her drop. "Why don't you, then?" was on his lips; but a frown from Polly restrained him, and he sat himself down on the rug to contemplate the corpulent victim.

"Have a cup of tea, aunt?" said Mrs. Snow.

"I will."

"Lie down and rest a little," suggested Polly.

"I won't."

"Can we do anything for you?" said both.

"Take my things away, and have dinner early."

Both departed to perform these behests, and, leaning back in her chair, Aunt Kipp reposed.

"I say, what's a bore?" asked Toady from the rug, where he sat rocking meditatively to and fro, holding on by his shoe-strings.

"It's a kind of a pig, very fierce, and folks are afraid of 'em," said Aunt Kipp, whose knowledge of Natural History was limited.

"Good for Polly! so you are!" sung out the boy, with the hearty child's laugh so pleasant to most ears.

"What do you mean, sir?" demanded the old lady, irefully poking at him with her umbrella.

"Why, Polly said you were a bore," explained Toady, with artless frankness. "You *are* fat, you know, and fierce sometimes, and folks are afraid of you. Good, wasn't it?"

"Very! Mary is a nice, grateful, respectful, loving niece, and I shan't forget her, she may depend on that," and Aunt Kipp laughed grimly.

"May she? well, that's jolly now. She was afraid you wouldn't give her the money; so I'll tell her it's all right;" and innocent Toady nodded approvingly.

"Oh, she expects some of my money, does she?"

"Course she does; ain't you always saying you'll remember us in your will, because father was your favorite nephew, and all that? I'll tell you a secret, if you won't let Polly know I spoke first. You'll find it out to-night, for you'd see Van and she were sweethearts in a minute."

"Sweethearts?" cried Aunt Kipp, turning red in the face.

"Yes'm. Van settled it last week, and Polly's been so happy ever since. Mother likes it, and *I* like it, for I'm fond of Van, though I do call him Baa-baa, because he looks like a sheep. We all like it, and we'd all say so, if we were not afraid of you. Mother and Polly, I mean; of course we men don't mind, but we don't want a fuss. You won't make one, will you, now?"

Anything more expressive of brotherly good-will, persuasive frankness, and a placid consciousness of having "fixed it," than Toady's dirty little face, it would be hard to find. Aunt Kipp eyed him so fiercely that even before she spoke a dim suspicion that something was wrong began to dawn on his too-confiding soul.

"*I* don't like it, and I'll put a stop to it. I won't have any ridiculous baa-baas in my family. If Mary counts on my money to begin housekeeping with, she'll find herself mistaken; for not one penny shall she have, married or single, and you may tell her so."

Toady was so taken aback by this explosion that he let go his shoe-strings, fell over with a crash, and lay flat, with shovel and tongs spread upon him like a pall. In rushed Mrs. Snow and Polly, to find the boy's spirits quite quenched, for once, and Aunt Kipp in a towering passion. It all came out in one overwhelming flood of words, and Toady fled from the storm to wander round the house, a prey to the deepest remorse. The meekness of that boy at dinner-time was so angelic that Mrs. Snow would have feared speedy translation for him, if she had not been very angry. Polly's red eyes, and Aunt Kipp's griffinesque expression of countenance, weighed upon his soul so heavily, that even roly-poly pudding failed to assuage his trouble, and, taking his mother into the china-closet, he anxiously inquired "if it was all up with Polly?"

"I'm afraid so, for aunt vows she will make a new will to-morrow, and leave every penny to the Charitable Rag-bag Society," sighed Mrs. Snow.

"I didn't mean to do it, I truly didn't! I thought I'd just 'give her a hint,' as you say. She looked all right, and laughed when I told her about being a bore, and I thought she liked it. If she was a man, I'd thrash her for making Polly cry;" and Toady shook his fist at Aunt Kipp's umbrella, which was an immense relief to his perturbed spirit.

"Bless the boy! I do believe he would!" cried Mrs. Snow, watching the little turkey-cock with maternal pride. "You can't do that: so just be careful and not make any more mischief, dear."

"I'll try, mother; but I'm always getting into scrapes with Aunt Kipp. She's worse than measles, any day,—such an old aggrawater! Van's coming this afternoon, won't he make her pleasant again?"

"Oh, dear, no! He will probably make things ten times worse, he's so bashful and queer. I'm afraid our last chance is gone, deary, and we must rub along as we have done."

One sniff of emotion burst from Toady, and for a moment he laid his head in the knife-tray, overcome with disappointment and regret. But scorning to yield to unmanly tears, he was soon himself again. Thrusting his beloved jack-knife, with three blades and a file, into Polly's hand, he whispered, brokenly, —

"Keep it forever'n'ever; I'm awful sorry!" Then, feeling that the magnitude of this sacrifice atoned for everything, he went to watch for Van, — the forlorn hope to which he now clung.

II

"Sophy, I'm surprised at your want of judgment. Do you really mean to let your girl marry this Lamb? Why, the man's a fool!" began Aunt Kipp, after dinner, by way of opening a pleasant conversation with her relatives.

"Dear me, aunt! how can you know that, when you never saw him?" mildly returned Mrs. Snow.

"I've heard of him, and that's enough for me. I've a deal of penetration in judging character, and I tell you Van Bahr Lamb is a fool."

The amiable old lady thought this would rouse Polly, against whom her anger still burned hotly. But Polly also possessed penetration; and, well knowing that contradiction would delight Aunt Kipp, she completely took the wind out of her sails, by coolly remarking, —

"I like fools."

"Bless my heart! what does the girl mean?" ejaculated Aunt Kipp.

"Just what I say. If Van is a fool, I prefer simpletons to wiseacres. I know he is shy and awkward, and does absurd things now and then. But I also know that he has the kindest heart that ever was; is unselfish, faithful and loving; that he took good care of his old parents till they died, and never thought of himself while they needed him. He loves me dearly; will wait for me a dozen years, if I say so, and work all his days to make me happy. He's a help and comfort to mother, a good friend to Toady, and I love and respect and am proud of him, though you do say he is a fool," cried Polly heartily.

"And you insist on marrying him?" demanded Aunt Kipp.

"Yes, I do."

"Then I wish a carriage immediately," was the somewhat irrelevant reply.

"Why, aunt, you don't mean to go so soon?" cried Mrs. Snow, with a reproachful glance at the rebellious Polly.

"Far from it. I wish to see Judge Banks about altering my will," was the awful answer.

Polly's face fell; her mother gave a despairing sigh; Toady, who had hovered about the door, uttered a suppressed whistle of dismay; and Mrs. Kipp looked about her with vengeful satisfaction.

"Get the big carryall and old Bob, so the boy can drive, and all of you come; the trip will do you good."

It was like Aunt Kipp to invite her poor relations to go and "nip their own noses off," as she elegantly expressed it. It was a party of pleasure that just suited her, for all the fun was on her side. She grew affable at once, was quite pressing in her invitation, regretted that Sophy was too busy to go, praised Polly's hat; and professed herself quite satisfied with "that dear boy" for a driver. The "dear boy" distorted his young countenance frightfully behind her back, but found a balm for every wound in the delight of being commander of the expedition.

The big carryall appeared, and, with much creaking and swaying Mrs. Kipp was got into the back seat, where the big bonnet gloomed like a thunder-cloud. Polly, in a high state of indignation, which only made her look ten times prettier, sat in front with Toady, who was a sight to see as he drove off with his short legs planted against the boot, his elbows squared, and the big whip scientifically cracking now and then. Away they went, leaving poor Mrs. Snow to bewail herself dismally after she had smiled and nodded them out of sight.

"Don't go over any bridges or railroad crossings or by any saw-mills," said the old lady, as if the town could be suddenly remodelled to suit her taste.

"Yes'm," returned Toady, with a crack which would have done honor to a French postilion.

It was a fine day, and the young people would have enjoyed the ride in spite of the breakers ahead, if Aunt Kipp hadn't entertained the girl with a glowing account of the splendors of her own wedding, and aggravated the boy by frequent pokes and directions in the art of driving, of which she was of course, profoundly ignorant. Polly couldn't restrain a tear or two, in thinking of her own poor little prospects, and Toady was goaded to desperation.

"I'll give her a regular shaking up; it'll make her hold her tongue and do her good," he said to himself, as a stony hill sloped temptingly before him.

A sly chuck, and some mysterious manœuvre with the reins, and Bob started off at a brisk trot, as if he objected to the old lady as much as her mischievous little nephew.

"Hold him in! Keep a taut rein! Lord 'a mercy, he's running away!" shrieked Aunt Kipp, or tried to shriek, for the bouncing and bumping jerked the words out of her mouth with ludicrous incoherency.

"I am holding him, but he *will* go," said Toady, with a wicked triumph in his eye as he glanced back at Polly.

The next minute the words were quite true; for, as he spoke, two or three distracted hens flew squalling over the wall and scattered about, under, over, and before the horse, as only distracted hens could do. It was too much for Bob's nerves; and, taking matters into his own hands, or feet, rather, he broke into a run, and rattled the old lady over the stones with a velocity which left her speechless.

Polly laughed, and Toady chuckled, as they caught glimpses of the awful bonnet vibrating wildly in the background, and felt the frantic clutchings of the old lady's hands. But both grew sober as a shrill car-whistle sounded not far off; and Bob, as if possessed by an evil spirit, turned suddenly into the road that led to the railroad crossing.

"That will do, Toady; now pull up, for we can't get over in time," said Polly, glancing anxiously toward the rapidly approaching puffs of white smoke.

"I can't, Polly,—I really can't," cried the boy, tugging with all his might, and beginning to look scared.

Polly lent her aid; but Bob scarcely seemed to feel it, for he had been a racer once, and when his blood was up he was hard to handle. His own good sense might have checked him, if Aunt Kipp hadn't unfortunately recovered her voice at this crisis, and uttered a succession of the shrillest screams that ever saluted mortal ears. With a snort and a bound Bob dashed straight on toward the crossing, as the train appeared round the bend.

"Let me out! Let me out! Jump! Jump!" shrieked Aunt Kipp, thrusting her head out of the window, while she fumbled madly for the door-handle.

"O Toady, save us! save us!" gasped Polly, losing her presence of mind, and dropping the reins to cling to her brother, with a woman's instinctive faith in the stronger sex.

But Toady held on manfully, though his arms were nearly pulled off, for "Never say die," was his motto, and the plucky little lad wouldn't show fear before the women.

"Don't howl; we'll do it! Hi, Bob!" and with a savage slash of the whip, an exciting cry, a terrible reeling and rattling, they *did* do it; for Bob cleared the track at a breakneck pace, just in time for the train to sweep swiftly by behind them.

Aunt Kipp dropped in a heap, Polly looked up at her brother, with a look which he never forgot; and Toady tried to say, stoutly, "It's all right!" with lips that were white and dry in spite of himself.

"We shall smash up at the bridge," he muttered, as they tore through the town, where every one obligingly shouted, waved their hats, and danced about on the sidewalks, doing nothing but add to Bob's fright and the party's danger. But Toady was wrong,—they did not smash up at the bridge; for, before they reached the perilous spot, one man had the sense to fly straight at the horse's head and hold on till the momentary check enabled others to lend a hand.

The instant they were safe, Polly, like a regular heroine, threw herself into the arms of her dishevelled preserver, who of course was Van, and would have refreshed herself with hysterics if the sight of Toady hadn't steadied her. The boy sat as stiff and rigid as a wooden figure till they took the reins from him; then all the strength seemed to go out of him, and he leaned against his sister, as white and trembling as she, whispering with an irrepressible sob,—

"O Polly, wasn't it horrid? Tell mother I stood by you like a man. Do tell her that!"

If any one had had time or heart to laugh, they certainly would have done it when, after much groping, heaving, and hoisting, Mrs. Kipp was extricated and restored to consciousness; for a more ludicrously deplorable spectacle was seldom seen. Quite unhurt, though much shaken, the old lady insisted on believing herself to be dying, and kept the town in a ferment till three doctors had pronounced her perfectly well able to go home. Then the perversity of her nature induced her to comply, that she might have the satisfaction of dying on the way, and proving herself in the right.

Unfortunately she did not expire, but, having safely arrived, went to bed in high dudgeon, and led Polly and her mother a sad life of it for two weary days. Having heard of Toady's gallant behavior, she solemnly ordered him up to receive her blessing. But the sight of Aunt Kipp's rubicund visage, surrounded by the stiff frills of an immense nightcap, caused the irreverent boy to explode with laughter in his handkerchief, and to be hustled away by his mother before Aunt Kipp discovered the true cause of his convulsed appearance.

"Ah! poor dear, his feelings are too much for him. He sees my doom in my face, and is overcome by what you refuse to believe. I shan't forget that boy's devotion. Now leave me to the meditations befitting these solemn hours."

Mrs. Snow retired, and Aunt Kipp tried to sleep; but the murmur of voices, and the sound of stifled laughter in the next room disturbed her repose.

"They are rejoicing over my approaching end, knowing that I haven't changed my will. Mercenary creatures, don't exult too soon! there's time yet," she muttered; and presently, unable to control her curiosity, she crept out of bed to listen and peep through the key-hole.

Van Bahr Lamb did look rather like a sheep. He had a blond curly head, a long face, pale, mild eyes, a plaintive voice, and a general expression of innocent timidity strongly suggestive of animated mutton. But Baa-baa was a "trump," as Toady emphatically declared, and though every one laughed at him, every one liked him, and that is more than can be said of many saints and sages. He adored Polly, was dutifully kind to her mother, and had stood by T. Snow, Jr., in many an hour of tribulation with fraternal fidelity. Though he had long blushed, sighed, and cast sheep's eyes at the idol of his affections, only till lately had he dared to bleat forth his passion. Polly loved him because she couldn't help it; but she was proud, and wouldn't marry till Aunt Kipp's money was hers, or at least a sure prospect of it; and now even the prospect of a prospect was destroyed by that irrepressible Toady. They were talking of this as the old lady suspected, and of course the following conversation afforded her intense satisfaction.

"It's a shame to torment us as she does, knowing how poor we are and how happy a little of her money would make us. I'm tired of being a slave to a cruel old woman just because she's rich. If it was not for mother, I declare I'd wash my hands of her entirely, and do the best I could for myself."

"Hooray for Polly! I always said let her money go and be jolly without it," cried Toady, who, in his character of wounded hero, reposed with a lordly air on the sofa, enjoying the fragrance of the opedeldoc with which his strained wrists were bandaged.

"It's on your account, children, that I bear with aunt's temper as I do. I don't want anything for myself, but I really think she owes it to your dear father, who was devoted to her while he lived, to provide for his children when he couldn't;" after which remarkably spirited speech for her, Mrs. Snow dropped a tear, and stitched away on a small trouser-leg which was suffering from a complicated compound fracture.

"Don't you worry about me, mother; I'll take care of myself and you too," remarked Toady, with the cheery belief in impossibilities which makes youth so charming.

"Now, Van, tell us what to do, for things have come to such a pass that we must either break away altogether or be galley-slaves as long as Aunt Kipp lives," said Polly, who was a good deal excited about the matter.

"Well, really, my dear, I don't know," hesitated Van, who did know what *he* wanted, but thought it might be selfish to urge it. "Have you tried to soften your aunt's heart?" he asked, after a moment's meditation.

"Good gracious, Van, she hasn't got any," cried Polly, who firmly believed it.

"It's hossified," thoughtfully remarked Toady, quite unconscious of any approach to a joke till every one giggled.

"You've had hossification enough for one while, my lad," laughed Van. "Well, Polly, if the old lady has no heart you'd better let her go, for people without hearts are not worth much."

"That's a beautiful remark, Van, and a wise one. I just wish she could hear you make it, for she called you a fool," said Polly, irefully.

"Did she? Well, I don't mind, I'm used to it," returned Van, placidly; and so he was, for Polly called him a goose every day of her life, and he enjoyed it immensely.

"Then you think, dear, if we stopped worrying about aunt and her money, and worked instead of waiting, that we shouldn't be any poorer and might be a great deal happier than we are now?" asked Polly, making a pretty little tableau as she put her hand through Van's arm and looked up at him with as much love, respect, and reliance as if he had been six feet tall, with the face of an Apollo and the manners of a Chesterfield.

"Yes, my dear, I do, for it has troubled me a good deal to see you so badgered by that very uncomfortable old lady. Independence is a very nice thing, and poverty isn't half as bad as this sort of slavery. But you are not going to be poor, nor worry about anything. We'll just be married and take mother and Toady home and be as jolly as grigs, and never think of Mrs. K. again,—unless she loses her fortune, or gets sick, or comes to grief in any way. We'd lend her a hand then, wouldn't we, Polly?" and Van's mild face was pleasant to behold as he made the kindly proposition.

"Well, we'd think of it," said Polly, trying not to relent, but feeling that she was going very fast.

"Let's do it!" cried Toady, fired with the thought of privy conspiracy and rebellion. "Mother would be so comfortable with Polly, and I'd help Van in the store, when I've learned that confounded multiplication table," he added with a groan; "and if Aunt Kipp comes a visiting, we'll just say 'Not at home,' and let her trot off again."

"It sounds very nice, but aunt will be dreadfully offended and I don't wish to be ungrateful," said Mrs. Snow, brightening visibly.

"There's no ingratitude about it," cried Van. "She might have done everything to make you love, and respect, and admire her, and been a happy, useful, motherly, old soul; but she didn't choose to, and now she must take the consequences. No one cares for her, because she cares for nobody; her money's the plague of her life, and not a single heart will ache when she dies."

"Poor Aunt Kipp!" said Polly, softly.

Mrs. Snow echoed the words, and for a moment all thought pitifully of the woman whose life had given so little happiness, whose age had won so little reverence, and whose death would cause so little regret. Even Toady had a kind thought for her, as he broke the silence, saying soberly, —

"You'd better put tails on my jackets, mother; then the next time we get run away with, Aunt Kipp will have something to hold on by."

It was impossible to help laughing at the recollection of the old lady clutching at the boy till he had hardly a button left, and at the paternal air with which he now proposed a much-desired change of costume, as if intent on Aunt Kipp's future accommodation.

Under cover of the laugh, the old lady stole back to bed, wide awake, and with subjects enough to meditate upon now. The shaking up had certainly done her good, for somehow the few virtues she possessed came to the surface, and the mental shower-bath just received had produced a salutary change. Polly wouldn't have doubted her aunt's possession of a heart, if she could have known the pain and loneliness that made it ache, as the old woman crept away; and Toady wouldn't have laughed if he had seen the tears on the face, between the big frills, as Aunt Kipp laid it on the pillow, muttering, drearily, —

"I might have been a happy, useful woman, but I didn't choose to, and now it's too late."

It *was* too late to be all she might have been, for the work of seventy selfish years couldn't be undone in a minute. But with regret, rose the sincere wish to earn a little love before the end came, and the old perversity gave a relish to the reformation, for even while she resolved to do the just and generous thing, she said to herself, —

"They say I've got no heart; I'll show 'em that I have: they don't want my money; I'll *make* 'em take it: they turn their backs on me; I'll just render myself so useful and agreeable that they can't do without me."

III

Aunt Kipp sat bolt upright in the parlor, hemming a small handkerchief, adorned with a red ship, surrounded by a border of green monkeys. Toady suspected that this elegant article of dress was intended for him, and yearned to possess it; so, taking advantage of his mother's and Polly's absence, he strolled into the room, and, seating himself on a high, hard chair, folded his hands, crossed his legs, and asked for a story with the thirsting-for-knowledge air which little boys wear in the moral story-books.

Now Aunt Kipp had one soft place in her heart, though it *was* partially ossified, as she very truly declared, and Toady was enshrined therein. She thought there never was such a child, and loved him as she had done his father before him, though the rack wouldn't have forced her to confess it. She scolded, snubbed, and predicted he'd come to a bad end in public; but she forgave his naughtiest pranks, always brought him something when she came, and privately intended to make his future comfortable with half of her fortune. There was a dash and daring, a generosity and integrity, about the little fellow, that charmed her. Sophy was weak and low-spirited, Polly pretty and head-strong, and Aunt Kipp didn't think much of either of them; but Toady defied, distracted, and delighted her, and to Toady she clung, as the one sunshiny thing in her sour, selfish old age.

When he made his demure request, she looked at him, and her eyes began to twinkle, for the child's purpose was plainly seen in the loving glances cast upon the pictorial pocket-handkerchief.

"A story? Yes, I'll tell you one about a little boy who had a kind old—ahem!—grandma. She was rich, and hadn't made up her mind who she'd leave her money to. She was fond of the boy,—a deal fonder than he deserved,—for he was as mischievous a monkey as any that ever lived in a tree, with a curly tail. He put pepper in her snuff-box,"—here Toady turned scarlet,—"he cut up her best frisette to make a mane for his rocking-horse,"—Toady opened his mouth impulsively, but shut it again without betraying himself—"he repeated rude things to her, and called her 'an old aggrawater,'"—here Toady wriggled in his chair, and gave a little gasp.

"If you are tired I won't go on," observed Aunt Kipp, mildly.

"I'm not tired, 'm; it's a very interesting story," replied Toady, with a gravity that nearly upset the old lady.

"Well, in spite of all this, that kind, good, forgiving grandma left that bad boy twenty thousand dollars when she died. What do you think of that?" asked Aunt Kipp, pausing suddenly with her sharp eye on him.

"I—I think she was a regular dear," cried Toady, holding on to the chair with both hands, as if that climax rather took him off his legs.

"And what did the boy do about it?" continued Aunt Kipp, curiously.

"He bought a velocipede, and gave his sister half, and paid his mother's rent, and put a splendid marble cherakin over the old lady, and had a jolly good time, and—"

"What in the world is a cherakin?" laughed Aunt Kipp, as Toady paused for breath.

"Why, don't you know? It's a angel crying, or pointing up, or flapping his wings. They have them over graves; and I'll give you the biggest one I can find when you die. But I'm not in a *very* great hurry to have you."

"Thankee, dear; I'm in no hurry, myself. But, Toady, the boy did wrong in giving his sister half; she didn't deserve *any*; and the grandma left word she wasn't to have a penny of it."

"Really?" cried the boy, with a troubled face.

"Yes, really. If he gave her any he lost it all; the old lady said so. Now what do you think?" asked Aunt Kipp, who found it impossible to pardon Polly,—perhaps because she was young, and pretty, and much beloved.

Toady's eyes kindled, and his red cheeks grew redder still, as he cried out defiantly,—

"I think she was a selfish pig,—don't you?"

"No, I don't, sir; and I'm sure that little boy wasn't such a fool as to lose the money. He minded his grandma's wishes, and kept it all."

"No, he didn't," roared Toady, tumbling off his chair in great excitement. "He just threw it out a winder, and smashed the old cherakin all to bits."

Aunt Kipp dropped her work with a shrill squeak, for she thought the boy was dangerous, as he stood before her, sparring away at nothing as the only vent for his indignation.

"It isn't an interesting story," he cried; "and I won't hear any more; and I won't have your money if I mayn't go halves with Polly; and I'll work to earn more than that, and we'll all be jolly together, and you may give your twenty thousand to the old rag-bags, and so I tell you, Aunt Kipp."

"Why, Toady, my boy, what's the matter?" cried a mild voice at the door, as young Lamb came trotting up to the rescue.

"Never you mind, Baa-baa; I shan't do it; and it's a mean shame Polly can't have half; then she could marry you and be so happy," blubbered Toady, running to try to hide his tears of disappointment in the coat-skirts of his friend.

"Mr. Lamb, I suppose you *are* that misguided young man?" said Aunt Kipp, as if it was a personal insult to herself.

"Van Bahr Lamb, ma'am, if you please. Yes, thank you," murmured Baa-baa, bowing, blushing, and rumpling his curly fleece in bashful trepidation.

"Don't thank me," cried the old lady. "I'm not going to give you anything, — far from it. I object to you altogether. What business have you to come courting my niece?"

"Because I love her, ma'am," returned Van, with unexpected spirit.

"No, you don't; you want her money, or rather my money. She depends on it; but you'll both be disappointed, for she won't have a penny of it," cried Aunt Kipp, who, in spite of her good resolutions, found it impossible to be amiable all at once.

"I'm glad of it!" burst out Van, indignant at her accusation. "I didn't want Polly for the money; I always doubted if she got it; and I never wished her to make herself a slave to anybody. I've got enough for all, if we're careful; and when my share of the Van Bahr property comes, we shall live in clover."

"What's that? What property are you talking of?" demanded Aunt Kipp, pricking up her ears.

"The great Van Bahr estate, ma'am. There has been a long lawsuit about it, but it's nearly settled, and there isn't much doubt that we shall get it. I am the last of our branch, and my share will be a large one."

"Oh, indeed! I wish you joy," said Aunt Kipp, with sudden affability; for she adored wealth, like a few other persons in the world. "But suppose you don't get it, how then?"

"Then I shall try to be contented with my salary of two thousand, and make Polly as happy as I can. Money doesn't *always* make people happy or agreeable, I find." And Van looked at Aunt Kipp in a way that would have made her hair stand erect if she had possessed any. She stared at him a moment, then, obeying one of the odd whims that made an irascible weathercock of her, she said, abruptly, —

"If you had capital should you go into business for yourself, Mr. Lambkin?"

"Yes, ma'am, at once," replied Van, promptly.

"Suppose you lost the Van Bahr money, and some one offered you a tidy little sum to start with, would you take it?"

"It would depend upon who made the offer, ma'am," said Van, looking more like a sheep than ever, as he stood staring in blank surprise.

"Suppose it was me, wouldn't you take it?" asked Aunt Kipp, blandly, for the new fancy pleased her.

"No, thank you, ma'am," said Van, decidedly.

"And why not, pray?" cried the old lady, with a shrillness that made him jump, and Toady back to the door precipitately.

"Because, if you'll excuse my speaking plainly, I think you owe anything you may have to spare to your niece, Mrs. Snow;" and, having freed his mind, Van joined Toady, ready to fly if necessary.

"You're an idiot, sir," began Aunt Kipp, in a rage again.

"Thank you, ma'am." And Van actually laughed and bowed in return for the compliment.

"Hold your tongue, sir," snapped the old lady. "You're a fool and Sophy is another. She's no strength of mind, no sense about anything; and would make ducks and drakes of my money in less than no time if I gave it to her, as I've thought of doing."

"Mrs. Kipp, you forget who you are speaking to. Mrs. Snow's sons love and respect her if you don't, and they won't hear anything untrue or unkind said of a good woman, a devoted mother, and an almost friendless widow."

Van wasn't a dignified man at all, but as he said that with a sudden flash of his mild eyes, there was something in his face and manner that daunted Aunt Kipp more than the small fist belligerently shaken at her from behind the sofa. The poor old soul was cross, and worried, and ashamed of herself, and being as feeble-minded as Sophy in many respects, she suddenly burst into tears, and, covering her face with the gay handkerchief, cried as if bent on floating the red ship in a sea of salt water without delay.

"I'm a poor, lonely, abused old woman," she moaned, with a green monkey at each eye. "No one loves me, or minds me, or thanks me when I want to help 'em. My money's only a worryment and a burden, and I don't know what to do with it, for people I don't want to leave it to ought to have it, and people I do like won't take it. Oh, deary me, what *shall* I do! what shall I do!"

"Shall I tell you, ma'am?" asked Van, gently, for, though she was a very provoking old lady, he pitied and wished to help her.

A nod and a gurgle seemed to give consent, and, boldly advancing, Van said, with blush and a stammer, but a very hearty voice, —

"I think, ma'am, if you'd do the right thing with your money you'd be at ease and find it saved a deal of worry all round. Give it to Mrs. Snow; she deserves it, poor lady, for she's had a hard time, and done her duty faithfully. Don't wait till you are — that is, till you — well, till you in point of fact die, ma'am. Give it now, and enjoy the happiness it will make. Give it kindly, let them see you're glad to do it, and I am sure you'll find them grateful; I'm sure you won't be lonely any more, or feel that you are not loved and thanked. Try it, ma'am, just try it," cried Van, getting excited by the picture he drew. "And I give you my word I'll do my best to respect and love you like a son, ma'am."

He knew that he was promising a great deal, but for Polly's sake he felt that he could make even that Herculean effort. Aunt Kipp was surprised and touched; but the contrary old lady couldn't make up her mind to yield so soon, and wouldn't have done it if Toady hadn't taken her by storm. Having a truly masculine horror of tears, a very tender heart under his tail-less jacket, and being much "tumbled up and down in his own mind" by the events of the week, the poor little lad felt nerved to attempt any novel enterprise, even that of voluntarily embracing Aunt Kipp. First a grimy little hand came on her shoulder, as she sat sniffing behind the handkerchief; then, peeping out, she saw an apple-cheeked face very near her own, with eyes full of pity, penitence, and affection; and then she heard a choky little voice say earnestly, —

"Don't cry, aunty; I'm sorry I was rude. Please be good to Mother and Polly, and I'll love and take care of you, and stand by you all my life. Yes, I'll — I'll *kiss* you, I will, by George!" And with one promiscuous plunge the Spartan boy cast himself into her arms.

That finished Aunt Kipp; she hugged him close, and cried out with a salute that went off like a pistol-shot,—

"Oh, my dear, my dear! this is better than a dozen cherakins!"

When Toady emerged, somewhat flushed and tumbled, Mrs. Snow, Polly, and Van were looking on with faces full of wonder, doubt, and satisfaction. To be an object of interest was agreeable to Aunt Kipp; and, as her old heart was really softened, she met them with a gracious smile, and extended the olive-branch generally.

"Sophy, I shall give my money to *you* at once and entirely, only asking that you'll let me stay with you when Polly's gone. I'll do my best to be agreeable, and you'll bear with me because I'm a cranky, solitary old woman, and I loved your husband."

Mrs. Snow hugged her on the spot, and gushed, of course, murmuring thanks, welcomes, and promises in one grateful burst.

"Polly, I forgive you; I consent to your marriage, and will provide your wedding finery. Mr. Lamb, you are not a fool, but a very excellent young man. I thank you for saving my life, and I wish you well with all my heart. You needn't say anything. I'm far from strong, and all this agitation is shortening my life."

Polly and Van shook her hand heartily, and beamed upon each other like a pair of infatuated turtle-doves with good prospects.

"Toady, you are as near an angel as a boy can be. Put a name to whatever you most wish for in the world, and it's yours," said Aunt Kipp, dramatically waving the rest away.

With his short legs wide apart, his hands behind him, and his rosy face as round and radiant as a rising sun, Toady stood before the fire surveying the scene with the air of a man who has successfully carried through a difficult and dangerous undertaking, and wasn't proud. His face brightened, then fell, as he heaved a sigh, and answered, with a shake of his curly head,—

"You can't give me what I want most. There are three things, and I've got to wait for them all."

"Gracious me, what are they?" cried the old lady, good-naturedly, for she felt better already.

"A mustache, a beaver, *and* a sweetheart," answered Toady, with his eyes fixed wistfully on Baa-baa, who possessed all these blessings, and was particularly enjoying the latter at that moment.

How Aunt Kipp did laugh at this early budding of romance in her pet! And all the rest joined her, for Toady's sentimental air was irresistible.

"You precocious chick! I dare say you will have them all before we know where we are. Never mind, deary; you shall have my little watch, and the silver-headed cane with a *boar's* head on it," answered the old lady, in high good-humor. "You needn't blush, dear; I don't bear malice; so let's forget and forgive. I shall settle things to-morrow, and have a free mind. You are welcome to my money, and I hope I shall live to see you all enjoy it."

So she did; for she lived to see Sophy plump, cheery, and care-free; Polly surrounded by a flock of Lambkins; Van in possession of a generous slice of the Van Bahr fortune; Toady revelling in the objects of his desire; and, best of all, she lived to find that it is never too late to make oneself useful, happy, and beloved.

PSYCHE'S ART

"Handsome is that handsome does."

I

ONCE upon a time there raged in a certain city one of those fashionable epidemics which occasionally attack our youthful population. It wasn't the music mania, nor gymnastic convulsions, nor that wide-spread malady, croquet. Neither was it one of the new dances which, like a tarantula-bite, set every one a twirling, nor stage madness, nor yet that American lecturing influenza which yearly sweeps over the land. No, it was a new disease called the Art fever, and it attacked the young women of the community with great violence.

Nothing but time could cure it, and it ran its course to the dismay, amusement, or edification of the beholders, for its victims did all manner of queer things in their delirium. They besieged potteries for clay, drove Italian plaster-workers out of their wits with unexecutable orders, got neuralgia and rheumatism sketching perched on fences and trees like artistic hens, and caused a rise in the price of bread, paper, and charcoal, by their ardor in crayoning. They covered canvas with the expedition of scene-painters, had classes, lectures, receptions, and exhibitions, made models of each other, and rendered their walls hideous with bad likenesses of all their friends. Their conversation ceased to be intelligible to the uninitiated, and they prattled prettily of "chiaro oscuro, French sauce, refraction of the angle of the eye, seventh spinus process, depth and juiciness of color, tender touch, and a good tone." Even in dress the artistic disorder was visible; some cast aside crinoline altogether, and stalked about with a severe simplicity of outline worthy of Flaxman. Others flushed themselves with scarlet, that no landscape which they adorned should be without some touch of Turner's favorite tint. Some were *blue* in every sense of the word, and the heads of all were adorned with classic braids, curls tied Hebe-wise, or hair dressed à la hurricane.

It was found impossible to keep them safe at home, and, as the fever grew, these harmless maniacs invaded the sacred retreats where artists of the other sex did congregate, startling those anchorites with visions of large-eyed damsels bearing portfolios in hands delicately begrimed with crayon, chalk, and clay, gliding through the corridors hitherto haunted only by shabby paletots, shadowy hats, and cigar smoke. This irruption was borne with manly fortitude, not to say cheerfulness, for studio doors stood hospitably open as the fair invaders passed, and studies from life were generously offered them in glimpses of picturesque gentlemen posed before easels, brooding over master-pieces in "a divine despair," or attitudinizing upon couches as if exhausted by the soarings of genius.

An atmosphere of romance began to pervade the old buildings when the girls came, and nature and art took turns. There were peepings and whisperings, much stifled laughter and whisking in and out; not to mention the accidental rencontres, small services, and eye telegrams, which somewhat lightened the severe studies of all parties.

Half a dozen young victims of this malady met daily in one of the cells of a great art bee-hive called "Raphael's Rooms," and devoted their shining hours to modelling fancy heads, gossiping the while; for the poor things found the road to fame rather dull and dusty without such verbal sprinklings.

"Psyche Dean, you've had an adventure! I see it in your face; so tell it at once, for we are as stupid as owls here to-day," cried one of the sisterhood, as a bright-eyed girl entered with some precipitation.

"I dropped my portfolio, and a man picked it up, that's all," replied Psyche, hurrying on her gray linen pinafore.

"That won't do; I know something interesting happened, for you've been blushing, and you look brisker than usual this morning," said the first speaker, polishing off the massive nose of her Homer.

"It wasn't anything," began Pysche a little reluctantly. "I was coming up in a hurry when I ran against a man coming down in a hurry. My portfolio slipped, and my papers went flying all about the landing. Of course we both laughed and begged pardon, and I began to pick them up, but he wouldn't let me; so I held the book while he collected the sketches. I saw him glance at them as he did so, and that made me blush, for they are wretched things, you know."

"Not a bit of it; they are capital, and you are a regular genius, as we all agree," cut in the Homeric Miss Cutter.

"Never tell people they are geniuses unless you wish to spoil them," returned Psyche severely. "Well, when the portfolio was put to rights I was going on, but he fell to picking up a little bunch of violets I had dropped; you know I always wear a posy into town to give me inspiration. I didn't care for the dusty flowers, and told him so, and hurried away before any one came. At the top of the stairs I peeped over the railing, and there he was, gathering up every one of those half-dead violets as carefully as if they had been tea-roses."

"Psyche Dean, you have met your fate this day!" exclaimed a third damsel, with straw-colored tresses, and a good deal of weedy shrubbery in her hat, which gave an Ophelia-like expression to her sentimental countenance.

Psyche frowned and shook her head, as if half sorry she had told her little story.

"Was he handsome?" asked Miss Larkins, the believer in fate.

"I didn't particularly observe."

"It was the red-headed man, whom we call Titian: he's always on the stairs."

"No, it wasn't; his hair was brown and curly," cried Psyche, innocently falling into the trap.

"Like Peerybingle's baby when its cap was taken off," quoted Miss Dickenson, who pined to drop the last two letters of her name.

"Was it Murillo, the black-eyed one?" asked the fair Cutter, for the girls had a name for all the attitudinizers and promenaders whom they oftenest met.

"No, he had gray eyes, and very fine ones they were too," answered Psyche, adding, as if to herself, "he looked as I imagine Michael Angelo might have looked when young."

"Had he a broken nose, like the great Mike?" asked an irreverent damsel.

"If he had, no one would mind it, for his head is splendid; he took his hat off, so I had a fine view. He isn't handsome, but he'll *do* something," said Psyche, prophetically, as she recalled the strong, ambitious face which she had often observed, but never mentioned before.

"Well, dear, considering that you didn't 'particularly look' at the man, you've given us a very good idea of his appearance. We'll call him Michael Angelo, and he shall be your idol. I prefer stout old Rembrandt myself, and Larkie adores that dandified Raphael," said the lively Cutter, slapping away at Homer's bald pate energetically, as she spoke.

"Raphael is a dear, but Rubens is more to my taste now," returned Miss Larkins. "He was in the hall yesterday talking with Sir Joshua, who had his inevitable umbrella, like a true Englishman. Just as I came up, the umbrella fell right before me. I started back; Sir Joshua laughed, but Rubens said, 'Deuce take it!' and caught up the umbrella, giving me a never-to-be-forgotten look. It was perfectly thrilling."

"Which,—the umbrella, the speech, or the look?" asked Psyche, who was not sentimental.

"Ah, you have no soul for art in nature, and nature in art," sighed the amber-tressed Larkins. "I have, for I feed upon a glance, a tint, a curve, with exquisite delight. Rubens is adorable (*as a study*); that lustrous eye, that night of hair, that sumptuous cheek, are perfect. He only needs a cloak, lace collar, and slouching hat to be the genuine thing."

"This isn't the genuine thing by any means. What *does* it need?" said Psyche, looking with a despondent air, at the head on her stand.

Many would have pronounced it a clever thing; the nose was strictly Greek, the chin curved upward gracefully, the mouth was sweetly haughty, the brow classically smooth and low, and the breezy hair well done. But something was wanting; Psyche felt that, and could have taken her Venus by the dimpled shoulders, and given her a hearty shake, if that would have put strength and spirit into the lifeless face.

"Now *I* am perfectly satisfied with my Apollo, though you all insist that it is the image of Theodore Smythe. He says so himself, and assures me it will make a sensation when we exhibit," remarked Miss Larkins, complacently caressing the ambrosial locks of her Smythified Phebus.

"What shall you do if it does not?" asked Miss Cutter, with elegance.

"I shall feel that I have mistaken my sphere, shall drop my tools, veil my bust, and cast myself into the arms of Nature, since Art rejects me;" replied Miss Larkins, with a tragic gesture and an expression which strongly suggested that in her eyes nature meant Theodore.

"She must have capacious arms if she is to receive all Art's rejected admirers. Shall I be one of them?"

Psyche put the question to herself as she turned to work, but somehow ambitious aspirations were not in a flourishing condition that morning; her heart was not in tune, and head and hands sympathized. Nothing went well, for certain neglected home-duties had dogged her into town, and now worried her more than dust, or heat, or the ceaseless clatter of tongues. Tom, Dick, and Harry's unmended hose persisted in dancing a spectral jig before her mental eye, mother's querulous complaints spoilt the song she hummed to cheer herself, and little May's wistful face put the goddess of beauty entirely out of countenance.

"It's no use; I can't work till the clay is wet again. Where is Giovanni?" she asked, throwing down her tools with a petulant gesture and a dejected air.

"He is probably playing truant in the empty upper rooms, as usual. I can't wait for him any longer, so I'm doing his work myself," answered Miss Dickenson, who was tenderly winding a wet bandage round her Juno's face, one side of which was so much plumper than the other that it looked as if the Queen of Olympus was being hydropathically treated for a severe fit of ague.

"I'll go and find the little scamp; a run will do me good; so will a breath of air and a view of the park from the upper windows."

Doffing her apron, Psyche strolled away up an unfrequented staircase to the empty apartments, which seemed to be too high even for the lovers of High Art. On the western side they were shady and cool, and, leaning from one of the windows, Psyche watched the feathery tree-tops ruffled by the balmy wind, that brought spring odors from the hills, lying green and sunny far away. Silence and solitude were such pleasant companions that the girl forgot herself, till a shrill whistle disturbed her day-dreams, and reminded her what she came for. Following the sound she found the little Italian errand-boy busily uncovering a clay model which stood in the middle of a scantily furnished room near by.

"He is not here; come and look; it is greatly beautiful," cried Giovanni, beckoning with an air of importance.

Psyche did look and speedily forgot both her errand and herself. It was the figure of a man, standing erect, and looking straight before him with a wonderfully life-like expression. It was neither a mythological nor a historical character, Psyche thought, and was glad of it, being tired to death of gods and heroes. She soon ceased to wonder what it was, feeling only the indescribable charm of something higher than beauty. Small as her knowledge was, she could see and enjoy the power visible in every part of it; the accurate anatomy of the vigorous limbs, the grace of the pose, the strength and spirit in the countenance, clay though it was. A majestic figure, but the spell lay in the face, which, while it suggested the divine, was full of human truth and tenderness, for pain and passion seemed to have passed over it, and a humility half pathetic, a courage half heroic seemed to have been born from some great loss or woe.

How long she stood there Psyche did not know. Giovanni went away unseen, to fill his water-pail, and in the silence she just stood and looked. Her eyes kindled, her color rose, despondency and discontent vanished, and her soul was in her face, for she loved beauty passionately, and all that was best and truest in her did honor to the genius of the unknown worker.

"If I could do a thing like that, I'd die happy!" she exclaimed impetuously, as a feeling of despair came over her at the thought of her own poor attempts.

"Who did it, Giovanni?" she asked, still looking up at the grand face with unsatisfied eyes.

"Paul Gage."

It was not the boy's voice, and, with a start, Psyche turned to see her Michael Angelo, standing in the doorway, attentively observing her. Being too full of artless admiration to think of herself just yet, she neither blushed nor apologized, but looked straight at him, saying heartily,—

"You have done a wonderful piece of work, and I envy you more than I can tell!"

The enthusiasm in her face, the frankness of her manner, seemed to please him, for there was no affectation about either. He gave her a keen, kind glance out of the "fine gray eyes," a little bow, and a grateful smile, saying quietly,—

"Then my Adam is not a failure in spite of his fall?"

Psyche turned from the sculptor to his model with increased admiration in her face, and earnestness in her voice, as she exclaimed delighted,—

"Adam! I might have known it was he. O sir, you have indeed succeeded, for you have given that figure the power and pathos of the first man who sinned and suffered, and began again."

"Then I am satisfied." That was all he said, but the look he gave his work was a very eloquent one, for it betrayed that he had paid the price of success in patience and privation, labor and hope.

"What can one do to learn your secret?" asked the girl wistfully, for there was nothing in the man's manner to disturb her self-forgetful mood, but much to foster it, because to the solitary worker this confiding guest was as welcome as the doves who often hopped in at his window.

"Work and wait, and meantime feed heart, soul, and imagination with the best food one can get," he answered slowly, finding it impossible to give a receipt for genius.

"I can work and wait a long time to gain my end; but I don't know where to find the food you speak of?" she answered, looking at him like a hungry child.

"I wish I could tell you, but each needs different fare, and each must look for it in different places."

The kindly tone and the sympathizing look, as well as the lines in his forehead, and a few gray hairs among the brown, gave Psyche courage to say more.

"I love beauty so much that I not only want to possess it myself, but to gain the power of seeing it in all things, and the art of reproducing it with truth. I have tried very hard to do it, but something is wanting; and in spite of my intense desire I never get on."

As she spoke the girl's eyes filled and fell in spite of herself, and turning a little with sudden shamefacedness she saw, lying on the table beside her among other scraps in manuscript and print, the well-known lines,—

> "I slept, and dreamed that life was beauty;
>
> I woke, and found that life was duty.
>
> Was thy dream then a shadowy lie?
>
> Toil on, sad heart, courageously,
>
> And thou shalt find thy dream to be
>
> A noonday light and truth to thee."

She knew them at a glance, had read them many times, but now they came home to her with sudden force, and, seeing that his eye had followed hers, she said in her impulsive fashion,—

"Is doing one's duty a good way to feed heart, soul, and imagination?"

As if he had caught a glimpse of what was going on in her mind, Paul answered emphatically,—

"Excellent; for if one is good, one is happy, and if happy, one can work well. Moulding character is the highest sort of sculpture, and all of us should learn that art before we touch clay or marble."

He spoke with the energy of a man who believed what he said, and did his best to be worthy of the rich gift bestowed upon him. The sight of her violets in a glass of water, and Giovanni staring at her with round eyes, suddenly recalled Psyche to a sense of the proprieties which she had been innocently outraging for the last ten minutes. A sort of panic seized her; she blushed deeply, retreated precipitately to the door, and vanished, murmuring thanks and apologies as she went.

"Did you find him? I thought you had forgotten," said Miss Dickenson, now hard at work.

"Yes, I found him. No, I shall not forget," returned Psyche, thinking of Gage, not Giovanni.

She stood before her work eying it intently for several minutes; then, with an expression of great contempt for the whole thing, she suddenly tilted her cherished Venus on to the floor, gave the classical face a finishing crunch, and put on her hat in a decisive manner, saying briefly to the dismayed damsels, —

"Good-by, girls; I shan't come any more, for I'm going to work at home hereafter."

II

THE prospect of pursuing artistic studies at home was not brilliant, as one may imagine when I mention that Psyche's father was a painfully prosaic man, wrapt in flannel, so to speak; for his woollen mills left him no time for anything but sleep, food, and newspapers. Mrs. Dean was one of those exasperating women who pervade their mansions like a domestic steam-engine one week and take to their sofas the next, absorbed by fidgets and foot-stoves, shawls and lamentations. There were three riotous and robust young brothers, whom it is unnecessary to describe except by stating that they were *boys* in the broadest sense of that delightful word. There was a feeble little sister, whose patient, suffering face demanded constant love and care to mitigate the weariness of a life of pain. And last, but not least by any means, there were two Irish ladies, who, with the best intentions imaginable, produced a universal state of topsy-turviness when left to themselves for a moment.

But being very much in earnest about doing her duty, not because it *was* her duty, but as a means toward an end, Psyche fell to work with a will, hoping to serve both masters at once. So she might have done, perhaps, if flesh and blood had been as plastic as clay, but the live models were so exacting in their demands upon her time and strength, that the poor statues went to the wall. Sculpture and sewing, calls and crayons, Ruskin and receipt-books, didn't work well together, and poor Psyche found duties and desires desperately antagonistic. Take a day as a sample.

"The washing and ironing are well over, thank goodness, mother quiet, the boys out of the way, and May comfortable, so I'll indulge myself in a blissful day after my own heart," Psyche said, as she shut herself into her little studio, and prepared to enjoy a few hours of hard study and happy day-dreams.

With a book on her lap, and her own round white arm going through all manner of queer evolutions, she was placidly repeating, "Deltoides, Biceps, Triceps, Pronator, Supinator, Palmanis, Flexor carpi ulnaris—"

"Here's Flexis what-you-call-ums for you," interrupted a voice, which began in a shrill falsetto and ended in a gruff bass, as a flushed, dusty, long-legged boy burst in, with a bleeding hand obligingly extended for inspection.

"Mercy on us, Harry! what have you done to yourself now? Split your fingers with a cricket-ball again?" cried Psyche, as her arms went up and her book went down.

"I just thrashed one of the fellows because he got mad and said father was going to fail."

"O Harry, is he?"

"Of course he isn't! It's hard times for every one, but father will pull through all right. No use to try and explain it all; girls can't understand business; so you just tie me up, and don't worry," was the characteristic reply of the young man, who, being three years her junior, of course treated the weaker vessel with lordly condescension.

"What a dreadful wound! I hope nothing is broken, for I haven't studied the hand much yet, and may do mischief doing it up," said Psyche, examining the great grimy paw with tender solicitude.

"Much good your biceps, and deltoids, and things do you, if you can't right up a little cut like that," squeaked the ungrateful hero.

"I'm not going to be a surgeon, thank heaven; I intend to make perfect hands and arms, not mend damaged ones," retorted Psyche, in a dignified tone, somewhat marred by a great piece of court-plaster on her tongue.

"I should say a surgeon could improve *that* perfect thing, if he didn't die a-laughing before he began," growled Harry, pointing with a scornful grin at a clay arm humpy with muscles, all carefully developed in the wrong places.

"Don't sneer Hal, for you don't know anything about it. Wait a few years and see if you're not proud of me."

"Sculp away and do something, then I'll hurrah for your mud-pies like a good one;" with which cheering promise the youth departed, having effectually disturbed his sister's peaceful mood.

Anxious thoughts of her father rendered "biceps, deltoids, and things" uninteresting, and hoping to compose her mind, she took up The Old

Painters and went on with the story of Claude Lorraine. She had just reached the tender scene where,—

"Calista gazed with enthusiasm, while she looked like a being of heaven rather than earth. 'My friend,' she cried, 'I read in thy picture thy immortality!' As she spoke, her head sunk upon his bosom, and it was several moments before Claude perceived that he supported a lifeless form."

"How sweet!" said Psyche, with a romantic sigh.

"Faith, and swate it is, thin!" echoed Katy, whose red head had just appeared round the half opened door. "It's gingy-bread I'm making the day, miss, and will I be puttin' purlash or sallyrathis into it, if ye plase?"

"Purlash, by all means," returned the girl, keeping her countenance, fearing to enrage Katy by a laugh; for the angry passions of the red-haired one rose more quickly than her bread. As she departed with alacrity to add a spoonful of starch and a pinch of whiting to her cake, Psyche, feeling better for her story and her smile, put on her bib and paper cap and fell to work on the deformed arm. An hour of bliss, then came a ring at the door-bell, followed by Biddy to announce callers, and add that as "the mistress was in her bed, miss must go and take care of 'em." Whereat "miss" cast down her tools in despair, threw her cap one way, her bib another, and went in to her guests with anything but a rapturous welcome.

Dinner being accomplished after much rushing up and down stairs with trays and messages for Mrs. Dean, Psyche fled again to her studio, ordering no one to approach under pain of a scolding. All went well till, going in search of something, she found her little sister sitting on the floor with her cheek against the studio door.

"I didn't mean to be naughty, Sy, but mother is asleep, and the boys all gone, so I just came to be near you; it's so lonely everywhere," she said, apologetically, as she lifted up the heavy head that always ached.

"The boys are very thoughtless. Come in and stay with me; you are such a mouse you won't disturb me. Wouldn't you like to play be a model and let me draw your arm, and tell you all about the nice little bones and muscles?" asked Psyche, who had the fever very strong upon her just then.

May didn't look as if the proposed amusement overwhelmed her with delight, but meekly consented to be perched upon a high stool with one arm propped up by a dropsical plaster cherub, while Psyche drew busily, feeling that duty and pleasure were being delightfully combined.

"Can't you hold your arm still, child? It shakes so I can't get it right," she said, rather impatiently.

"No, it will tremble 'cause it's weak. I try hard, Sy, but there doesn't seem to be much strongness in me lately."

"That's better; keep it so a few minutes and I'll be done," cried the artist, forgetting that a few minutes may seem ages.

"My arm is so thin you can see the bunches nicely,—can't you?"

"Yes, dear."

Psyche glanced up at the wasted limb, and when she drew again there was a blur before her eyes for a minute.

"I wish I was as fat as this white boy; but I get thinner every day somehow, and pretty soon there won't be any of me left but my little bones," said the child, looking at the winged cherub with sorrowful envy.

"Don't, my darling; don't say that," cried Psyche, dropping her work with a sudden pang at her heart. "I'm a sinful, selfish girl to keep you here! you're weak for want of air; come out and see the chickens, and pick dandelions, and have a good romp with the boys."

The weak arms were strong enough to clasp Psyche's neck, and the tired face brightened beautifully as the child exclaimed, with grateful delight,—

"Oh, I'd like it very much! I wanted to go dreadfully; but everybody is so busy all the time. I don't want to play, Sy; but just to lie on the grass with my head in your lap while you tell stories and draw me pretty things as you used to."

The studio was deserted all that afternoon, for Psyche sat in the orchard drawing squirrels on the wall, pert robins hopping by, buttercups and mosses, elves and angels; while May lay contentedly enjoying sun and air, sisterly care, and the "pretty things" she loved so well. Psyche did not find the task a hard one; for this time her heart was in it, and if she needed any reward she surely found it; for the little face on her knee lost its weary look, and the peace and beauty of nature soothed her own troubled spirit, cheered her heart, and did her more good than hours of solitary study.

Finding, much to her own surprise, that her fancy was teeming with lovely conceits, she did hope for a quiet evening. But mother wanted a bit of gossip, father must have his papers read to him, the boys had lessons and rips and grievances to be attended to, May's lullaby could not be forgotten, and the maids had to be looked after, lest burly "cousins" should be hidden in the boiler, or lucifer matches among the shavings. So Psyche's day ended, leaving her very tired, rather discouraged, and almost heart-sick with the shadow of a coming sorrow.

All summer she did her best, but accomplished very little, as she thought; yet this was the teaching she most needed, and in time she came to see it. In the autumn May died, whispering, with her arms about her sister's neck, —

"You make me so happy, Sy, I wouldn't mind the pain if I could stay a little longer. But if I can't, good-by, dear, good-by."

Her last look and word and kiss were all for Psyche, who felt then with grateful tears that her summer had not been wasted; for the smile upon the little dead face was more to her than any marble perfection her hands could have carved.

In the solemn pause which death makes in every family, Psyche said, with the sweet self-forgetfulness of a strong yet tender nature, —

"I must not think of myself, but try to comfort them;" and with this resolution she gave herself heart and soul to duty, never thinking of reward.

A busy, anxious, humdrum winter, for, as Harry said, "it was hard times for every one." Mr. Dean grew gray with the weight of business cares about which he never spoke; Mrs. Dean, laboring under the delusion that an invalid was a necessary appendage to the family, installed herself in the place the child's death left vacant, and the boys needed much comforting, for the poor lads never knew how much they loved "the baby" till the little chair stood empty. All turned to Sy for help and consolation, and her strength seemed to increase with the demand upon it. Patience and cheerfulness, courage and skill came at her call like good fairies who had bided their time. Housekeeping ceased to be hateful, and peace reigned in parlor and kitchen while Mrs. Dean, shrouded in shawls, read Hahnemann's Lesser Writings on her sofa. Mr. Dean sometimes forgot his mills when a bright face came to meet him, a gentle hand smoothed the wrinkles out of his anxious forehead, and a daughterly heart sympathized with all his cares. The boys found home very pleasant with Sy always there ready to "lend a hand," whether it was to make fancy ties, help conjugate "a confounded verb," pull candy, or sing sweetly in the twilight when all thought of little May and grew quiet.

The studio door remained locked till her brothers begged Psyche to open it and make a bust of the child. A flush of joy swept over her face at the request, and her patient eyes grew bright and eager, as a thirsty traveller's might at the sight or sound of water. Then it faded as she shook her head, saying with a regretful sigh, "I'm afraid I've lost the little skill I ever had."

But she tried, and with great wonder and delight discovered that she could work as she had never done before. She thought the newly found power lay in her longing to see the little face again; for it grew like magic under her loving hands, while every tender memory, sweet thought, and devout hope she had ever cherished, seemed to lend their aid. But when it was done and welcomed with tears and smiles, and praise more precious than any the world could give, then Psyche said within herself, like one who saw light at last, —

"He was right; doing one's duty *is* the way to feed heart, soul, and imagination; for if one is good, one is happy, and if happy, one can work well."

III

"She broke her head and went home to come no more," was Giovanni's somewhat startling answer when Paul asked about Psyche, finding that he no longer met her on the stairs or in the halls. He understood what the boy meant, and with an approving nod turned to his work again, saying, "I like that! If there is any power in her, she has taken the right way to find it out, I suspect."

How she prospered he never asked; for, though he met her more than once that year, the interviews were brief ones in street, concert-room, or picture-gallery, and she carefully avoided speaking of herself. But, possessing the gifted eyes which can look below the surface of things, he detected in the girl's face something better than beauty, though each time he saw it, it looked older and more thoughtful, often anxious and sad.

"She is getting on," he said to himself with a cordial satisfaction which gave his manner a friendliness as grateful to Psyche as his wise reticence.

Adam was finished at last, proved a genuine success, and Paul heartily enjoyed the well-earned reward for years of honest work. One blithe May morning, he slipped early into the art-gallery, where the statue now stood, to look at his creation with paternal pride. He was quite alone with the stately figure that shone white against the purple draperies and seemed to offer him a voiceless welcome from its marble lips. He gave it one loving look, and then forgot it, for at the feet of his Adam lay a handful of wild violets, with the dew still on them. A sudden smile broke over his face as he took them up, with the thought, "She has been here and found my work good."

For several moments he stood thoughtfully turning the flowers to and fro in his hands; then, as if deciding some question within himself, he said, still smiling, —

"It is just a year since she went home; she must have accomplished something in that time; I'll take the violets as a sign that I may go and ask her what."

He knew she lived just out of the city, between the river and the mills, and as he left the streets behind him, he found more violets blooming all along the way like flowery guides to lead him right. Greener grew the road, balmier blew the wind, and blither sang the birds, as he went on, enjoying his holiday with the zest of a boy, until he reached a most attractive little path winding away across the fields. The gate swung invitingly open, and all the ground before it was blue with violets. Still following their guidance he took the narrow path, till, coming to a mossy stone beside a brook, he sat down to listen to the blackbirds singing deliciously in the willows over head. Close by the stone, half hidden in the grass lay a little book, and, taking it up he found it was a pocket-diary. No name appeared on the flyleaf, and, turning the pages to find some clue to its owner, he read here and there enough to give him glimpses into an innocent and earnest heart which seemed to be learning some hard lesson patiently. Only near the end did he find the clue in words of his own, spoken long ago, and a name. Then, though longing intensely to know more, he shut the little book and went on, showing by his altered face that the simple record of a girl's life had touched him deeply.

Soon an old house appeared nestling to the hillside with the river shining in the low green meadows just before it.

"She lives there," he said, with as much certainty as if the pansies by the door-stone spelt her name, and, knocking he asked for Psyche.

"She's gone to town, but I expect her home every minute. Ask the gentleman to walk in and wait, Katy," cried a voice from above, where the whisk of skirts was followed by the appearance of an inquiring eye over the banisters.

The gentleman did walk in, and while he waited looked about him. The room, though very simply furnished, had a good deal of beauty in it, for the pictures were few and well chosen, the books such as never grow old, the music lying on the well-worn piano of the sort which is never out of fashion, and standing somewhat apart was one small statue in a recess full of flowers. Lovely in its simple grace and truth was the figure of a child looking upward as if watching the airy flight of some butterfly which had evidently escaped from the chrysalis still lying in the little hand.

Paul was looking at it with approving eyes when Mrs. Dean appeared with his card in her hand, three shawls on her shoulders, and in her face a somewhat startled expression, as if she expected some novel demonstration from the man whose genius her daughter so much admired.

"I hope Miss Psyche is well," began Paul, with great discrimination if not originality.

The delightfully commonplace remark tranquillized Mrs. Dean at once, and, taking off the upper shawl with a fussy gesture, she settled herself for a chat.

"Yes, thank heaven, Sy is well. I don't know what would become of us if she wasn't. It has been a hard and sorrowful year for us with Mr. Dean's business embarrassments, my feeble health, and May's death. I don't know that you were aware of our loss, sir;" and unaffected maternal grief gave sudden dignity to the faded, fretful face of the speaker.

Paul murmured his regrets, understanding better now the pathetic words on a certain tear-stained page of the little book still in his pocket.

"Poor dear, she suffered everything, and it came very hard upon Sy, for the child wasn't happy with any one else, and almost lived in her arms," continued Mrs. Dean, dropping the second shawl to get her handkerchief.

"Miss Psyche has not had much time for art-studies this year, I suppose?" said Paul, hoping to arrest the shower, natural as it was.

"How could she with two invalids, the housekeeping, her father and the boys to attend to? No, she gave that up last spring, and though it was a great disappointment to her at the time, she has got over it now, I hope," added her mother, remembering as she spoke that Psyche even now went about the house sometimes pale and silent, with a hungry look in her eyes.

"I am glad to hear it," though a little shadow passed over his face as Paul spoke, for he was too true an artist to believe that any work could be as happy as that which he loved and lived for. "I thought there was much promise in Miss Psyche, and I sincerely believe that time will prove me a true prophet," he said, with mingled regret and hope in his voice, as he glanced about the room, which betrayed the tastes still cherished by the girl.

"I'm afraid ambition isn't good for women; I mean the sort that makes them known by coming before the public in any way. But Sy deserves some reward, I'm sure, and I know she'll have it, for a better daughter never lived."

Here the third shawl was cast off, as if the thought of Psyche, or the presence of a genial guest had touched Mrs. Dean's chilly nature with a comfortable warmth.

Further conversation was interrupted by the avalanche of boys which came tumbling down the front stairs, as Tom, Dick, and Harry shouted in a sort of chorus, —

"Sy, my balloon has got away; lend us a hand at catching him!"

"Sy, I want a lot of paste made, right off."

"Sy, I've split my jacket down the back; come sew me up, there's a dear!"

On beholding a stranger the young gentlemen suddenly lost their voices, found their manners, and with nods and grins took themselves away as quietly as could be expected of six clumping boots and an unlimited quantity of animal spirits in a high state of effervescence. As they trooped off, an unmistakable odor of burnt milk pervaded the air, and the crash of china, followed by an Irish wail, caused Mrs. Dean to clap on her three shawls again and excuse herself in visible trepidation.

Paul laughed quietly to himself, then turned sober and said, "Poor Psyche!" with a sympathetic sigh. He roamed about the room impatiently till the sound of voices drew him to the window to behold the girl coming up the walk with her tired old father leaning on one arm, the other loaded with baskets and bundles, and her hands occupied by a remarkably ugly turtle.

"Here we are!" cried a cheery voice, as they entered without observing the new-comer. "I've done all my errands and had a lovely time. There is Tom's gunpowder, Dick's fish-hooks, and one of Professor Gazzy's famous turtles for Harry. Here are your bundles, mother dear, and, best of all, here's father home in time for a good rest before dinner. I went to the mill and got him."

Psyche spoke as if she had brought a treasure; and so she had, for though Mr. Dean's face usually was about as expressive as the turtle's, it woke and warmed with the affection which his daughter had fostered till no amount of flannel could extinguish it. His big hand patted her cheek very gently as he said, in a tone of fatherly love and pride, —

"My little Sy never forgets old father, does she?"

"Good gracious me, my dear, there's such a mess in the kitchen! Katy's burnt up the pudding, put castor-oil instead of olive in the salad, smashed the best meat-dish, and here's Mr. Gage come to dinner," cried Mrs. Dean in accents of despair as she tied up her head in a fourth shawl.

"Oh, I'm so glad; I'll go in and see him a few minutes, and then I'll come and attend to everything; so don't worry, mother."

"How did you find me out?" asked Psyche as she shook hands with her guest and stood looking up at him with all the old confiding frankness in her face and manner.

"The violets showed me the way."

She glanced at the posy in his button-hole and smiled.

"Yes, I gave them to Adam, but I didn't think you would guess. I enjoyed your work for an hour to-day, and I have no words strong enough to express my admiration."

"There is no need of any. Tell me about yourself; what have you been doing all this year?" he asked, watching with genuine satisfaction the serene and sunny face before him, for discontent, anxiety, and sadness were no longer visible there.

"I've been working and waiting," she began.

"And succeeding, if I may believe what I see and hear and read," he said, with an expressive little wave of the book as he laid it down before her.

"My diary! I didn't know I had lost it. Where did you find it?"

"By the brook where I stopped to rest. The moment I saw your name I shut it up. Forgive me, but I can't ask pardon for reading a few pages of that little gospel of patience, love, and self-denial."

She gave him a reproachful look, and hurried the tell-tale book out of sight as she said, with a momentary shadow on her face, —

"It has been a hard task; but I think I have learned it, and am just beginning to find that my dream *is* 'a noonday light and truth,' to me."

"Then you do not relinquish your hopes, and lay down your tools?" he asked, with some eagerness.

"Never! I thought at first that I could not serve two masters, but in trying to be faithful to one I find I am nearer and dearer to the other. My cares and duties are growing lighter every day (or I have learned to bear them better), and when my leisure does come I shall know how to use it, for my head is full of ambitious plans, and I feel that I can do something *now*."

All the old enthusiasm shone in her eyes, and a sense of power betrayed itself in voice and gesture as she spoke.

"I believe it," he said heartily. "You have learned the secret, as that proves."

Psyche looked at the childish image as he pointed to it, and into her face there came a motherly expression that made it very sweet.

"That little sister was so dear to me I could not fail to make her lovely, for I put my heart into my work. The year has gone, but I don't regret it, though this is all I have done."

"You forget your three wishes; I think the year has granted them."

"What were they?"

"To possess beauty in yourself, the power of seeing it in all things, and the art of reproducing it with truth."

She colored deeply under the glance which accompanied the threefold compliment, and answered with grateful humility,—

"You are very kind to say so; I wish I could believe it." Then, as if anxious to forget herself, she added rather abruptly,—

"I hear you think of giving your Adam a mate,—have you begun yet?"

"Yes, my design is finished, all but the face."

"I should think you could image Eve's beauty, since you have succeeded so well with Adam's."

"The features perhaps, but not the expression. That is the charm of feminine faces, a charm so subtle that few can catch and keep it. I want a truly womanly face, one that shall be sweet and strong without being either weak or hard. A hopeful, loving, earnest face with a tender touch of motherliness in it, and perhaps the shadow of a grief that has softened but not saddened it."

"It will be hard to find a face like that."

"I don't expect to find it in perfection; but one sometimes sees faces which suggest all this, and in rare moments give glimpses of a lovely possibility."

"I sincerely hope you will find one then," said Psyche, thinking of the dinner.

"Thank you; *I* think I have."

Now, in order that every one may be suited, we will stop here, and leave our readers to finish the story as they like. Those who prefer the good old fashion may believe that the hero and heroine fell in love, were married, and lived happily ever afterward. But those who can conceive of a world outside of a wedding-ring may believe that the friends remained faithful friends all their lives, while Paul won fame and fortune, and Psyche grew beautiful with the beauty of a serene and sunny nature, happy in duties which became pleasures, rich in the art which made life lovely to herself and others, and brought rewards in time.

A COUNTRY CHRISTMAS

"A handful of good life is worth a bushel of learning."

"DEAR EMILY,—I have a brilliant idea, and at once hasten to share it with you. Three weeks ago I came up here to the wilds of Vermont to visit my old aunt, also to get a little quiet and distance in which to survey certain new prospects which have opened before me, and to decide whether I will marry a millionnaire and become a queen of society, or remain 'the charming Miss Vaughan' and wait till the conquering hero comes.

"Aunt Plumy begs me to stay over Christmas, and I have consented, as I always dread the formal dinner with which my guardian celebrates the day.

"My brilliant idea is this. I'm going to make it a real old-fashioned frolic, and won't you come and help me? You will enjoy it immensely I am sure, for Aunt is a character, Cousin Saul worth seeing, and Ruth a far prettier girl than any of the city rose-buds coming out this season. Bring Leonard Randal along with you to take notes for his new book; then it will be fresher and truer than the last, clever as it was.

"The air is delicious up here, society amusing, this old farmhouse full of treasures, and your bosom friend pining to embrace you. Just telegraph yes or no, and we will expect you on Tuesday.

"Ever yours,

"Sophie Vaughan."

"They will both come, for they are as tired of city life and as fond of change as I am," said the writer of the above, as she folded her letter and went to get it posted without delay.

Aunt Plumy was in the great kitchen making pies; a jolly old soul, with a face as ruddy as a winter apple, a cheery voice, and the kindest heart that ever beat under a gingham gown. Pretty Ruth was chopping the mince, and singing so gaily as she worked that the four-and-twenty immortal blackbirds could not have put more music into a pie than she did. Saul was piling wood into the big oven, and Sophie paused a moment on the threshold to look at him, for she always enjoyed the sight of this stalwart cousin, whom she likened to a Norse viking, with his fair hair and beard, keen blue eyes, and six feet of manly height, with shoulders that looked broad and strong enough to bear any burden.

His back was toward her, but he saw her first, and turned his flushed face to meet her, with the sudden lighting up it always showed when she approached.

"I've done it, Aunt; and now I want Saul to post the letter, so we can get a speedy answer."

"Just as soon as I can hitch up, cousin;" and Saul pitched in his last log, looking ready to put a girdle round the earth in less than forty minutes.

"Well, dear, I ain't the least mite of objection, as long as it pleases you. I guess we can stan' it ef your city folks can. I presume to say things will look kind of sing'lar to 'em, but I s'pose that's what they come for. Idle folks do dreadful queer things to amuse 'em;" and Aunt Plumy leaned on the rolling-pin to smile and nod with a shrewd twinkle of her eye, as if she enjoyed the prospect as much as Sophie did.

"I shall be afraid of 'em, but I'll try not to make you ashamed of me," said Ruth, who loved her charming cousin even more than she admired her.

"No fear of that, dear. They will be the awkward ones, and you must set them at ease by just being your simple selves, and treating them as if they were everyday people. Nell is very nice and jolly when she drops her city ways, as she must here. She will enter into the spirit of the fun at once, and I know you'll all like her. Mr. Randal is rather the worse for too much praise and petting, as successful people are apt to be, so a little plain talk and rough work will do him good. He is a true gentleman in spite of his airs and elegance, and he will take it all in good part, if you treat him like a man and not a lion."

"I'll see to him," said Saul, who had listened with great interest to the latter part of Sophie's speech, evidently suspecting a lover, and enjoying the idea of supplying him with a liberal amount of "plain talk and rough work."

"I'll keep 'em busy if that's what they need, for there will be a sight to do, and we can't get help easy up here. Our darters don't hire out much. Work to home till they marry, and don't go gaddin' 'round gettin' their heads full of foolish notions, and forgettin' all the useful things their mothers taught 'em."

Aunt Plumy glanced at Ruth as she spoke, and a sudden color in the girl's cheeks proved that the words hit certain ambitious fancies of this pretty daughter of the house of Basset.

"They shall do their parts and not be a trouble; I'll see to that, for you certainly are the dearest aunt in the world to let me take possession of you and yours in this way," cried Sophie, embracing the old lady with warmth.

Saul wished the embrace could be returned by proxy, as his mother's hands were too floury to do more than hover affectionately round the delicate face that looked so fresh and young beside her wrinkled one. As it could not be done, he fled temptation and "hitched up" without delay.

The three women laid their heads together in his absence, and Sophie's plan grew apace, for Ruth longed to see a real novelist and a fine lady, and Aunt Plumy, having plans of her own to further, said "Yes, dear," to every suggestion.

Great was the arranging and adorning that went on that day in the old farmhouse, for Sophie wanted her friends to enjoy this taste of country pleasures, and knew just what additions would be indispensable to their comfort; what simple ornaments would be in keeping with the rustic stage on which she meant to play the part of prima donna.

Next day a telegram arrived accepting the invitation, for both the lady and the lion. They would arrive that afternoon, as little preparation was needed for this impromptu journey, the novelty of which was its chief charm to these *blasé* people.

Saul wanted to get out the double sleigh and span, for he prided himself on his horses, and a fall of snow came most opportunely to beautify the landscape and add a new pleasure to Christmas festivities.

But Sophie declared that the old yellow sleigh, with Punch, the farm-horse, must be used, as she wished everything to be in keeping; and Saul obeyed, thinking he had never seen anything prettier than his cousin when she appeared in his mother's old-fashioned camlet cloak and blue silk pumpkin hood. He looked remarkably well himself in his fur coat, with hair and beard brushed till they shone like spun gold, a fresh color in his cheek, and the sparkle of amusement in his eyes, while excitement gave his usually grave face the animation it needed to be handsome.

Away they jogged in the creaking old sleigh, leaving Ruth to make herself pretty, with a fluttering heart, and Aunt Plumy to dish up a late dinner fit to tempt the most fastidious appetite.

"She has not come for us, and there is not even a stage to take us up. There must be some mistake," said Emily Herrick, as she looked about the shabby little station where they were set down.

"That is the never-to-be-forgotten face of our fair friend, but the bonnet of her grandmother, if my eyes do not deceive me," answered Randal, turning to survey the couple approaching in the rear.

"Sophie Vaughan, what do you mean by making such a guy of yourself?" exclaimed Emily, as she kissed the smiling face in the hood and stared at the quaint cloak.

"I'm dressed for my part, and I intend to keep it up. This is our host, my cousin, Saul Basset. Come to the sleigh at once, he will see to your luggage," said Sophie, painfully conscious of the antiquity of her array as her eyes rested on Emily's pretty hat and mantle, and the masculine elegance of Randal's wraps.

They were hardly tucked in when Saul appeared with a valise in one hand and a large trunk on his shoulder, swinging both on to a wood-sled that stood near by as easily as if they had been hand-bags.

"That is your hero, is it? Well, he looks it, calm and comely, taciturn and tall," said Emily, in a tone of approbation.

"He should have been named Samson or Goliath; though I believe it was the small man who slung things about and turned out the hero in the end," added Randal, surveying the performance with interest and a touch of envy, for much pen work had made his own hands as delicate as a woman's.

"Saul doesn't live in a glass house, so stones won't hurt him. Remember sarcasm is forbidden and sincerity the order of the day. You are country folks now, and it will do you good to try their simple, honest ways for a few days."

Sophie had no time to say more, for Saul came up and drove off with the brief remark that the baggage would "be along right away."

Being hungry, cold and tired, the guests were rather silent during the short drive, but Aunt Plumy's hospitable welcome, and the savory fumes of the dinner awaiting them, thawed the ice and won their hearts at once.

"Isn't it nice? Aren't you glad you came?" asked Sophie, as she led her friends into the parlor, which she had redeemed from its primness by putting bright chintz curtains to the windows, hemlock boughs over the old portraits, a china bowl of flowers on the table, and a splendid fire on the wide hearth.

"It is perfectly jolly, and this is the way I begin to enjoy myself," answered Emily, sitting down upon the home-made rug, whose red flannel roses bloomed in a blue list basket.

"If I may add a little smoke to your glorious fire, it will be quite perfect. Won't Samson join me?" asked Randal, waiting for permission, cigar-case in hand.

"He has no small vices, but you may indulge yours," answered Sophie, from the depths of a grandmotherly chair.

Emily glanced up at her friend as if she caught a new tone in her voice, then turned to the fire again with a wise little nod, as if confiding some secret to the reflection of herself in the bright brass andiron.

"His Delilah does not take this form. I wait with interest to discover if he has one. What a daisy the sister is. Does she ever speak?" asked Randal, trying to lounge on the haircloth sofa, where he was slipping uncomfortably about.

"Oh yes, and sings like a bird. You shall hear her when she gets over her shyness. But no trifling, mind you, for it is a jealously guarded daisy and not to be picked by any idle hand," said Sophie warningly, as she recalled Ruth's blushes and Randal's compliments at dinner.

"I should expect to be annihilated by the big brother if I attempted any but the 'sincerest' admiration and respect. Have no fears on that score, but tell us what is to follow this superb dinner. An apple bee, spinning match, husking party, or primitive pastime of some sort, I have no doubt."

"As you are new to our ways I am going to let you rest this evening. We will sit about the fire and tell stories. Aunt is a master hand at that, and Saul has reminiscences of the war that are well worth hearing if we can only get him to tell them."

"Ah, he was there, was he?"

"Yes, all through it, and is Major Basset, though he likes his plain name best. He fought splendidly and had several wounds, though only a mere boy when he earned his scars and bars. I'm very proud of him for that," and Sophie looked so as she glanced at the photograph of a stripling in uniform set in the place of honor on the high mantel-piece.

"We must stir him up and hear these martial memories. I want some new incidents, and shall book all I can get, if I may."

Here Randal was interrupted by Saul himself, who came in with an armful of wood for the fire.

"Anything more I can do for you, cousin?" he asked, surveying the scene with a rather wistful look.

"Only come and sit with us and talk over war times with Mr. Randal."

"When I've foddered the cattle and done my chores I'd be pleased to. What regiment were you in?" asked Saul, looking down from his lofty height upon the slender gentleman, who answered briefly,—

"In none. I was abroad at the time."

"Sick?"

"No, busy with a novel."

"Took four years to write it?"

"I was obliged to travel and study before I could finish it. These things take more time to work up than outsiders would believe."

"Seems to me our war was a finer story than any you could find in Europe, and the best way to study it would be to fight it out. If you want heroes and heroines you'd have found plenty of 'em there."

"I have no doubt of it, and shall be glad to atone for my seeming neglect of them by hearing about your own exploits, Major."

Randal hoped to turn the conversation gracefully; but Saul was not to be caught, and left the room, saying, with a gleam of fun in his eye,—

"I can't stop now; heroes can wait, pigs can't."

The girls laughed at this sudden descent from the sublime to the ridiculous, and Randal joined them, feeling his condescension had not been unobserved.

As if drawn by the merry sound Aunt Plumy appeared, and being established in the rocking-chair fell to talking as easily as if she had known her guests for years.

"Laugh away, young folks, that's better for digestion than any of the messes people use. Are you troubled with dyspepsy, dear? You didn't seem to take your vittles very hearty, so I mistrusted you was delicate," she said, looking at Emily, whose pale cheeks and weary eyes told the story of late hours and a gay life.

"I haven't eaten so much for years, I assure you, Mrs. Basset; but it was impossible to taste all your good things. I am not dyspeptic, thank you, but a little seedy and tired, for I've been working rather hard lately."

"Be you a teacher? or have you a 'perfessun,' as they call a trade nowadays?" asked the old lady in a tone of kindly interest, which prevented a laugh at the idea of Emily's being anything but a beauty and a belle. The others kept their countenances with difficulty, and she answered demurely, —

"I have no trade as yet, but I dare say I should be happier if I had."

"Not a doubt on't, my dear."

"What would you recommend, ma'am?"

"I should say dressmakin' was rather in your line, ain't it. Your clothes is dreadful tasty, and do you credit if you made 'em yourself," and Aunt Plumy surveyed with feminine interest the simple elegance of the travelling dress which was the masterpiece of a French modiste.

"No, ma'am, I don't make my own things, I'm too lazy. It takes so much time and trouble to select them that I have only strength left to wear them."

"Housekeepin' used to be the favorite perfessun in my day. It ain't fashionable now, but it needs a sight of trainin' to be perfect in all that's required, and I've an idee it would be a sight healthier and usefuller than the paintin' and music and fancy work young women do nowadays."

"But every one wants some beauty in their lives, and each one has a different sphere to fill, if one can only find it."

"'Pears to me there's no call for so much art when nater is full of beauty for them that can see and love it. As for 'spears' and so on, I've a notion if each of us did up our own little chores smart and thorough we needn't go wanderin' round to set the world to rights. That's the Lord's job, and I presume to say He can do it without any advice of ourn."

Something in the homely but true words seemed to rebuke the three listeners for wasted lives, and for a moment there was no sound but the crackle of the fire, the brisk click of the old lady's knitting needles, and Ruth's voice singing overhead as she made ready to join the party below.

"To judge by that sweet sound you have done one of your 'chores' very beautifully, Mrs. Basset, and in spite of the follies of our day, succeeded in keeping one girl healthy, happy and unspoiled," said Emily, looking up into the peaceful old face with her own lovely one full of respect and envy.

"I do hope so, for she's my ewe lamb, the last of four dear little girls; all the rest are in the burying ground 'side of father. I don't expect to keep her long, and don't ought to regret when I lose her, for Saul is the best of sons; but daughters is more to mothers somehow, and I always yearn over girls that is left without a broodin' wing to keep 'em safe and warm in this world of tribulation."

Aunt Plumy laid her hand on Sophie's head as she spoke, with such a motherly look that both girls drew nearer, and Randal resolved to put her in a book without delay.

Presently Saul returned with little Ruth hanging on his arm and shyly nestling near him as he took the three-cornered leathern chair in the chimney nook, while she sat on a stool close by.

"Now the circle is complete and the picture perfect. Don't light the lamps yet, please, but talk away and let me make a mental study of you. I seldom find so charming a scene to paint," said Randal, beginning to enjoy himself immensely, with a true artist's taste for novelty and effect.

"Tell us about your book, for we have been reading it as it comes out in the magazine, and are much exercised about how it's going to end," began Saul, gallantly throwing himself into the breach, for a momentary embarrassment fell upon the women at the idea of sitting for their portraits before they were ready.

"Do you really read my poor serial up here, and do me the honor to like it?" asked the novelist, both flattered and amused, for his work was of the æsthetic sort, microscopic studies of character, and careful pictures of modern life.

"Sakes alive, why shouldn't we," cried Aunt Plumy. "We have some eddication, though we ain't very genteel. We've got a town libry, kep up by the women mostly, with fairs and tea parties and so on. We have all the magazines reg'lar, and Saul reads out the pieces while Ruth sews and I knit, my eyes bein' poor. Our winter is long and evenins would be kinder lonesome if we didn't have novils and newspapers to cheer 'em up."

"I am very glad I can help to beguile them for you. Now tell me what you honestly think of my work? Criticism is always valuable, and I should really like yours, Mrs. Basset," said Randal, wondering what the good woman would make of the delicate analysis and worldly wisdom on which he prided himself.

Short work, as Aunt Plumy soon showed him, for she rather enjoyed freeing her mind at all times, and decidedly resented the insinuation that country folk could not appreciate light literature as well as city people.

"I ain't no great of a jedge about anything but nat'ralness of books, and it really does seem as if some of your men and women was dreadful uncomfortable creaters. 'Pears to me it ain't wise to be always pickin' ourselves to pieces and pryin' into things that ought to come gradual by way of experience and the visitations of Providence. Flowers won't blow worth a cent ef you pull 'em open. Better wait and see what they can do alone. I do relish the smart sayins, the odd ways of furrin parts, and the sarcastic slaps at folkses weak spots. But, massy knows, we can't live on spice-cake and Charlotte Ruche, and I do feel as if books was more sustainin' ef they was full of every-day people and things, like good bread and butter. Them that goes to the heart and ain't soon forgotten is the kind I hanker for. Mis Terry's books now, and Mis Stowe's, and Dickens's Christmas pieces,— them is real sweet and cheerin', to my mind."

As the blunt old lady paused it was evident she had produced a sensation, for Saul smiled at the fire, Ruth looked dismayed at this assault upon one of her idols, and the young ladies were both astonished and amused at the keenness of the new critic who dared express what they had often felt. Randal, however, was quite composed and laughed good-naturedly, though secretly feeling as if a pail of cold water had been poured over him.

"Many thanks, madam; you have discovered my weak point with surprising accuracy. But you see I cannot help 'picking folks to pieces,' as you have expressed it; that is my gift, and it has its attractions, as the sale of my books will testify. People like the 'spice-bread,' and as that is the only sort my oven will bake, I must keep on in order to make my living."

"So rumsellers say, but it ain't a good trade to foller, and I'd chop wood 'fore I'd earn my livin' harmin' my feller man. 'Pears to me I'd let my oven cool a spell, and hunt up some homely, happy folks to write about; folks that don't borrer trouble and go lookin' for holes in their neighbors' coats, but take their lives brave and cheerful; and rememberin' we are all human, have pity on the weak, and try to be as full of mercy, patience and lovin' kindness as Him who made us. That sort of a book would do a heap of good; be real warmin' and strengthenin', and make them that read it love the man that wrote it, and remember him when he was dead and gone."

"I wish I could!" and Randal meant what he said, for he was as tired of his own style, as a watch-maker might be of the magnifying glass through which he strains his eyes all day. He knew that the heart was left out of his work, and that both mind and soul were growing morbid with dwelling on the faulty, absurd and metaphysical phases of life and character. He often threw down his pen and vowed he would write no more; but he loved ease and the books brought money readily; he was accustomed to the stimulant of praise and missed it as the toper misses his wine, so that which had once been a pleasure to himself and others was fast becoming a burden and a disappointment.

The brief pause which followed his involuntary betrayal of discontent was broken by Ruth, who exclaimed, with a girlish enthusiasm that overpowered girlish bashfulness, —

"*I* think all the novels are splendid! I hope you will write hundreds more, and I shall live to read 'em."

"Bravo, my gentle champion! I promise that I will write one more at least, and have a heroine in it whom your mother will both admire and love," answered Randal, surprised to find how grateful he was for the girl's approval, and how rapidly his trained fancy began to paint the background on which he hoped to copy this fresh, human daisy.

Abashed by her involuntary outburst, Ruth tried to efface herself behind Saul's broad shoulder, and he brought the conversation back to its starting-point by saying in a tone of the most sincere interest, —

"Speaking of the serial, I am very anxious to know how your hero comes out. He is a fine fellow, and I can't decide whether he is going to spoil his life marrying that silly woman, or do something grand and generous, and not be made a fool of."

"Upon my soul, I don't know myself. It is very hard to find new finales. Can't you suggest something, Major? then I shall not be obliged to leave my story without an end, as people complain I am rather fond of doing."

"Well, no, I don't think I've anything to offer. Seems to me it isn't the sensational exploits that show the hero best, but some great sacrifice quietly made by a common sort of man who is noble without knowing it. I saw a good many such during the war, and often wish I could write them down, for it is surprising how much courage, goodness and real piety is stowed away in common folks ready to show when the right time comes."

"Tell us one of them, and I'll bless you for a hint. No one knows the anguish of an author's spirit when he can't ring down the curtain on an effective tableau," said Randal, with a glance at his friends to ask their aid in eliciting an anecdote or reminiscence.

"Tell about the splendid fellow who held the bridge, like Horatius, till help came up. That was a thrilling story, I assure you," answered Sophie, with an inviting smile.

But Saul would not be his own hero, and said briefly:

"Any man can be brave when the battle-fever is on him, and it only takes a little physical courage to dash ahead." He paused a moment, with his eyes on the snowy landscape without, where twilight was deepening;

then, as if constrained by the memory that winter scene evoked, he slowly continued,—

"One of the bravest things I ever knew was done by a poor fellow who has been a hero to me ever since, though I only met him that night. It was after one of the big battles of that last winter, and I was knocked over with a broken leg and two or three bullets here and there. Night was coming on, snow falling, and a sharp wind blew over the field where a lot of us lay, dead and alive, waiting for the ambulance to come and pick us up. There was skirmishing going on not far off, and our prospects were rather poor between frost and fire. I was calculating how I'd manage, when I found two poor chaps close by who were worse off, so I braced up and did what I could for them. One had an arm blown away, and kept up a dreadful groaning. The other was shot bad, and bleeding to death for want of help, but never complained. He was nearest, and I liked his pluck, for he spoke cheerful and made me ashamed to growl. Such times make dreadful brutes of men if they haven't something to hold on to, and all three of us were most wild with pain and cold and hunger, for we'd fought all day fasting, when we heard a rumble in the road below, and saw lanterns bobbing round. That meant life to us, and we all tried to holler; two of us, were pretty faint, but I managed a good yell, and they heard it.

"'Room for one more. Hard luck, old boys, but we are full and must save the worst wounded first. Take a drink, and hold on till we come back,' says one of them with the stretcher.

"'Here's the one to go,' I says, pointin' out my man, for I saw by the light that he was hard hit.

"'No, that one. He's got more chances than I, or this one; he's young and got a mother; I'll wait,' said the good feller, touchin' my arm, for he'd heard me mutterin' to myself about this dear old lady. We always want mother when we are down, you know."

Saul's eyes turned to the beloved face with a glance of tenderest affection, and Aunt Plumy answered with a dismal groan at the recollection of his need that night, and her absence.

"Well, to be short, the groaning chap was taken, and my man left. I was mad, but there was no time for talk, and the selfish one went off and left that poor feller to run his one chance. I had my rifle, and guessed I could hobble up to use it if need be; so we settled back to wait without much hope of help, everything being in a muddle. And wait we did till morning, for that ambulance did not come back till next day, when most of us were past needing it.

"I'll never forget that night. I dream it all over again as plain as if it was real. Snow, cold, darkness, hunger, thirst, pain, and all round us cries and cursing growing less and less, till at last only the wind went moaning over that meadow. It was awful! so lonesome, helpless, and seemingly God-forsaken. Hour after hour we lay there side by side under one coat, waiting to be saved or die, for the wind grew strong and we grew weak."

Saul drew a long breath, and held his hands to the fire as if he felt again the sharp suffering of that night.

"And the man?" asked Emily, softly, as if reluctant to break the silence.

"He *was* a man! In times like that men talk like brothers and show what they are. Lying there, slowly freezing, Joe Cummings told me about his wife and babies, his old folks waiting for him, all depending on him, yet all ready to give him up when he was needed. A plain man, but honest and true, and loving as a woman; I soon saw that as he went on talking, half to me and half to himself, for sometimes he wandered a little toward the end. I've read books, heard sermons, and seen good folks, but nothing ever came so close or did me so much good as seeing this man die. He had one chance and gave it cheerfully. He longed for those he loved, and let 'em go with a good-by they couldn't hear. He suffered all the pains we most shrink from without a murmur, and kept my heart warm while his own was growing cold. It's no use trying to tell that part of it; but I heard prayers that night that meant something, and I saw how faith could hold a soul up when everything was gone but God."

Saul stopped there with a sudden huskiness in his deep voice, and when he went on it was in the tone of one who speaks of a dear friend.

"Joe grew still by and by, and I thought he was asleep, for I felt his breath when I tucked him up, and his hand held on to mine. The cold sort of numbed me, and I dropped off, too weak and stupid to think or feel. I never should have waked up if it hadn't been for Joe. When I came to, it was morning, and I thought I was dead, for all I could see was that great field of white mounds, like graves, and a splendid sky above. Then I looked for Joe, remembering; but he had put my coat back over me, and lay stiff and still under the snow that covered him like a shroud, all except his face. A bit of my cape had blown over it, and when I took it off and the sun shone on his dead face, I declare to you it was so full of heavenly peace I felt as if that common man had been glorified by God's light, and rewarded by God's 'Well done.' That's all."

No one spoke for a moment, while the women wiped their eyes, and Saul dropped his as if to hide something softer than tears.

"It was very noble, very touching. And you? how did you get off at last?" asked Randal, with real admiration and respect in his usually languid face.

"Crawled off," answered Saul, relapsing into his former brevity of speech.

"Why not before, and save yourself all that misery?"

"Couldn't leave Joe."

"Ah, I see; there were two heroes that night."

"Dozens, I've no doubt. Those were times that made heroes of men, and women, too."

"Tell us more;" begged Emily, looking up with an expression none of her admirers ever brought to her face by their softest compliments or wiliest gossip.

"I've done my part. It's Mr. Randal's turn now;" and Saul drew himself out of the ruddy circle of firelight, as if ashamed of the prominent part he was playing.

Sophie and her friend had often heard Randal talk, for he was an accomplished *raconteur*, but that night he exerted himself, and was unusually brilliant and entertaining, as if upon his mettle. The Bassets were charmed. They sat late and were very merry, for Aunt Plumy got up a little supper for them, and her cider was as exhilarating as champagne. When they parted for the night and Sophie kissed her aunt, Emily did the same, saying heartily,—

"It seems as if I'd known you all my life, and this is certainly the most enchanting old place that ever was."

"Glad you like it, dear. But it ain't all fun, as you'll find out to-morrow when you go to work, for Sophie says you must," answered Mrs. Basset, as her guests trooped away, rashly promising to like everything.

They found it difficult to keep their word when they were called at half past six next morning. Their rooms were warm, however, and they managed to scramble down in time for breakfast, guided by the fragrance of coffee and Aunt Plumy's shrill voice singing the good old hymn—

"Lord, in the morning Thou shalt hear

My voice ascending high."

An open fire blazed on the hearth, for the cooking was done in the lean-to, and the spacious, sunny kitchen was kept in all its old-fashioned perfection, with the wooden settle in a warm nook, the tall clock behind the door, copper and pewter utensils shining on the dresser, old china in the corner closet and a little spinning wheel rescued from the garret by Sophie to adorn the deep window, full of scarlet geraniums, Christmas roses, and white chrysanthemums.

The young lady, in a checked apron and mob-cap, greeted her friends with a dish of buckwheats in one hand, and a pair of cheeks that proved she had been learning to fry these delectable cakes.

"You do 'keep it up' in earnest, upon my word; and very becoming it is, dear. But won't you ruin your complexion and roughen your hands if you do so much of this new fancy-work?" asked Emily, much amazed at this novel freak.

"I like it, and really believe I've found my proper sphere at last. Domestic life seems so pleasant to me that I feel as if I'd better keep it up for the rest of my life," answered Sophie, making a pretty picture of herself as she cut great slices of brown bread, with the early sunshine touching her happy face.

"The charming Miss Vaughan in the rôle of a farmer's wife. I find it difficult to imagine, and shrink from the thought of the wide-spread dismay such a fate will produce among her adorers," added Randal, as he basked in the glow of the hospitable fire.

"She might do worse; but come to breakfast and do honor to my handiwork," said Sophie, thinking of her worn-out millionnaire, and rather nettled by the satiric smile on Randal's lips.

"What an appetite early rising gives one. I feel equal to almost anything, so let me help wash cups," said Emily, with unusual energy, when the hearty meal was over and Sophie began to pick up the dishes as if it was her usual work.

Ruth went to the window to water the flowers, and Randal followed to make himself agreeable, remembering her defence of him last night. He was used to admiration from feminine eyes, and flattery from soft lips, but found something new and charming in the innocent delight which showed itself at his approach in blushes more eloquent than words, and shy glances from eyes full of hero-worship.

"I hope you are going to spare me a posy for to-morrow night, since I can be fine in no other way to do honor to the dance Miss Sophie proposes for us," he said, leaning in the bay window to look down on the little girl, with the devoted air he usually wore for pretty women.

"Anything you like! I should be so glad to have you wear my flowers. There will be enough for all, and I've nothing else to give to people who have made me as happy as cousin Sophie and you," answered Ruth, half drowning her great calla as she spoke with grateful warmth.

"You must make her happy by accepting the invitation to go home with her which I heard given last night. A peep at the world would do you good, and be a pleasant change, I think."

"Oh, very pleasant! but would it do me good?" and Ruth looked up with sudden seriousness in her blue eyes, as a child questions an elder, eager, yet wistful.

"Why not?" asked Randal, wondering at the hesitation.

"I might grow discontented with things here if I saw splendid houses and fine people. I am very happy now, and it would break my heart to lose that happiness, or ever learn to be ashamed of home."

"But don't you long for more pleasure, new scenes and other friends than these?" asked the man, touched by the little creature's loyalty to the things she knew and loved.

"Very often, but mother says when I'm ready they will come, so I wait and try not to be impatient." But Ruth's eyes looked out over the green leaves as if the longing was very strong within her to see more of the unknown world lying beyond the mountains that hemmed her in.

"It is natural for birds to hop out of the nest, so I shall expect to see you over there before long, and ask you how you enjoy your first flight," said Randal, in a paternal tone that had a curious effect on Ruth.

To his surprise, she laughed, then blushed like one of her own roses, and answered with a demure dignity that was very pretty to see.

"I intend to hop soon, but it won't be a very long flight or very far from mother. She can't spare me, and nobody in the world can fill her place to me."

"Bless the child, does she think I'm going to make love to her," thought Randal, much amused, but quite mistaken. Wiser women had thought so when he assumed the caressing air with which he beguiled them into the little revelations of character he liked to use, as the south wind makes flowers open their hearts to give up their odor, then leaves them to carry it elsewhere, the more welcome for the stolen sweetness.

"Perhaps you are right. The maternal wing is a safe shelter for confiding little souls like you, Miss Ruth. You will be as comfortable here as your flowers in this sunny window," he said, carelessly pinching geranium leaves, and ruffling the roses till the pink petals of the largest fluttered to the floor.

As if she instinctively felt and resented something in the man which his act symbolized, the girl answered quietly, as she went on with her work, "Yes, if the frost does not touch me, or careless people spoil me too soon."

Before Randal could reply Aunt Plumy approached like a maternal hen who sees her chicken in danger.

"Saul is goin' to haul wood after he's done his chores, mebbe you'd like to go along? The view is good, the roads well broke, and the day uncommon fine."

"Thanks; it will be delightful, I dare say," politely responded the lion, with a secret shudder at the idea of a rural promenade at 8 A.M. in the winter.

"Come on, then; we'll feed the stock, and then I'll show you how to yoke oxen," said Saul, with a twinkle in his eye as he led the way, when his new aide had muffled himself up as if for a polar voyage.

"Now, that's too bad of Saul! He did it on purpose, just to please you, Sophie," cried Ruth presently, and the girls ran to the window to behold Randal bravely following his host with a pail of pigs' food in each hand, and an expression of resigned disgust upon his aristocratic face.

"To what base uses may we come," quoted Emily, as they all nodded and smiled upon the victim as he looked back from the barn-yard, where he was clamorously welcomed by his new charges.

"It is rather a shock at first, but it will do him good, and Saul won't be too hard upon him, I'm sure," said Sophie, going back to her work, while Ruth turned her best buds to the sun that they might be ready for a peace-offering to-morrow.

There was a merry clatter in the big kitchen for an hour; then Aunt Plumy and her daughter shut themselves up in the pantry to perform some culinary rites, and the young ladies went to inspect certain antique costumes laid forth in Sophie's room.

"You see, Em, I thought it would be appropriate to the house and season to have an old-fashioned dance. Aunt has quantities of ancient finery stowed away, for great-grandfather Basset was a fine old gentleman and his family lived in state. Take your choice of the crimson, blue or silver-gray damask. Ruth is to wear the worked muslin and quilted white satin skirt, with that coquettish hat."

"Being dark, I'll take the red and trim it up with this fine lace. You must wear the blue and primrose, with the distracting high-heeled shoes. Have you any suits for the men?" asked Emily, throwing herself at once into the all-absorbing matter of costume.

"A claret velvet coat and vest, silk stockings, cocked hat and snuff-box for Randal. Nothing large enough for Saul, so he must wear his uniform. Won't Aunt Plumy be superb in this plum-colored satin and immense cap?"

A delightful morning was spent in adapting the faded finery of the past to the blooming beauty of the present, and time and tongues flew till the toot of a horn called them down to dinner.

The girls were amazed to see Randal come whistling up the road with his trousers tucked into his boots, blue mittens on his hands, and an unusual amount of energy in his whole figure, as he drove the oxen, while Saul laughed at his vain attempts to guide the bewildered beasts.

"It's immense! The view from the hill is well worth seeing, for the snow glorifies the landscape and reminds one of Switzerland. I'm going to make a sketch of it this afternoon; better come and enjoy the delicious freshness, young ladies."

Randal was eating with such an appetite that he did not see the glances the girls exchanged as they promised to go.

"Bring home some more winter-green, I want things to be real nice, and we haven't enough for the kitchen," said Ruth, dimpling with girlish delight as she imagined herself dancing under the green garlands in her grandmother's wedding gown.

It was very lovely on the hill, for far as the eye could reach lay the wintry landscape sparkling with the brief beauty of sunshine on virgin snow. Pines sighed overhead, hardy birds flitted to and fro, and in all the trodden spots rose the little spires of evergreen ready for its Christmas duty. Deeper in the wood sounded the measured ring of axes, the crash of falling trees, while the red shirts of the men added color to the scene, and a fresh wind brought the aromatic breath of newly cloven hemlock and pine.

"How beautiful it is! I never knew before what winter woods were like. Did you, Sophie?" asked Emily, sitting on a stump to enjoy the novel pleasure at her ease.

"I've found out lately; Saul lets me come as often as I like, and this fine air seems to make a new creature of me," answered Sophie, looking about her with sparkling eyes, as if this was a kingdom where she reigned supreme.

"Something is making a new creature of you, that is very evident. I haven't yet discovered whether it is the air or some magic herb among that green stuff you are gathering so diligently;" and Emily laughed to see the color deepen beautifully in her friend's half-averted face.

"Scarlet is the only wear just now, I find. If we are lost like babes in the woods there are plenty of Red-breasts to cover us with leaves," and Randal joined Emily's laugh, with a glance at Saul, who had just pulled his coat off.

"You wanted to see this tree go down, so stand from under and I'll show you how it's done," said the farmer, taking up his axe, not unwilling to gratify his guests and display his manly accomplishments at the same time.

It was a fine sight, the stalwart man swinging his axe with magnificent strength and skill, each blow sending a thrill through the stately tree, till its heart was reached and it tottered to its fall. Never pausing for breath Saul shook his yellow mane out of his eyes, and hewed away, while the drops stood on his forehead and his arm ached, as bent on distinguishing himself as if he had been a knight tilting against his rival for his lady's favor.

"I don't know which to admire most, the man or his muscle. One doesn't often see such vigor, size and comeliness in these degenerate days," said Randal, mentally booking the fine figure in the red shirt.

"I think we have discovered a rough diamond. I only wonder if Sophie is going to try and polish it," answered Emily, glancing at her friend, who stood a little apart, watching the rise and fall of the axe as intently as if her fate depended on it.

Down rushed the tree at last, and, leaving them to examine a crow's nest in its branches, Saul went off to his men, as if he found the praises of his prowess rather too much for him.

Randal fell to sketching, the girls to their garland-making, and for a little while the sunny woodland nook was full of lively chat and pleasant laughter, for the air exhilarated them all like wine. Suddenly a man came running from the wood, pale and anxious, saying, as he hastened by for help, "Blasted tree fell on him! Bleed to death before the doctor comes!"

"Who? who?" cried the startled trio.

But the man ran on, with some breathless reply, in which only a name was audible—"Basset."

"The deuce it is!" and Randal dropped his pencil, while the girls sprang up in dismay. Then, with one impulse, they hastened to the distant group, half visible behind the fallen trees and corded wood.

Sophie was there first, and forcing her way through the little crowd of men, saw a red-shirted figure on the ground, crushed and bleeding, and threw herself down beside it with a cry that pierced the hearts of those who heard it. In the act she saw it was not Saul, and covered her bewildered face as if to hide its joy. A strong arm lifted her, and the familiar voice said cheeringly,—

"I'm all right, dear. Poor Bruce is hurt, but we've sent for help. Better go right home and forget all about it."

"Yes, I will, if I can do nothing;" and Sophie meekly returned to her friends who stood outside the circle over which Saul's head towered, assuring them of his safety.

Hoping they had not seen her agitation, she led Emily away, leaving Randal to give what aid he could and bring them news of the poor wood-chopper's state.

Aunt Plumy produced the "camphire" the moment she saw Sophie's pale face, and made her lie down, while the brave old lady trudged briskly off with bandages and brandy to the scene of action. On her return she brought comfortable news of the man, so the little flurry blew over and was forgotten by all but Sophie, who remained pale and quiet all the evening, tying evergreen as if her life depended on it.

"A good night's sleep will set her up. She ain't used to such things, dear child, and needs cossetin'," said Aunt Plumy, purring over her until she was in her bed, with a hot stone at her feet and a bowl of herb tea to quiet her nerves.

An hour later, when Emily went up, she peeped in to see if Sophie was sleeping nicely, and was surprised to find the invalid wrapped in a dressing-gown writing busily.

"Last will and testament, or sudden inspiration, dear? How are you? faint or feverish, delirious or in the dumps! Saul looks so anxious, and Mrs. Basset hushes us all up so, I came to bed, leaving Randal to entertain Ruth."

As she spoke Emily saw the papers disappear in a portfolio, and Sophie rose with a yawn.

"I was writing letters, but I'm sleepy now. Quite over my foolish fright, thank you. Go and get your beauty sleep that you may dazzle the natives to-morrow."

"So glad, good night;" and Emily went away, saying to herself, "Something is going on, and I must find out what it is before I leave. Sophie can't blind *me*."

But Sophie did all the next day, being delightfully gay at the dinner, and devoting herself to the young minister who was invited to meet the distinguished novelist, and evidently being afraid of him, gladly basked in the smiles of his charming neighbor. A dashing sleigh-ride occupied the afternoon, and then great was the fun and excitement over the costumes.

Aunt Plumy laughed till the tears rolled down her cheeks as the girls compressed her into the plum-colored gown with its short waist, leg-of-mutton sleeves, and narrow skirt. But a worked scarf hid all deficiencies, and the towering cap struck awe into the soul of the most frivolous observer.

"Keep an eye on me, girls, for I shall certainly split somewheres or lose my head-piece off when I'm trottin' round. What would my blessed mother say if she could see me rigged out in her best things?" and with a smile and a sigh the old lady departed to look after "the boys," and see that the supper was all right.

Three prettier damsels never tripped down the wide staircase than the brilliant brunette in crimson brocade, the pensive blonde in blue, or the rosy little bride in old muslin and white satin.

A gallant court gentleman met them in the hall with a superb bow, and escorted them to the parlor, where Grandma Basset's ghost was discovered dancing with a modern major in full uniform.

Mutual admiration and many compliments followed, till other ancient ladies and gentlemen arrived in all manner of queer costumes, and the old house seemed to wake from its humdrum quietude to sudden music and merriment, as if a past generation had returned to keep its Christmas there.

The village fiddler soon struck up the good old tunes, and then the strangers saw dancing that filled them with mingled mirth and envy; it was so droll, yet so hearty. The young men, unusually awkward in their grandfathers' knee-breeches, flapping vests, and swallow-tail coats, footed it bravely with the buxom girls who were the prettier for their quaintness, and danced with such vigor that their high combs stood awry, their furbelows waved wildly, and their cheeks were as red as their breast-knots, or hose.

It was impossible to stand still, and one after the other the city folk yielded to the spell, Randal leading off with Ruth, Sophie swept away by Saul, and Emily being taken possession of by a young giant of eighteen, who spun her around with a boyish impetuosity that took her breath away. Even Aunt Plumy was discovered jigging it alone in the pantry, as if the music was too much for her, and the plates and glasses jingled gaily on the shelves in time to Money Musk and Fishers' Hornpipe.

A pause came at last, however, and fans fluttered, heated brows were wiped, jokes were made, lovers exchanged confidences, and every nook and corner held a man and maid carrying on the sweet game which is never out of fashion. There was a glitter of gold lace in the back entry, and a train of blue and primrose shone in the dim light. There was a richer crimson than that of the geraniums in the deep window, and a dainty shoe tapped the bare floor impatiently as the brilliant black eyes looked everywhere for the court gentleman, while their owner listened to the gruff prattle of an enamored boy. But in the upper hall walked a little white ghost as if waiting for some shadowy companion, and when a dark form appeared ran to take its arm, saying, in a tone of soft satisfaction,—

"I was so afraid you wouldn't come!"

"Why did you leave me, Ruth?" answered a manly voice in a tone of surprise, though the small hand slipping from the velvet coat-sleeve was replaced as if it was pleasant to feel it there.

A pause, and then the other voice answered demurely,—

"Because I was afraid my head would be turned by the fine things you were saying."

"It is impossible to help saying what one feels to such an artless little creature as you are. It does me good to admire anything so fresh and sweet, and won't harm you."

"It might if—"

"If what, my daisy?"

"I believed it," and a laugh seemed to finish the broken sentence better than the words.

"You may, Ruth, for I do sincerely admire the most genuine girl I have seen for a long time. And walking here with you in your bridal white I was just asking myself if I should not be a happier man with a home of my own and a little wife hanging on my arm than drifting about the world as I do now with only myself to care for."

"I know you would!" and Ruth spoke so earnestly that Randal was both touched and startled, fearing he had ventured too far in a mood of unwonted sentiment, born of the romance of the hour and the sweet frankness of his companion.

"Then you don't think it would be rash for some sweet woman to take me in hand and make me happy, since fame is a failure?"

"Oh, no; it would be easy work if she loved you. I know some one—if I only dared to tell her name."

"Upon my soul, this is cool," and Randal looked down, wondering if the audacious lady on his arm could be shy Ruth.

If he had seen the malicious merriment in her eyes he would have been more humiliated still, but they were modestly averted, and the face under the little hat was full of a soft agitation rather dangerous even to a man of the world.

"She is a captivating little creature, but it is too soon for anything but a mild flirtation. I must delay further innocent revelations or I shall do something rash."

While making this excellent resolution Randal had been pressing the hand upon his arm and gently pacing down the dimly lighted hall with the sound of music in his ears, Ruth's sweetest roses in his button-hole, and a loving little girl beside him, as he thought.

"You shall tell me by and by when we are in town. I am sure you will come, and meanwhile don't forget me."

"I am going in the spring, but I shall not be with Sophie," answered Ruth, in a whisper.

"With whom then? I shall long to see you."

"With my husband. I am to be married in May."

"The deuce you are!" escaped Randal, as he stopped short to stare at his companion, sure she was not in earnest.

But she was, for as he looked the sound of steps coming up the back stairs made her whole face flush and brighten with the unmistakable glow of happy love, and she completed Randal's astonishment by running into the arms of the young minister, saying with an irrepressible laugh, "Oh! John, why didn't you come before?"

The court gentleman was all right in a moment, and the coolest of the three as he offered his congratulations and gracefully retired, leaving the lovers to enjoy the tryst he had delayed. But as he went down stairs his brows were knit, and he slapped the broad railing smartly with his cocked hat as if some irritation must find vent in a more energetic way than merely saying, "Confound the little baggage!" under his breath.

Such an amazing supper came from Aunt Plumy's big pantry that the city guests could not eat for laughing at the queer dishes circulating through the rooms, and copiously partaken of by the hearty young folks.

Doughnuts and cheese, pie and pickles, cider and tea, baked beans and custards, cake and cold turkey, bread and butter, plum pudding and French bonbons, Sophie's contribution.

"May I offer you the native delicacies, and share your plate. Both are very good, but the china has run short, and after such vigorous exercise as you have had you must need refreshment. I'm sure I do!" said Randal, bowing before Emily with a great blue platter laden with two doughnuts, two wedges of pumpkin pie and two spoons.

The smile with which she welcomed him, the alacrity with which she made room beside her and seemed to enjoy the supper he brought, was so soothing to his ruffled spirit that he soon began to feel that there is no friend like an old friend, that it would not be difficult to name a sweet woman who would take him in hand and would make him happy if he cared to ask her, and he began to think he would by and by, it was so pleasant to sit in that green corner with waves of crimson brocade flowing over his feet, and a fine face softening beautifully under his eyes.

The supper was not romantic, but the situation was, and Emily found that pie ambrosial food eaten with the man she loved, whose eyes talked more eloquently than the tongue just then busy with a doughnut. Ruth kept away, but glanced at them as she served her company, and her own happy experience helped her to see that all was going well in that quarter. Saul and Sophie emerged from the back entry with shining countenances, but carefully avoided each other for the rest of the evening. No one observed this but Aunt Plumy from the recesses of her pantry, and she folded her hands as if well content, as she murmured fervently over a pan full of crullers, "Bless the dears! Now I can die happy."

Every one thought Sophie's old-fashioned dress immensely becoming, and several of his former men said to Saul with blunt admiration, "Major, you look to-night as you used to after we'd gained a big battle."

"I feel as if I had," answered the splendid Major, with eyes much brighter than his buttons, and a heart under them infinitely prouder than when he was promoted on the field of honor, for his Waterloo was won.

There was more dancing, followed by games, in which Aunt Plumy shone pre-eminent, for the supper was off her mind and she could enjoy herself. There were shouts of merriment as the blithe old lady twirled the platter, hunted the squirrel, and went to Jerusalem like a girl of sixteen; her cap in a ruinous condition, and every seam of the purple dress straining like sails in a gale. It was great fun, but at midnight it came to an end, and the young folks, still bubbling over with innocent jollity, went jingling away along the snowy hills, unanimously pronouncing Mrs. Basset's party the best of the season.

"Never had such a good time in my life!" exclaimed Sophie, as the family stood together in the kitchen where the candles among the wreaths were going out, and the floor was strewn with wrecks of past joy.

"I'm proper glad, dear. Now you all go to bed and lay as late as you like to-morrow. I'm so kinder worked up I couldn't sleep, so Saul and me will put things to rights without a mite of noise to disturb you;" and Aunt Plumy sent them off with a smile that was a benediction, Sophie thought.

"The dear old soul speaks as if midnight was an unheard-of hour for Christians to be up. What would she say if she knew how we seldom go to bed till dawn in the ball season? I'm so wide awake I've half a mind to pack a little. Randal must go at two, he says, and we shall want his escort," said Emily, as the girls laid away their brocades in the great press in Sophie's room.

"I'm not going. Aunt can't spare me, and there is nothing to go for yet," answered Sophie, beginning to take the white chrysanthemums out of her pretty hair.

"My dear child, you will die of ennui up here. Very nice for a week or so, but frightful for a winter. We are going to be very gay, and cannot get on without you," cried Emily, dismayed at the suggestion.

"You will have to, for I'm not coming. I am very happy here, and so tired of the frivolous life I lead in town, that I have decided to try a better one," and Sophie's mirror reflected a face full of the sweetest content.

"Have you lost your mind? experienced religion? or any other dreadful thing? You always were odd, but this last freak is the strangest of all. What will your guardian say, and the world?" added Emily in the awe-stricken tone of one who stood in fear of the omnipotent Mrs. Grundy.

"Guardy will be glad to be rid of me, and I don't care that for the world," cried Sophie, snapping her fingers with a joyful sort of recklessness which completed Emily's bewilderment.

"But Mr. Hammond? Are you going to throw away millions, lose your chance of making the best match in the city, and driving the girls of our set out of their wits with envy?"

Sophie laughed at her friend's despairing cry, and turning round said quietly,—

"I wrote to Mr. Hammond last night, and this evening received my reward for being an honest girl. Saul and I are to be married in the spring when Ruth is."

Emily fell prone upon the bed as if the announcement was too much for her, but was up again in an instant to declare with prophetic solemnity,—

"I knew something was going on, but hoped to get you away before you were lost. Sophie, you will repent. Be warned, and forget this sad delusion."

"Too late for that. The pang I suffered yesterday when I thought Saul was dead showed me how well I loved him. To-night he asked me to stay, and no power in the world can part us. Oh! Emily, it is all so sweet, so beautiful, that *everything* is possible, and I know I shall be happy in this dear old home, full of love and peace and honest hearts. I only hope you may find as true and tender a man to live for as my Saul."

Sophie's face was more eloquent than her fervent words, and Emily beautifully illustrated the inconsistency of her sex by suddenly embracing her friend, with the incoherent exclamation, "I think I have, dear! Your brave Saul is worth a dozen old Hammonds, and I do believe you are right."

It is unnecessary to tell how, as if drawn by the irresistible magic of sympathy, Ruth and her mother crept in one by one to join the midnight conference and add their smiles and tears, tender hopes and proud delight to the joys of that memorable hour. Nor how Saul, unable to sleep, mounted guard below, and meeting Randal prowling down to soothe his nerves with a surreptitious cigar found it impossible to help confiding to his attentive ear the happiness that would break bounds and overflow in unusual eloquence.

Peace fell upon the old house at last, and all slept as if some magic herb had touched their eyelids, bringing blissful dreams and a glad awakening.

"Can't we persuade you to come with us, Miss Sophie?" asked Randal next day, as they made their adieux.

"I'm under orders now, and dare not disobey my superior officer," answered Sophie, handing her Major his driving gloves, with a look which plainly showed that she had joined the great army of devoted women who enlist for life and ask no pay but love.

"I shall depend on being invited to your wedding, then, and yours, too, Miss Ruth," added Randal, shaking hands with "the little baggage," as if he had quite forgiven her mockery and forgotten his own brief lapse into sentiment.

Before she could reply Aunt Plumy said, in a tone of calm conviction, that made them all laugh, and some of them look conscious, —

"Spring is a good time for weddin's, and I shouldn't wonder if there was quite a number."

"Nor I;" and Saul and Sophie smiled at one another as they saw how carefully Randal arranged Emily's wraps.

Then with kisses, thanks and all the good wishes that happy hearts could imagine, the guests drove away, to remember long and gratefully that pleasant country Christmas.

ON PICKET DUTY

"Better late than never."

"WHAT air you thinkin' of, Phil?"

"My wife, Dick."

"So was I! Ain't it odd how fellers fall to thinkin' of thar little women, when they get a quiet spell like this?"

"Fortunate for us that we do get it, and have such memories to keep us brave and honest through the trials and temptations of a life like ours."

October moonlight shone clearly on the solitary tree, draped with gray moss, scarred by lightning and warped by wind, looking like a venerable warrior, whose long campaign was nearly done; and underneath was posted the guard of four. Behind them twinkled many camp-fires on a distant plain, before them wound a road ploughed by the passage of an army, strewn with the relics of a rout. On the right, a sluggish river glided, like a serpent, stealthy, sinuous, and dark, into a seemingly impervious jungle; on the left, a Southern swamp filled the air with malarial damps, swarms of noisome life, and discordant sounds that robbed the hour of its repose. The men were friends as well as comrades, for though gathered from the four quarters of the Union, and dissimilar in education, character, and tastes, the same spirit animated all; the routine of camp-life threw them much together, and mutual esteem soon grew into a bond of mutual good fellowship.

Thorn was a Massachusetts volunteer; a man who seemed too early old, too early embittered by some cross, for, though grim of countenance, rough of speech, cold of manner, a keen observer would have soon discovered traces of a deeper, warmer nature hidden behind the repellent front he turned upon the world. A true New Englander, thoughtful, acute, reticent, and opinionated; yet earnest withal, intensely patriotic, and often humorous, despite a touch of Puritan austerity.

Phil, the "romantic chap," as he was called, looked his character to the life. Slender, swarthy, melancholy-eyed, and darkly-bearded; with feminine features, mellow voice, and alternately languid or vivacious manners. A child of the South in nature as in aspect, ardent and proud; fitfully aspiring and despairing; without the native energy which moulds character and ennobles life. Months of discipline and devotion had done much for him, and some deep experience was fast ripening the youth into a man.

Flint, the long-limbed lumberman, from the wilds of Maine, was a conscript who, when government demanded his money or his life, calculated the cost, and decided that the cash would be a dead loss and the claim might be repeated, whereas the conscript would get both pay and plunder out of government, while taking excellent care that government got very little out of him. A shrewd, slow-spoken, self-reliant specimen, was Flint; yet something of the fresh flavor of the backwoods lingered in him still, as if Nature were loath to give him up, and left the mark of her motherly hand upon him, as she leaves it in a dry, pale lichen, on the bosom of the roughest stone.

Dick "hailed" from Illinois, and was a comely young fellow, full of dash and daring; rough and rowdy, generous and jolly, overflowing with spirits and ready for a free fight with all the world.

Silence followed the last words, while the friendly moon climbed up the sky. Each man's eye followed it, and each man's heart was busy with remembrances of other eyes and hearts that might be watching and wishing as theirs watched and wished. In the silence, each shaped for himself that vision of home that brightens so many camp-fires, haunts so many dreamers under canvas roofs, and keeps so many turbulent natures tender by memories which often are both solace and salvation.

Thorn paced to and fro, his rifle on his shoulder, vigilant and soldierly, however soft his heart might be. Phil leaned against the tree, one hand in the breast of his blue jacket, on the painted presentment of the face his fancy was picturing in the golden circle of the moon. Flint lounged on the sward, whistling softly as he whittled at a fallen bough. Dick was flat on his back, heels in air, cigar in mouth, and some hilarious notion in his mind, for suddenly he broke into a laugh.

"What is it, lad?" asked Thorn, pausing in his tramp, as if willing to be drawn from the disturbing thought that made his black brows lower and his mouth look grim.

"Thinkin' of my wife, and wishin' she was here, bless her heart! set me rememberin' how I see her fust, and so I roared, as I always do when it comes into my head."

"How was it? Come, reel off a yarn, and let's hear houw yeou hitched teams," said Flint, always glad to get information concerning his neighbors, if it could be cheaply done.

"Tellin' how we found our wives wouldn't be a bad game, would it, Phil?"

"I'm agreeable; but let's have your romance first."

"Devilish little of that about me or any of my doin's. I hate sentimental bosh as much as you hate slang, and should have been a bachelor to this day if I hadn't seen Kitty jest as I did. You see, I'd been too busy larkin' round to get time for marryin', till a couple of years ago, when I did up the job double-quick, as I'd like to do this thunderin' slow one, hang it all!"

"Halt a minute till I give a look, for this picket isn't going to be driven in or taken while I'm on guard."

Down his beat went Thorn, reconnoitring river, road, and swamp, as thoroughly as one pair of keen eyes could do it, and came back satisfied, but still growling like a faithful mastiff on the watch; performances which he repeated at intervals till his own turn came.

"I didn't have to go out of my own State for a wife, you'd better believe," began Dick, with a boast, as usual; "for we raise as fine a crop of girls thar as any State in or out of the Union, and don't mind raisin' Cain with any man who denies it. I was out on a gunnin' tramp with Joe Partridge, a cousin of mine,—poor old chap! he fired his last shot at Gettysburg, and died game in a way he didn't dream of the day we popped off the birds together. It ain't right to joke that way; I won't if I can help it; but a feller gets awfully kind of heathenish these times, don't he?"

"Settle up them scores byme-by; fightin' Christians is scurse raound here. Fire away, Dick."

"Well, we got as hungry as hounds half a dozen mile from home, and when a farmhouse hove in sight, Joe said he'd ask for a bite, and leave some of the plunder for pay. I was visitin' Joe, didn't know folks round, and backed out of the beggin' part of the job; so he went ahead alone. We'd come out of the woods behind the house, and while Joe was foragin', I took a reconnaissance. The view was fust-rate, for the main part of it was a girl airin' beds on the roof of a stoop. Now, jest about that time, havin' a leisure spell, I'd begun to think of marryin', and took a look at all the girls I met, with an eye to business. I s'pose every man has some sort of an idee or pattern of the wife he wants; pretty and plucky, good and gay was mine, but I'd never found it till I see Kitty; and as she didn't see me, I had the advantage and took an extra long stare."

"What was her good p'ints, hey?"

"Oh, well, she had a wide-awake pair of eyes, a bright, jolly sort of a face, lots of curly hair tumblin' out of her net, a trig little figger, and a pair of the neatest feet and ankles that ever stepped. 'Pretty,' thinks I; 'so far so good.' The way she whacked the pillers, shook the blankets, and pitched into the beds was a caution; specially one blunderin' old feather-bed that wouldn't do nothin' but sag round in a pig-headed sort of way, that would have made most girls get mad and give up. Kitty didn't, but just wrastled with it like a good one, till she got it turned, banged, and spread to suit her; then she plumped down in the middle of it, with a sarcy little nod and chuckle to herself, that tickled me mightily. 'Plucky,' thinks I, 'better 'n' better.' Jest then an old woman came flyin' out the back-door, callin', 'Kitty! Kitty! Squire Partridge's son's here, 'long with a friend; been gunnin', want luncheon, and I'm all in the suds; do come down and see to 'em.'

"'Where are they?' says Kitty, scrambling up her hair and settlin' her gown in a jiffy, as women have a knack of doin', you know.

"'Mr. Joe's in the front entry; the other man's somewheres round, Billy says, waitin' till I send word whether they can stop. I darsn't till I'd seen you, for I can't do nothin', I'm in such a mess,' says the old lady.

"'So am I, for I can't get in except by the entry window, and he'll see me,' says Kitty, gigglin' at the thoughts of Joe.

"'Come down the ladder, there's a dear. I'll pull it round and keep it stiddy,' says her mother.

"'Oh, ma, don't ask me!' says Kitty, with a shiver. 'I'm dreadfully scared of ladders since I broke my arm off this very one. It's so high, it makes me dizzy jest to think of.'

"'Well, then, I'll do the best I can; but I wish them boys was to Jericho!' says the old lady, with a groan, for she was fat and hot, had her gown pinned up, and was in a fluster generally. She was goin' off rather huffy, when Kitty called out,—

"'Stop, ma! I'll come down and help you, only ketch me if I tumble.'

"She looked scared but stiddy, and I'll bet it took as much grit for her to do it as for one of us to face a battery. It don't seem much to tell of, but I wish I may be hit if it wasn't a right down dutiful and clever thing to see done. When the old lady took her off at the bottom, with a good motherly hug, 'Good,' thinks I; 'what more do you want?'"

"A snug little property wouldn't a ben bad, I reckon," said Flint.

"Well, she had it, old skin-flint, though I didn't know or care about it then. What a jolly row she'd make if she knew I was tellin' the ladder part of the story! She always does when I get to it, and makes believe cry, with her head in my breast-pocket, or any such handy place, till I take it out and swear I'll never do so ag'in. Poor little Kit, I wonder what she's doin' now. Thinkin' of me, I'll bet."

Dick paused, pulled his cap lower over his eyes, and smoked a minute with more energy than enjoyment, for his cigar was out and he did not perceive it.

"That's not all, is it?" asked Thorn, taking a fatherly interest in the younger man's love passages.

"Not quite. 'Fore long, Joe whistled, and as I always take short cuts everywhar, I put in at the back-door, jest as Kitty come trottin' out of the pantry with a big berry-pie in her hand. I startled her, she tripped over the sill and down she come; the dish flew one way, the pie flopped into her lap, the juice spatterin' my boots and her clean gown. I thought she'd cry, scold, have hysterics, or some confounded thing or other; but she jest sat still a minute, then looked up at me with a great blue splash on her face, and went off into the good-naturedest gale of laughin' you ever heard in your life. That finished me. 'Gay,' thinks I; 'go in and win.' So I did; made love hand over hand, while I stayed with Joe; pupposed a fortnight after, married her in three months, and there she is, a tip-top little woman, with a pair of stunnin' boys in her arms!"

Out came a well-worn case, and Dick proudly displayed the likeness of a stout, much bejewelled young woman with two staring infants on her knee. In his sight, the poor picture was a more perfect work of art than any of Sir Joshua's baby-beauties, or Raphael's Madonnas, and the little story needed no better sequel than the young father's praises of his twins, the covert kiss he gave their mother when he turned as if to get a clearer light upon the face. Ashamed to show the tenderness that filled his honest heart, he hummed "Kingdom Coming," while relighting his cigar, and presently began to talk again.

"Now, then, Flint, it's your turn to keep guard, and Thorn's to tell his romance. Come, don't try to shirk; it does a man good to talk of such things, and we're all mates here."

"In some cases it don't do any good to talk of such things; better let 'em alone," muttered Thorn, as he reluctantly sat down, while Flint as reluctantly departed.

With a glance and gesture of real affection, Phil laid his hand upon his comrade's knee, saying in his persuasive voice, "Old fellow, it *will* do you good, because I know you often long to speak of something that weighs upon you. You've kept us steady many a time, and done us no end of kindnesses; why be too proud to let us give our sympathy in return, if nothing more?"

Thorn's big hand closed over the slender one upon his knee, and the mild expression, so rarely seen upon his face, passed over it as he replied, —

"I think I could tell you almost anything if you asked me that way, my boy. It isn't that I am too proud, — and you're right about my sometimes wanting to free my mind, — but it's because a man of forty don't just like to open out to young fellows, if there is any danger of their laughing at him, though he may deserve it. I guess there isn't now; and I'll tell you how I found my wife."

Dick sat up, and Phil drew nearer, for the earnestness that was in the man dignified his plain speech, and inspired an interest in his history, even before it was begun. Looking gravely at the river and never at his hearers, as if still a little shy of confidants, yet grateful for the relief of words, Thorn began abruptly: —

"I never hear the number eighty-four without clapping my hand to my left breast and missing my badge. You know I was on the police in New York, before the war, and that's about all you do know yet. One bitter cold night I was going my rounds for the last time, when, as I turned a corner, I saw there was a trifle of work to be done. It was a bad part of the city, full of dirt and deviltry; one of the streets led to a ferry, and at the corner an old woman had an apple-stall. The poor soul had dropped asleep, worn out with the cold, and there were her goods left with no one to watch 'em. Somebody was watching 'em, however; a girl, with a ragged shawl over her head, stood at the mouth of an alley close by, waiting for a chance to grab something. I'd seen her there when I went by before, and mistrusted she was up to some mischief; as I turned the corner, she put out her hand and cribbed an apple. She saw me the minute she did it, but neither dropped it nor ran, only stood stock still with the apple in her hand till I came up.

"'This won't do, my girl,' said I. I never could be harsh with 'em, poor things! She laid it back and looked up at me with a miserable sort of a smile, that made me put my hand in my pocket to fish for a nine-pence before she spoke.

"'I know it won't,' she says. 'I didn't want to do it, it's so mean, but I'm awful hungry, sir.'

"'Better run home and get your supper, then.'

"'I've got no home.'

"'Where do you live?'

"'In the street.'

"'Where do you sleep?'

"'Anywhere; last night in the lock-up, and I thought I'd get in there again, if I did that when you saw me. I like to go there, it's warm and safe.'

"'If I don't take you there, what will you do?'

"'Don't know. I could go over there and dance again as I used to, but being sick has made me ugly, so they won't have me, and no one else will take me because I have been there once.'

"I looked where she pointed, and thanked the Lord that they wouldn't take her. It was one of those low theatres that do so much damage to the like of her; there was a gambling place one side of it, an eating saloon the other. I was new to the work then, but though I'd heard about hunger and homelessness often enough, I'd never had this sort of thing, nor seen that look on a girl's face. A white, pinched face hers was, with frightened, tired-looking eyes, but so innocent! She wasn't more than sixteen, had been pretty once, I saw, looked sick and starved now, and seemed just the most helpless, hopeless little thing that ever was.

"'You'd better come to the Station for to-night, and we'll see to you to-morrow,' says I.

"'Thank you, sir,' says she, looking as grateful as if I'd asked her home. I suppose I did speak kind of fatherly. I ain't ashamed to say I felt so, seeing what a child she was; nor to own that when she put her little hand in mine, it hurt me to feel how thin and cold it was. We passed the eating-house where the red lights made her face as rosy as it ought to have been; there was meat and pies in the window, and the poor thing stopped to look. It was too much for her; off came her shawl, and she said in that coaxing way of hers,—

"'I wish you'd let me stop at the place close by and sell this; they'll give a little for it, and I'll get some supper. I've had nothing since yesterday morning, and maybe cold is easier to bear than hunger.'

"'Have you nothing better than that to sell?' I says, not quite sure that she wasn't all a humbug, like so many of 'em. She seemed to see that, and looked up at me again with such innocent eyes, I couldn't doubt her when she said, shivering with something beside the cold,—

"'Nothing but myself.' Then the tears came, and she laid her head down on my arm, sobbing,—'Keep me! oh, do keep me safe somewhere!'"

Thorn choked here, steadied his voice with a resolute hem! but could only add one sentence more, —

"That's how I found my wife."

"Come, don't stop thar. I told the whole o' mine, you do the same. Whar did you take her? how'd it all come round?"

"Please tell us, Thorn."

The gentler request was answered presently, very steadily, very quietly.

"I was always a soft-hearted fellow, though you wouldn't think it now, and when that little girl asked me to keep her safe, I just did it. I took her to a good woman whom I knew, for I hadn't any women folks belonging to me, nor any place but that to put her in. She stayed there till spring working for her keep, growing brighter, prettier, every day, and fonder of me, I thought. If I believed in witchcraft, I shouldn't think myself such a fool as I do now, but I don't believe in it, and to this day I can't understand how I came to do it. To be sure I was a lonely man, without kith or kin, had never had a sweetheart in my life, or been much with women since my mother died. Maybe that's why I was so bewitched with Mary, for she had little ways with her that took your fancy and made you love her whether you would or no. I found her father was an honest fellow enough, a fiddler in some theatre; that he'd taken good care of Mary till he died, leaving precious little but advice for her to live on. She'd tried to get work, failed, spent all she had, got sick, and was going to the bad, as the poor souls can hardly help doing with so many ready to give them a shove. It's no use trying to make a bad job better; so the long and short of it was, I thought she loved me; God knows I loved her! and I married her before the year was out."

"Show us her picture; I know you've got one; all the fellows have, though half of 'em won't own up."

"I've only got part of one. I once saved my little girl, and her picture once saved me."

From an inner pocket Thorn produced a woman's housewife, carefully untied it, though all its implements were missing but a little thimble, and from one of its compartments took a flattened bullet and the remnants of a picture.

"I gave her that the first Christmas after I found her. She wasn't as tidy about her clothes as I liked to see, and I thought if I gave her a handy thing like this, she'd be willing to sew. But she only made one shirt for me, and then got tired, so I keep it like an old fool, as I am. Yes, that's the bit of lead that would have done for me, if Mary's likeness hadn't been just where it was."

"You'll like to show her this when you go home, won't you?" said Dick, as he took up the bullet, while Phil examined the marred picture, and Thorn poised the little thimble on his big finger, with a sigh.

"How can I, when I don't know where she is, and camp is all the home I've got!"

The words broke from him like a sudden groan, when some old wound is rudely touched. Both of the young men started, both laid back the relics they had taken up, and turned their eyes from Thorn's face, across which swept a look of shame and sorrow, too significant to be misunderstood. Their silence assured him of their sympathy, and, as if that touch of friendliness unlocked his heavy heart, he eased it by a full confession. When he spoke again, it was with the calmness of repressed emotion, a calmness more touching to his mates than the most passionate outbreak, the most pathetic lamentation; for the coarse camp-phrases seemed to drop from his vocabulary; more than once his softened voice grew tremulous, and to the words "my little girl," there went a tenderness that proved how dear a place she still retained in that deep heart of his.

"Boys, I've gone so far; I may as well finish; and you'll see I'm not without some cause for my stern looks and ways; you'll pity me, and from you I'll take the comfort of it. It's only the old story,—I married her, worked for her, lived for her, and kept my little girl like a lady. I should have known that I was too old and sober for a young thing like that, for the life she led before the pinch came just suited her. She liked to be admired, to dress, and dance and make herself pretty for all the world to see; not to keep house for a quiet man like me. Idleness wasn't good for her, it bred discontent; then some of her old friends, who'd left her in her trouble, found her out when better times came round, and tried to get her back again. I was away all day, I didn't know how things were going, and she wasn't open with me, afraid she said; I was so grave, and hated theatres so. She got courage finally to tell me that she wasn't happy; that she wanted to dance again, and asked me if she mightn't. I'd rather have had her ask me to put her in a fire, for I *did* hate theatres, and was bred to; others think they're no harm. I do; and knew it was a bad life for a girl like mine. It pampers vanity, and vanity is the Devil's help with such; so I said No, kindly at first, sharp and stern when she kept on teasing. That roused her spirit. 'I will go!' she said, one day. 'Not while you are my wife,' I answered back; and neither said any more, but she gave me a look I didn't think she could, and I resolved to take her away from temptation before worse came of it.

"I didn't tell her my plan; but I resigned my place, spent a week or more finding and fixing a little home for her out in the wholesome country, where she'd be safe from theatres and disreputable friends, and maybe learn to love me better when she saw how much she was to me. It was coming summer, and I made things look as home-like and as pretty as I could. She liked flowers, and I fixed a garden for her; she was fond of pets, and I got her a bird, a kitten, and a dog to play with her; she fancied gay colors and tasty little matters, so I filled her rooms with all the handsome things I could afford, and when it was done, I was as pleased as any boy, thinking what happy times we'd have together and how pleased she'd be. Boys, when I went to tell her and to take her to her little home, she was gone."

"Who with?"

"With those cursed friends of hers; a party of them left the city just then; she was wild to go; she had money now, and all her good looks back again. They teased and tempted her; I wasn't there to keep her, and she went, leaving a line behind to tell me that she loved the old life more than the new; that my house was a prison, and she hoped I'd let her go in peace. That almost killed me; but I managed to bear it, for I knew most of the fault was mine; but it was awful bitter to think I hadn't saved her, after all."

"Oh, Thorn! what did you do?"

"Went straight after her; found her dancing in Philadelphia, with paint on her cheeks, trinkets on her neck and arms, looking prettier than ever; but the innocent eyes were gone, and I couldn't see my little girl in the bold, handsome woman twirling there before the footlights. She saw me, looked scared at first, then smiled, and danced on with her eyes upon me, as if she said, —

"'See! I'm happy now; go away and let me be.'

"I couldn't stand that, and got out somehow. People thought me mad, or drunk; I didn't care, I only wanted to see her once in quiet and try to get her home. I couldn't do it then nor afterwards by fair means, and I wouldn't by force. I wrote to her, promised to forgive her, begged her to come back, or let me keep her honestly somewhere away from me. But she never answered, never came, and I have never tried again."

"She wasn't worthy of you, Thorn; you jest forgit her."

"I wish I could! I wish I could!" In his voice quivered an almost passionate regret, and a great sob heaved his chest, as he turned his away to hide the love and longing, still so tender and so strong.

"Don't say that, Dick; such fidelity should make us charitable for its own sake. There is always time for penitence, always certainty of pardon. Take heart, Thorn, you may not wait in vain, and she may yet return to you."

"I know she will! I've dreamed of it, I've prayed for it; every battle I come out of safe makes me surer that I was kept for that, and when I've borne enough to atone for my part of the fault, I'll be repaid for all my patience, all my pain, by finding her again. She knows how well I love her still, and if there comes a time when she is sick and poor and all alone again, then she'll remember her old John, then she'll come home and let me take her in."

Hope shone in Thorn's melancholy eyes, and long-suffering, all-forgiving love beautified the rough, brown face, as he folded his arms and bent his gray head on his breast, as if the wanderer were already come.

The emotion which Dick scorned to show on his own account was freely manifested for another, as he sniffed audibly, and, boy-like, drew his sleeve across his eyes. But Phil, with the delicate perception of a finer nature, felt that the truest kindness he could show his friend was to distract his thoughts from himself, to spare him any comments, and lessen the embarrassment which would surely follow such unwonted confidence.

"Now I'll relieve Flint, and he will give you a laugh. Come on, Hiram, and tell us about your Bewlah."

The gentleman addressed had performed his duty by sitting on a fence and "righting up" his pockets, to beguile the tedium of his exile. Before his multitudinous possessions could be restored to their native sphere, Thorn was himself again, and on his feet.

"Stay where you are, Phil; I like to tramp, it seems like old times, and I know you're tired. Just forget all this I've been saying, and go on as before. Thank you, boys! thank you," and with a grasp of the two hands extended to him, he strode away along the path already worn by his own restless feet.

"It's done him good, and I'm glad of that; but I'd like to see the little baggage that bewitched the poor old boy, wouldn't you, Phil?"

"Hush! here's Flint."

"What's up naow? want me tew address the meetin', hey? I'm willin', only the laugh's ruther ag'inst me, ef I tell that story; expect you'll like it all the better fer that." Flint coiled up his long limbs, put his hands in his pockets, chewed meditatively for a moment, and then began, with his slowest drawl: —

"Waal, sir, it's pretty nigh ten year ago, I was damster daown tew Oldtaown, clos't to Banggore. My folks lived tew Bethel; there was only the old man, and Aunt Siloam, keepin' house fer him, seein' as I was the only chick he hed. I hedn't heared from 'em fer a long spell, when there come a letter sayin' the old man was breakin' up. He'd said it every spring fer a number er years, and I didn't mind it no more'n the breakin' up er the river; not so much, jest then; fer the gret spring drive was comin' on, and my hands was tew full to quit work all tew oncet. I sent word I'd be 'long 'fore a gret while, and byme-by I went. I ought tew hev gone at fust; but they'd sung aout 'Wolf!' so often I warn't scared; an' sure 'nuff the wolf did come at last. Father hed been dead and berried a week when I got there, and aunt was so mad she wouldn't write, nor scurcely speak tew me for a consider'ble spell. I didn't blame her a mite, and felt jest the wust kind; so I give in every way, and fetched her raound. Yeou see I hed a cousin who'd kind er took my place tew hum while I was off, an' the old man hed left him a good slice er his money, an' me the farm, hopin' to keep me there. He'd never liked the lumberin' bizness, an' hankered arfter me a sight, I faound. Waal, seein' haow 'twas, I tried tew please him, late as it was; but ef there was ennything I did spleen ag'inst it was farmin', 'specially arfter the smart times I'd ben hevin', up Oldtaown way. Yeou don't know nothin' abaout it; but ef yeou want tew see high dewin's, jest hitch onto a timber-drive an' go it daown along them lakes and rivers, say from Kaumchenungamooth tew Punnobscot Bay. Guess yeou'd see a thing or tew, an' find livin' on a log come as handy as ef you was born a turtle.

"Waal, I stood it one summer; but it was the longest kind of a job. Come fall I turned contry, darned the farm, and vaowed I'd go back tew loggin'. Aunt hed got fond er me by that time, and felt dreadful bad abaout my leavin' on her. Cousin Siah, as we called Josiah, didn't cotton tew the old woman, though he did tew her cash; but we hitched along fust-rate. She was 'tached tew the place, hated tew hev it let or sold, thought I'd go to everlastin' rewin ef I took tew lumberin' ag'in, an' hevin' a tidy little sum er money all her own, she took a notion tew buy me off. 'Hiram,' sez she, 'ef yeou'll stay to hum, merry some smart girl, an' kerry on the farm, I'll leave yeou the hull er my fortin. Ef yeou don't, I'll leave every cent on't tew Siah, though he ain't done as waal by me as yeou hev. Come,' sez she, 'I'm breakin' up like brother; I shan't wurry any one a gret while, and 'fore spring I dessay you'll hev cause tew rejice that yeou done as Aunt Si counselled yeou.'

"Now, that idee kinder took me, seein' I hedn't no overpaourin' love fer cousin; but I brewdid over it a spell 'fore I 'greed. Fin'lly, I said I'd dew it, as it warn't a hard nor a bad trade; and begun to look raound fer Mis Flint, Jr. Aunt was dreadf'l pleased; but 'mazin pertickler as tew who was goin' tew stan' in her shoes, when she was fetched up ag'inst the etarnal boom. There was a sight er likely women-folks raound taown; but aunt she set her foot daown that Mis Flint must be smart, pious, an good-natered; harnsome she didn't say nothin' abaout, bein' the humliest woman in the State er Maine. I hed my own calk'lations on that p'int, an' went sparkin' two or three er the pootiest gals, all that winter. I warn't in no hurry, fer merryin' is an awful resky bizness; an' I wan't goan to be took in by nobuddy. Some haouw I couldn't make up my mind which I'd hev, and kept dodgin', all ready to slew raound, an' hitch on tew ary one that seemed likeliest. 'Long in March, Aunt, she ketched cold, took tew her bed, got wuss, an' told me tew hurry up, fer nary cent should I hev, ef I warn't safely married 'fore she stepped out. I thought that was ruther craoudin' a feller; but I see she was goan sure, an' I'd got inter a way er considerin' the cash mine, so that it come hard to hear abaout givin' on 't up. Off I went that evenin' an' asked Almiry Nash ef she'd hev me. No, she wouldn't; I'd shilly-shallyed so long, she'd got tired er waitin' and took tew keepin' company with a doctor daown ter Banggore, where she'd ben visitin' a spell. I didn't find that as hard a nub to swaller, as I'd a thought I would, though Almiry was the richest, pootiest, and good-naterest of the lot. Aunt larfed waal, an' told me tew try ag'in; so a couple er nights arfter, I spruced up, an' went over to Car'line Miles's; she was as smart as old cheese, an' waal off intew the barg'in. I was just as sure she'd hev me, as I be that I'm gittin' the rewmatiz a settin' in this ma'sh. But that minx, Almiry, hed ben and let on abaout her own sarsy way er servin' on me, an' Car'line jest up an' said she warn't goan to hev annybuddy's leavin's; so daown I come ag'in.

"Things was gettin' desper't by that time; fer aunt was failin' rapid, an' the story hed leaked aout some way, so the hull taown was gigglin' over it. I thought I'd better quit them parts; but aunt she showed me her will all done complete, 'sceptin the fust name er the legatee. 'There,' sez she, 'it all depends on yeou, whether that place is took by Hiram or Josiah. It's easy done, an' so it's goan tew stan till the last minit.' That riled me consid'able, an' I streaked off tew May Jane Simlin's. She wan't very waal off, nor extra harnsome, but she was pious the worst kind, an' dreadf'l clever to them she fancied. But I was daown on my luck ag'in; fer at the fust word I spoke of merryin', she showed me the door, an' give me to understan' that she couldn't think er hevin' a man that warn't a church-member, that hadn't experienced religion, or even ben struck with conviction, an' all the rest on 't. Ef anny one hed a wanted tew hev seen a walkin' hornet's nest, they could hev done it cheap that night, as I went hum. I jest bounced intew the kitchen, chucked my hat intew one corner, my coat intew 'nother, kicked the cat, cussed the fire, drawed up a chair, and set scaoulin' like sixty, bein' tew mad fer talkin'. The young woman that was nussin' aunt,—Bewlah Blish, by name,—was a cooking grewel on the coals, and 'peared tew understan' the mess I was in; but she didn't say nothin', only blowed up the fire, fetched me a mug er cider, an' went raound so kinder quiet, and sympathizin', that I found the wrinkles in my temper gettin' smoothed aout 'mazin' quick; an' 'fore long I made a clean breast er the hull thing. Bewlah larfed, but I didn't mind her doin' on't, for she sez, sez she, real sort o' cunnin',—

"'Poor Hiram! they didn't use yeou waal. Yeou ought to hev tried some er the poor an' humly girls; they'd a been glad an' grateful fer such a sweetheart as yeou be.'

"I was good-natered ag'in by that time, an' I sez, larfin' along with her, 'Waal, I've got three mittens, but I guess I might's waal hev 'nother, and that will make two pair complete. Say, Bewlah, will yeou hev me?'

"'Yes, I will,' sez she.

"'Reelly?' sez I.

"'Solemn trew,' sez she.

"Ef she'd up an' slapped me in the face, I shouldn't hev ben more throwed aback, fer I never mistrusted she cared two chips for me. I jest set an' gawped; fer she was 'solemn trew,' I see that with half an eye, an' it kinder took my breath away. Bewlah drawed the grewel off the fire, wiped her hands, an' stood lookin' at me a minnet, then she sez, slow an' quiet, but tremblin' a little, as women hev a way er doin', when they've consid'able steam aboard,—

"'Hiram, other folks think lumberin' has spilt yeou; *I* don't; they call you rough an' rewd; *I* know you've got a real kind heart fer them as knows haow tew find it. Them girls give yeou up so easy, 'cause they never loved yeou, an' yeou give them up 'cause you only thought abaout their looks an' money. I'm humly, an' I'm poor; but I've loved yeou ever sence we went a-nuttin' years ago, an' yeou shook daown fer me, kerried my bag, and kissed me tew the gate, when all the others shunned me, 'cause my father drank an' I was shabby dressed, ugly, an' shy. Yeou asked me in sport, I answered in airnest; but I don't expect nothin' unless yeou mean as I mean. Like me, Hiram, or leave me, it won't make no odds in my lovin' of yeou, nor helpin' of yeou, ef I kin.'

"'T ain't easy tew say haouw I felt, while she was goin' on that way, but my idees was tumblin' raound inside er me, as ef half a dozen dams was broke loose all tew oncet. One thing was rather stiddier 'n the rest, an' that was that I liked Bewlah more 'n I knew. I begun tew see what kep' me loafin' tew hum so much, sence aunt was took daown; why I wan't in no hurry tew git them other gals, an' haow I come tew pocket my mittens so easy arfter the fust rile was over. Bewlah *was* humly, poor in flesh, dreadful freckled, hed red hair, black eyes, an' a gret mold side of her nose. But I'd got wonted tew her; she knowed my ways, was a fust rate housekeeper, real good-tempered, and pious without flingin' on't in yer face. She was a lonely creeter,—her folks bein' all dead but one sister, who didn't use her waal, an' somehow I kinder yearned over her, as they say in Scripter. For all I set an' gawped, I was coming raound fast, though I felt as I used tew, when I was goin' to shoot the rapids, kinder breathless an' oncertin, whether I'd come aout right side up or not. Queer, warn't it?"

"Love, Flint; that was a sure symptom of it."

"Waal, guess 't was; anyway I jumped up all of a sudden, ketched Bewlah raound the neck, give her a hearty kiss, and sung aout, 'I'll dew it sure's my name's Hi Flint!' The words was scarcely out of my maouth, 'fore daown come Dr. Parr. He'd ben up tew see aunt, an' said she wouldn't last the night threw, prob'ly. That give me a scare er the wust kind; an' when I told doctor haow things was, he sez, kinder jokin',—

"'Better git married right away, then. Parson Dill is tew come an' see the old lady, an' he'll dew both jobs tew oncet.'

"'Will yeou, Bewlah?' sez I.

"'Yes, Hiram, to 'blige yeou,' sez she.

"With that, I put it fer the license; got it, an' was back in less 'n half an haour, most tuckered aout with the flurry of the hull concern. Quick as I'd been, Bewlah hed faound time tew whip on her best gaoun, fix up her hair, and put a couple er white chrissanthymums intew her hand'chif pin. Fer the fust time in her life, she looked harnsome,—leastways *I* thought so,—with a pretty color in her cheeks, somethin' brighter 'n a larf shinin' in her eyes, and her lips smilin' an' tremblin', as she come to me an' whispered so 's 't none er the rest could hear,—

"'Hiram, don't yeou dew it, ef yeou'd ruther not. I've stood it a gret while alone, an' I guess I can ag'in.'

"Never yeou mind what I said or done abaout that; but we was married ten minutes arfter, 'fore the kitchen fire, with Dr. Parr an' aour hired man, fer witnesses; an' then we all went up tew aunt. She was goan fast, but she understood what I told her, hed strength tew fill up the hole in the will, an' to say, a-kissin' Bewlah, 'Yeou'll be a good wife, an' naow yeou ain't a poor one.'

"I couldn't help givin' a peek tew the will, and there I see not Hiram Flint nor Josiah Flint, but Bewlah Flint, wrote every which way, but as plain as the nose on yer face. 'It won't make no odds, dear,' whispered my wife, peekin' over my shoulder. 'Guess it won't!' sez I, aout laoud; 'I'm glad on't, and it ain't a cent more'n yeou derserve.'

"That pleased aunt. 'Riz me, Hiram,' sez she; an' when I'd got her easy, she put her old arms raound my neck, an' tried to say, 'God bless you, dear—,' but died a doin' of it; an' I ain't ashamed tew say I boo-hooed real hearty, when I laid her daown, fer she was dreadf'l good tew me, an' I don't forgit her in a hurry."

"How's Bewlah?" asked Dick, after the little tribute of respect all paid to Aunt Siloam's memory, by a momentary silence.

"Fust-rate! that harum-scarum venter er mine was the best I ever made. She's done waal by me, hes Bewlah; ben a grand good haousekeeper, kin kerry on the farm better'n me, any time, an' is as dutif'l an' lovin' a wife as,—waal, as annything that *is* extra dutif'l and lovin'."

"Got any boys to brag of?"

"We don't think much o' boys daown aour way; they're 'mazin' resky stock to fetch up,—alluz breakin' baounds, gittin' intew the paound, and wurryin' your life aout somehaow 'nother. Gals naow doos waal; I've got six o' the likeliest the is goin', every one on 'em is the very moral of Bewlah,—red hair, black eyes, quiet ways, an' a mold 'side the nose. Baby's ain't growed yet; but I expect tew see it in a consid'able state o' forrardness, when I git hum, an' wouldn't miss it fer the world."

The droll expression of Flint's face, and the satisfied twang of his last words, were irresistible. Dick and Phil went off into a shout of laughter; and even Thorn's grave lips relapsed into a smile at the vision of six little Flints with their six little moles. As if the act were an established ceremony, the "paternal head" produced his pocket-book, selected a worn black-and-white paper, which he spread in his broad palm, and displayed with the air of a connoisseur.

"There, thet's Bewlah! we call it a cuttin'; but the proper name's a silly-hoot, I b'leeve. I've got a harnsome big degarrytype tew hum, but the heft on't makes it bad tew kerry raound, so I took this. I don't tote it abaout inside my shirt, as some dew,—it ain't my way; but I keep it in my wallet long with my other valleu'bles, and guess I set as much store by it as ef it was all painted up, and done off to kill."

The "silly-hoot" was examined with interest, and carefully stowed away again in the old brown wallet, which was settled in its place with a satisfied slap; then Flint said briskly,—

"Naouw, Phil, yeou close this interestin' and instructive meeting; and be spry, fer time's most up."

"I haven't much to tell, but must begin with a confession which I have often longed but never dared to make before, because I am a coward."

"Sho! who's goan to b'leeve that o' a man who fit like a wild-cat, wuz offered permotion on the field, and reported tew headquarters arfter his fust scrimmage. Try ag'in, Phil."

"Physical courage is as plentiful as brass buttons, nowadays, but moral courage is a rarer virtue; and I'm lacking in it, as I'll prove. You think me a Virginian; I'm an Alabamian by birth, and was a Rebel three months ago."

This confession startled his hearers, as he knew it would, for he had kept his secret well. Thorn laid his hand involuntarily upon his rifle, Dick drew off a little, and Flint illustrated one of his own expressions, for he "gawped." Phil laughed that musical laugh of his, and looked up at them with his dark face waking into sudden life, as he went on:—

"There's no treason in the camp, for I'm as fierce a Federalist as any of you now, and you may thank a woman for it. When Lee made his raid into Pennsylvania, I was a lieutenant in the—well, never mind what regiment, it hasn't signalized itself since, and I'd rather not hit my old neighbors when they are down. In one of the skirmishes during our retreat, I got a wound and was left for dead. A kind old Quaker found and took me home; but though I was too weak to talk, I had my senses by that time, and knew what went on about me. Everything was in confusion, even in that well-ordered place; no surgeon could be got at first, and a flock of frightened women thee'd and thou'd one another over me, but hadn't wit enough to see that I was bleeding to death. Among the faces that danced before my dizzy eyes was one that seemed familiar, probably because no cap surrounded it. I was glad to have it bending over me, to hear a steady voice say, 'Give me a bandage, quick!' and when none was instantly forthcoming to me, the young lady stripped up a little white apron she wore, and stanched the wound in my shoulder. I was not as badly hurt as I supposed, but so worn-out, and faint from loss of blood, they believed me to be dying, and so did I, when the old man took off his hat and said,—

"'Friend, if thee has anything to say, thee had better say it, for thee probably has not long to live.'

"I thought of my little sister, far away in Alabama, fancied she came to me, and muttered, 'Amy, kiss me good-by.' The women sobbed at that; but the girl bent her sweet compassionate face to mine, and kissed me on the forehead. That was my wife."

"So you seceded from Secession right away, to pay for that lip-service, hey?"

"No, Thorn, not right away,—to my shame be it spoken. I'll tell you how it came about. Margaret was not old Bent's daughter, but a Massachusetts girl on a visit, and a long one it proved, for she couldn't go till things were quieter. While she waited, she helped take care of me; for the good souls petted me like a baby when they found that a Rebel could be a gentleman. I held my tongue, and behaved my best to prove my gratitude, you know. Of course, I loved Margaret very soon. How could I help it? She was the sweetest woman I had ever seen, tender, frank, and spirited; all I had ever dreamed of and longed for. I did not speak of this, nor hope for a return, because I knew she was a hearty Unionist, and thought she only tended me from pity. But suddenly she decided to go home, and when I ventured to wish she would stay longer, she would not listen, and said, 'I must not stay; I should have gone before.'

"The words were nothing, but as she uttered them the color came up beautifully over all her face, and her eyes filled as they looked away from mine. Then I knew that she loved me, and my secret broke out against my will. Margaret was forced to listen, for I would not let her go, but she seemed to harden herself against me, growing colder, stiller, statelier, as I went on, and when I said in my desperate way,—

"'You should love me, for we are bid to love our enemies,' she flashed an indignant look at me and said,—

"'I will not love what I cannot respect! Come to me a loyal man, and see what answer I shall give you.'

"Then she went away. It was the wisest thing she could have done, for absence did more to change me than an ocean of tears, a year of exhortations. Lying there, I missed her every hour of the day, recalled every gentle act, kind word, and fair example she had given me. I contrasted my own belief with hers, and found a new significance in the words honesty and honor, and, remembering her fidelity to principle, was ashamed of my own treason to God and to herself. Education, prejudice, and interest, are difficult things to overcome, and that was the hottest fight I ever passed through, for as I tell you, I was a coward. But love and loyalty won the day, and, asking no quarter, the Rebel surrendered."

"Phil Beaufort, you're a brick!" cried Dick, with a sounding slap on his comrade's shoulder.

"A brand snatched from the burnin'. Hallelujah!" chanted Flint, seesawing with excitement.

"Then you went to find your wife? How? Where?" asked Thorn, forgetting vigilance in interest.

"Friend Bent hated war so heartily that he would have nothing to do with paroles, exchanges, or any martial process whatever, but bade me go when and where I liked, remembering to do by others as I had been done by. Before I was well enough to go, however, I managed, by means of Copperhead influence and returned prisoners, to send a letter to my father and receive an answer. You can imagine what both contained; and so I found myself penniless, but not poor, an outcast, but not alone. Old Bent treated me like a prodigal son, and put money in my purse; his pretty daughters loved me for Margaret's sake, and gave me a patriotic salute all round when I left them, the humblest, happiest man in Pennsylvania. Margaret once said to me that this was the time for deeds, not words; that no man should stand idle, but serve the good cause with head, heart, and hand, no matter in what rank; for in her eyes a private fighting for liberty was nobler than a dozen generals defending slavery. I remembered that, and, not having influential friends to get me a commission, enlisted in one of her own Massachusetts regiments, knowing that no act of mine would prove my sincerity like that. You should have seen her face when I walked in upon her, as she sat alone, busied with the army work, as I'd so often seen her sitting by my bed; it showed me all she had been suffering in silence, all I should have lost had I chosen darkness instead of light. She hoped and feared so much she could not speak, neither could I, but dropped my cloak, and showed her that, through love of her, I had become a soldier of the Union. How I love the coarse blue uniform! for when she saw it, she came to me without a word and kept her promise in a month."

"Thunder! what a harnsome woman!" exclaimed Flint, as Phil, opening the golden case that held his talisman, showed them the beautiful, beloved face of which he spoke.

"Yes! and a right noble woman too. I don't deserve her, but I will. We parted on our wedding-day, for orders to be off came suddenly, and she would not let me go until I had given her my name to keep. We were married in the morning, and at noon I had to go. Other women wept as we marched through the city, but my brave Margaret kept her tears till we were gone, smiling and waving her hand to me,—the hand that wore the wedding-ring,—till I was out of sight. That image of her is before me day and night, and day and night her last words are ringing in my ears,—

"'I give you freely, do your best. Better a true man's widow than a traitor's wife.'

"Boys, I've only stood on the right side for a month; I've only fought one battle, earned one honor; but I believe these poor achievements are an earnest of the long atonement I desire to make for five-and-twenty years of blind transgression. You say I fight well. Have I not cause to dare much?—for in owning many slaves, I too became a slave; in helping to make many freemen, I liberate myself. You wonder why I refused promotion. Have I any right to it yet? Are there not men who never sinned as I have done, and beside whose sacrifices mine look pitifully small? You tell me I have no ambition. I have the highest, for I desire to become God's noblest work,—an honest man,—living, to make Margaret happy in a love that every hour grows worthier of her own,—dying to make death proud to take me."

Phil had risen while he spoke, as if the enthusiasm of his mood lifted him into the truer manhood he aspired to attain. Straight and strong he stood up in the moonlight, his voice deepened by unwonted energy, his eye clear and steadfast, his whole face ennobled by the regenerating power of this late loyalty to country, wife, and self, and bright against the dark blue of his jacket shone the pictured face, the only medal he was proud to wear.

Ah, brave, brief moment, cancelling years of wrong! Ah, fair and fatal decoration, serving as a mark for a hidden foe! The sharp crack of a rifle broke the stillness of the night, and with those hopeful words upon his lips, the young man sealed his purpose with his life.

THE BARON'S GLOVES; OR, AMY'S ROMANCE

"All is fair in love and war."

I

HOW THEY WERE FOUND

"WHAT a long sigh! Are you tired, Amy?"

"Yes, and disappointed as well. I never would have undertaken this journey if I had not thought it would be full of novelty, romance, and charming adventures."

"Well, we have had several adventures."

"Bah! losing one's hat in the Rhine, getting left at a dirty little inn, and having our pockets picked, are not what *I* call adventures. I wish there were brigands in Germany—it needs something of that sort to enliven its stupidity."

"How can you call Germany stupid when you have a scene like this before you?" said Helen, with a sigh of pleasure, as she looked from the balcony which overhangs the Rhine at the hotel of the "Three Kings" at Coblentz. Ehrenbreitstein towered opposite, the broad river glittered below, and a mid-summer moon lent its enchantment to the landscape.

As she spoke, her companion half rose from the low chair where she lounged, and showed the pretty, piquant face of a young girl. She seemed in a half melancholy, half petulant mood; and traces of recent illness were visible in the languor of her movements and the pallor of her cheeks.

"Yes, it is lovely; but I want adventures and romance of some sort to make it quite perfect. I don't care what, if something would only happen."

"My dear, you are out of spirits and weary now, to-morrow you'll be yourself again. Do not be ungrateful to uncle or unjust to yourself. Something pleasant will happen, I've no doubt. In fact, something *has* happened that you may make a little romance out of, perhaps, for lack of a more thrilling adventure."

"What do you mean?" and Amy's listless face brightened.

"Speak low; there are balconies all about us, and we may be overheard," said Helen, drawing nearer after an upward glance.

"What is the beginning of a romance?" whispered Amy, eagerly.

"A pair of gloves. Just now, as I stood here, and you lay with your eyes shut, these dropped from the balcony overhead. Now amuse yourself by weaving a romance out of them and their owner."

Amy seized them, and stepping inside the window, examined them by the candle.

"A gentleman's gloves, scented with violets! Here's a little hole fretted by a ring on the third finger. Bless me! here are the initials, 'S. P.,' stamped on the inside, with a coat of arms below. What a fop to get up his gloves in this style! They are exquisite, though. Such a delicate color, so little soiled, and so prettily ornamented! Handsome hands wore these. I'd like to see the man."

Helen laughed at the girl's interest, and was satisfied if any trifle amused her *ennui*.

"I will send them back by the *kellner*, and in that way we may discover their owner," she said.

But Amy arrested her on the way to the door.

"I've a better plan; these waiters are so stupid you'll get nothing out of them. Here's the hotel book sent up for our names; let us look among the day's arrivals and see who 'S. P.' is. He came to-day, I'm sure, for the man said the rooms above were just taken, so we could not have them."

Opening the big book, Amy was soon intently poring over the long list of names, written in many hands and many languages.

"I've got it! Here he is—oh, Nell, he's a baron! Isn't that charming? 'Sigismund von Palsdorf, Dresden.' We *must* see him, for I know he's handsome, if he wears such distracting gloves."

"You'd better take them up yourself, then."

"You know I can't do that; but I shall ask the man a few questions, just to get an idea what sort of person the baron is. Then I shall change my mind and go down to dinner; shall look well about me, and if the baron is agreeable I shall make uncle return the gloves. He will thank us, and I can say I've known a real baron. That will be so nice when we go home. Now, don't be duennaish and say I'm silly, but let me do as I like, and come and dress."

Helen submitted, and when the gong pealed through the house, Major Erskine marched into the great *salle à manger*, with a comely niece on each arm. The long tables were crowded, and they had to run the gauntlet of many eyes as they made their way to the head of the upper table. Before she touched her soup, Amy glanced down the line of faces opposite, and finding none that answered the slight description elicited from the waiter, she leaned a little forward to examine those on her own side of the table. Some way down sat several gentlemen, and as she bent to observe them, one did the same, and she received an admiring glance from a pair of fine black eyes. Somewhat abashed, she busied herself with her soup; but the fancy had taken possession of her, and presently she whispered to Helen,—

"Do you see any signs of the baron?"

"On my left; look at the hands."

Amy looked and saw a white, shapely hand with an antique ring on the third finger. Its owner's face was averted, but as he conversed with animation, the hand was in full play, now emphasizing an opinion, now lifting a glass, or more frequently pulling at a blond beard which adorned the face of the unknown. Amy shook her head decidedly.

"I hate light men, and don't think that is the baron, for the gloves are a size too small for those hands. Lean back and look some four or five seats lower down on the right. See what sort of person the dark man with the fine eyes is."

Helen obeyed, but almost instantly bent to her plate again, smiling in spite of herself.

"That is an Englishman; he stares rudely, says 'By Jove!' and wears no jewelry or beard."

"Now, I'm disappointed. Well, keep on the watch, and tell me if you make any discoveries, for I *will* find the baron."

Being hungry, Amy devoted herself to her dinner, till dessert was on the table. She was languidly eating grapes, while Helen talked with the major, when the word "baron" caught her ear. The speakers sat at a table behind her, so that she could not see them without turning quite round, which was impossible; but she listened eagerly to the following scrap of chat:—

"Is the baron going on to-morrow?" asked a gay voice in French.

"Yes, he is bound for Baden-Baden. The season is at its height, and he must make his game while the ball is rolling, or it is all up with the open-handed Sigismund," answered a rough voice.

"Won't his father pardon the last escapade?" asked a third, with a laugh.

"No, and he is right. The duel was a bad affair, for the man almost died, and the baron barely managed to get out of the scrape through court influence. When is the wedding to be?"

"Never, Palsdorf says. There is everything but love in the bargain, and he swears he'll not agree to it. I like that."

"There is much nobleness in him, spite of his vagaries. He will sow his wild oats and make a grand man in time. By the by, if we are going to the fortress, we must be off. Give Sigismund the word; he is dining at the other table with Power," said the gay voice.

"Take a look at the pretty English girl as you go by; it will do your eyes good, after the fat Frauleins we have seen of late," added the rough one.

Three gentlemen rose, and as they passed Amy stole a glance at them; but seeing several pairs of eyes fixed on herself, she turned away blushing, with the not unpleasant consciousness that "the pretty English girl" was herself. Longing to see which Sigismund was, she ventured to look after the young men, who paused behind the man with the blond beard, and also touched the dark-eyed gentleman on the shoulder. All five went down the hall and stood talking near the door.

"Uncle, I wish to go," said Amy, whose will was law to the amiable major. Up he rose, and Amy added, as she took his arm, "I'm seized with a longing to go to Baden-Baden and see a little gambling. You are not a wild young man, so you can be trusted there."

"I hope so. Now you are a sensible little woman, and we'll do our best to have a gay time. Wait an instant till I get my hat."

While the major searched for the missing article the girls went on, and coming to the door, Amy tried to open it. The unwieldy foreign lock resisted her efforts, and she was just giving it an impatient little shake, when a voice said behind her, —

"Permit me, mademoiselle;" at the same moment a handsome hand turned the latch, the flash of a diamond shone before her, and the door opened.

"*Merci, monsieur,*" she murmured, turning as she went out; but Helen was close behind her, and no one else to be seen except the massive major in the rear.

"Did you see the baron?" she whispered eagerly, as they went up-stairs.

"No; where was he?"

"He opened the door for me. I knew him by his hand and ring. He was close to you."

"I did not observe him, being busy gathering up my dress. I thought the person was a waiter, and never looked at him," said Helen, with provoking indifference.

"How unfortunate! Uncle, you are going to see the fortress; we don't care for it; but I want you to take these gloves and inquire for Baron Sigismund Palsdorf. He will be there with a party of gentlemen. You can easily manage it, men are so free and easy. Mind what he is like, and come home in time to tell me all about it."

Away went the major, and the cousins sat on the balcony enjoying the lovely night, admiring the picturesque scene, and indulging in the flights of fancy all girls love, for Helen, in spite of her three-and-twenty years, was as romantic as Amy at eighteen. It was past eleven when the major came, and the only greeting he received was the breathless question,—

"Did you find him?"

"I found something much better than any baron, a courier. I've wanted one ever since we started; for two young ladies and their baggage are more than one man can do his duty by. Karl Hoffman had such excellent testimonials from persons I know, that I did not hesitate to engage him, and he comes to-morrow; so henceforth I've nothing to do but devote myself to you."

"How very provoking! Did you bring the gloves back?" asked Amy, still absorbed in the baron.

The major tossed them to her, and indulged in a hearty laugh at her girlish regrets; then bade them good-night, and went away to give orders for an early start next morning.

Tired of talking, the girls lay down in the two little white beds always found in German hotels, and Amy was soon continuing in sleep the romance she had begun awake. She dreamed that the baron proved to be the owner of the fine eyes; that he wooed and won her, and they were floating down the river to the chime of wedding-bells.

At this rapturous climax she woke to find the air full of music, and to see Helen standing tall and white in the moonlight that streamed in at the open window.

"Hush, hide behind the curtains and listen; it's a serenade," whispered Helen, as Amy stole to her side.

Shrouded in the drapery, they leaned and listened till the song ended, then Amy peeped; a dark group stood below; all were bare-headed, and now seemed whispering together. Presently a single voice rose, singing an exquisite little French canzonet, the refrain of which was a passionate repetition of the word "*Amie.*" She thought she recognized the voice, and the sound of her own name uttered in such ardent tones made her heart beat and her color rise, for it seemed to signify that the serenade was for them. As the last melodious murmur ceased, there came a stifled laugh from below, and something fell into the balcony. Neither dared stir till the sound of departing feet reassured them; then creeping forward Amy drew in a lovely bouquet of myrtle, roses, and great German forget-me-nots, tied with a white ribbon and addressed in a dashing hand to *La belle Helène.*

"Upon my life, the romance has begun in earnest," laughed Helen, as she examined the flowers. "You are serenaded by some unknown nightingale, and I have flowers tossed up to me in the charming old style. Of course it is the baron, Amy."

"I hope so; but whoever it is, they are regular troubadours, and I'm delighted. I know the gloves will bring us fun of some kind. Do you take one and I'll take the other, and see who will find the baron first. Isn't it odd that they knew our names?"

"Amy, the writing on this card is very like that in the big book. I may be bewitched by this mid-summer moonlight, but it really is very like it. Come and see."

The two charming heads bent over the card, looking all the more charming for the dishevelled curls and braids that hung about them as the girls laughed and whispered together in the softly brilliant light that filled the room.

"You are right; it is the same. The men who stared so at dinner are gay students perhaps, and ready for any prank. Don't tell uncle, but let us see what will come of it. I begin to enjoy myself heartily now—don't you?" said Amy, laying her glove carefully away.

"I enjoyed myself before, but I think 'La belle Helène' gives an added relish to life, *Amie,*" laughed Nell, putting her flowers in water; and then both went back to their pillows, to dream delightfully till morning.

II

KARL, THE COURIER

"Three days, at least, before we reach Baden. How tiresome it is that uncle won't go faster!" said Amy, as she tied on her hat next morning, wondering as she did so if the baron would take the same boat.

"As adventures have begun, I feel assured that they will continue to cheer the way; so resign yourself and be ready for anything," replied Helen, carefully arranging her bouquet in her travelling-basket.

A tap at the door, which stood half open, made both look up. A tall, brown, gentlemanly man, in a gray suit, with a leathern bag slung over his shoulder, stood there, hat in hand, and meeting Helen's eyes, bowed respectfully, saying in good English, but with a strong German accent,—

"Ladies, the major desired me to tell you the carriage waits."

"Why, who—" began Amy, staring with her blue eyes full of wonder at the stranger.

He bowed again, and said, simply,—

"Karl Hoffman, at your service, mademoiselle."

"The courier—oh, yes! I forgot all about it. Please take these things."

And Amy began to hand him her miscellaneous collection of bags, books, shawls and cushions.

"I'd no idea couriers were such decent creatures," whispered Amy, as they followed him along the hall.

"Don't you remember the raptures Mrs. Mortimer used to have over their Italian courier, and her funny description of him? 'Beautiful to behold, with a night of hair, eyes full of an infinite tenderness, and a sumptuous cheek.'"

Both girls laughed, and Amy averred that Karl's eyes danced with merriment as he glanced over his shoulder, as the silvery peal sounded behind him.

"Hush! he understands English; we must be careful," said Helen, and neither spoke again till they reached the carriage.

Everything was ready, and as they drove away, the major, leaning luxuriously back, exclaimed,—

"Now I begin to enjoy travelling, for I'm no longer worried by the thought of luggage, time-tables, trains, and the everlasting perplexity of thalers, kreutzers, and pfenniges. This man is a treasure; everything is done in the best manner, and his knowledge of matters is really amazing."

"He's a very gentlemanly-looking person," said Amy, eying a decidedly aristocratic foot through the front window of the carriage, for Karl sat up beside the driver.

"He *is* a gentleman, my dear. Many of these couriers are well born and educated, but, being poor, prefer this business to any other, as it gives them variety, and often pleasant society. I've had a long talk with Hoffman, and find him an excellent and accomplished fellow. He has lost his fortune, it seems, through no fault of his own, so being fond of a roving life, turned courier for a time, and we are fortunate to have secured him."

"But one doesn't know how to treat him," said Helen. "I don't like to address him as a servant, and yet it's not pleasant to order a gentleman about."

"Oh, it will be easy enough as we go on together. Just call him Hoffman, and behave as if you knew nothing about his past. He begged me not to mention it, but I thought you'd like the romance of the thing. Only don't either of you run away with him, as Ponsonby's daughter did with her courier, who wasn't a gentleman, by the way."

"Not handsome enough," said Amy. "I don't like blue eyes and black hair. His manners are nice, but he looks like a gipsy, with his brown face and black beard: doesn't he, Nell?"

"Not at all. Gipsies haven't that style of face; they are thin, sharp, and cunning in feature as in nature. Hoffman has large, well-moulded features, and a mild, manly expression, which gives one confidence in him."

"He has a keen, wicked look in his blue eyes, as you will see, Nell. I mean mischievously, not malignantly wicked. He likes fun, I'm sure, for he laughed about the 'sumptuous cheek' till his own were red, though he dared not show it, and was as grave as an owl when we met uncle," said Amy, smiling at the recollection.

"We shall go by boat to Biebrich, and then by rail to Heidelberg. We shall get in late to-morrow night, but can rest a day, and then on to Baden. Here we are; now make yourselves easy, as I do, and let Karl take care of everything."

And putting his hands in his pockets, the major strolled about the boat, while the courier made matters comfortable for the day. So easily and well did he do his duty, that both girls enjoyed watching him after he had established them on the shady side of the boat, with camp-stools for their feet, cushions to lean on, books and bags laid commodiously at hand.

As they sailed up the lovely Rhine they grew more and more enthusiastic in their admiration and curiosity, and finding the meagre description of the guide-books very unsatisfactory, Amy begged her uncle to tell her all the legends of picturesque ruin, rock and river, as they passed.

"Bless me, child, I know nothing; but here's Hoffman, a German born, who will tell you everything, I dare say. Karl, what's that old castle up there? The young ladies want to know about it."

Leaning on the railing, Hoffman told the story so well that he was kept explaining and describing for an hour, and when he went away to order lunch, Amy declared it was as pleasant as reading fairy tales to listen to his dramatic histories and legends.

At lunch the major was charmed to find his favorite wines and dishes without any need of consulting dictionary or phrase-book beforehand, or losing his temper in vain attempts to make himself understood.

On reaching Biebrich, tired and hungry, at nightfall, everything was ready for them, and all went to bed praising Karl, the courier, though Amy, with unusual prudence, added, —

"He is a new broom now; let us wait a little before we judge."

All went well next day till nightfall, when a most untoward accident occurred, and Helen's adventures began in earnest. The three occupied a *coupé*, and being weary with long sitting, Helen got out at one of the stations where the train paused for ten minutes. A rosy sunset tempted her to the end of the platform, and there she found, what nearly all foreign railway stations possess, a charming little garden.

Amy was very tired, rather cross, and passionately fond of flowers, so when an old woman offered to pull a nosegay for "the gracious lady," Helen gladly waited for it, hoping to please the invalid. Twice the whistle warned her, and at last she ran back, but only in time to see the train move away, with her uncle gesticulating wildly to the guard, who shook his stupid German head, and refused to see the dismayed young lady imploring him to wait for her.

Just as the train was vanishing from the station, a man leaped from a second-class carriage at the risk of his neck, and hurried back to find Helen looking pale and bewildered, as well she might, left alone and money-less at night in a strange town.

"Mademoiselle, it is I; rest easy; we can soon go on; a train passes in two hours, and we can telegraph to Heidelberg that they may not fear for you."

"Oh, Hoffman, how kind of you to stop for me! What should I have done without you, for uncle takes care of all the money, and I have only my watch."

Helen's usual self-possession rather failed her in the flurry of the moment, and she caught Karl's arm with a feminine little gesture of confidence very pleasant to see. Leading her to the waiting-room, he ordered supper, and put her into the care of the woman of the place, while he went to make inquiries and dispatch the telegram. In half an hour he was back again, finding Helen refreshed and cheerful, though a trace of anxiety was still visible in her watchful eyes.

"All goes excellently, mademoiselle. I have sent word to several posts along the road that we are coming by the night train, so that Monsieur le Major will rest tranquil till we meet. It is best that I give you some money, lest such a mishap should again occur; it is not likely so soon; nevertheless, here is both gold and silver. With this, one can make one's way everywhere. Now, if mademoiselle will permit me to advise, she will rest for an hour, as we must travel till dawn. I will keep guard without and watch for the train."

He left her, and having made herself comfortable on one of the sofas, she lay watching the tall shadow pass and repass door and window, as Karl marched up and down the platform, with the tireless tramp of a sentinel on duty. A pleasant sense of security stole over her, and with a smile at Amy's enjoyment of the adventure when it was over, Helen fell asleep.

A far-off shriek half woke her, and starting up, she turned to meet the courier coming in to wake her. Up thundered the train, every carriage apparently full of sleepy passengers, and the guard in a state of sullen wrath at some delay, the consequences of which would fall heaviest on him.

From carriage to carriage hurried Karl and his charge, to be met with everywhere by the cry, "All full," in many languages, and with every aspect of inhospitality. One carriage only showed two places; the other seats were occupied by six students, who gallantly invited the lady to enter. But Helen shrunk back, saying,—

"Is there no other place?"

"None, mademoiselle; this, or remain till morning," said Karl.

"Where will you go if I take this place?"

"Among the luggage,—anywhere; it is nothing. But we must decide at once."

"Come with me; I'm afraid to be locked in here alone," said Helen, desperately.

"Mademoiselle forgets I am her courier."

"I do not forget that you are a gentleman. Pray come in; my uncle will thank you."

"I will," and with a sudden brightening of the eyes, a grateful glance, and an air of redoubled respect, Hoffman followed her into the carriage.

They were off at once, and the thing was done before Helen had time to feel anything but the relief which the protection of his presence afforded her.

The young gentlemen stared at the veiled lady and her grim escort, joked under their breath, and looked wistfully at the suppressed cigars, but behaved with exemplary politeness till sleep overpowered them, and one after the other dropped off asleep to dream of their respective Gretchens.

Helen could not sleep, and for hours sat studying the unconscious faces before her, the dim landscape flying past the windows, or forgot herself in reveries.

Hoffman remained motionless and silent, except when she addressed him, wakeful also, and assiduous in making the long night as easy as possible.

It was past midnight, and Helen's heavy eyelids were beginning to droop, when suddenly there came an awful crash, a pang of mortal fear, then utter oblivion.

As her senses returned she found herself lying in a painful position under what had been the roof of the car; something heavy weighed down her lower limbs, and her dizzy brain rung with a wild uproar of shrieks and groans, eager voices, the crash of wood and iron, and the shrill whistle of the engine, as it rushed away for help.

Through the darkness she heard the pant as of some one struggling desperately, then a cry close by her, followed by a strong voice exclaiming, in an agony of suspense,—

"My God, will no one come!"

"Hoffman, are you there?" cried Helen, groping in the gloom, with a thrill of joy at the sound of a familiar voice.

"Thank heaven, you are safe. Lie still. I will save you. Help is coming. Have no fear!" panted the voice, with an undertone of fervent gratitude in its breathless accents.

"What has happened? Where are the rest?"

"We have been thrown down an embankment. The lads are gone for help. God only knows what harm is done."

Karl's voice died in a stifled groan, and Helen cried out in alarm, —

"Where are you? You are hurt?"

"Not much. I keep the ruins from falling in to crush us. Be quiet, they are coming."

A shout answered the faint halloo he gave as if to guide them to the spot, and a moment after, five of the students were swarming about the wreck, intent on saving the three whose lives were still in danger.

A lamp torn from some demolished carriage was held through an opening, and Helen saw a sight that made her blood chill in her veins. Across her feet, crushed and bleeding, lay the youngest of the students, and kneeling close beside him was Hoffman, supporting by main strength a mass of timber, which otherwise would fall and crush them all. His face was ghastly pale, his eyes haggard with suffering and suspense, and great drops stood upon his forehead. But as she looked, he smiled with a cheery, —

"Bear up, dear lady, we shall soon be out of danger. Now, lads, work with a will; my strength is going fast."

They did work like heroes, and even in her pain and peril, Helen admired the skill, energy, and courage of the young men, who, an hour ago, had seemed to have no ideas above pipes and beer. Soon Hoffman was free, the poor senseless youth lifted out, and then, as tenderly as if she were a child, they raised and set her down, faint but unhurt, in a wide meadow, already strewn with sad tokens of the wreck.

Karl was taken possession of as well as herself, forced to rest a moment, drink a cordial draught from some one's flask, and be praised, embraced, and enthusiastically blessed by the impetuous youths.

"Where is the boy who was hurt? Bring him to me. I am strong now. I want to help. I have salts in my pocket, and I can bind up his wounds," said Helen, soon herself again.

Karl and Helen soon brought back life and sense to the boy, and never had human face looked so lovely as did Helen's to the anxious comrades when she looked up in the moonlight with a joyful smile, and softly whispered, —

"He is alive."

For an hour terrible confusion reigned, then the panic subsided a little, and such of the carriages as were whole were made ready to carry away as many as possible; the rest must wait till a return train could be sent for them.

A struggle of course ensued, for every one wished to go on, and fear made many selfish. The wounded, the women and children, were taken, as far as possible, and the laden train moved away, leaving many anxious watchers behind.

Helen had refused to go, and had given her place to poor Conrad, thereby overwhelming his brother and comrades with gratitude. Two went on with the wounded lad; the rest remained, and chivalrously devoted themselves to Helen as a body-guard.

The moon shone clearly, the wide field was miles from any hamlet, and a desolate silence succeeded to the late uproar, as the band of waiters roamed about, longing for help and dawn.

"Mademoiselle, you shiver; the dew falls, and it is damp here; we must have a fire;" and Karl was away to a neighboring hedge, intent on warming his delicate charge if he felled a forest to do it.

The students rushed after him, and soon returned in triumph to build a glorious fire, which drew all forlorn wanderers to its hospitable circle. A motley assemblage; but mutual danger and discomfort produced mutual sympathy and good will, and a general atmosphere of friendship pervaded the party.

"Where is the brave Hoffman?" asked Wilhelm, the blond student, who, being in the Werther period of youth, was already madly in love with Helen, and sat at her feet catching cold in the most romantic manner.

"Behold me! The little ones cry for hunger, so I ransack the ruins and bring away my spoils. Eat, Kinder, eat and be patient."

As he spoke, Karl appeared with an odd collection of baskets, bags, and bottles, and with a fatherly air that won all the mothers, he gave the children whatever first appeared, making them laugh in spite of weariness and hunger by the merry speeches which accompanied his gifts.

"You too need something. Here is your own basket with the lunch I ordered you. In a sad state of confusion but still eatable. See, it is not bad," and he deftly spread on a napkin before Helen cold chicken, sandwiches, and fruit.

His care for the little ones as well as for herself touched her and made her eyes fill, as she remembered that she owed her life to him, and recalled the sight of his face in the overturned car.

Her voice trembled a little as she thanked him, and the moonlight betrayed her wet eyes. He fancied she was worn out with excitement and fatigue, and anxious to cheer her spirits, he whispered to Wilhelm and his mates,—

"Sing, then, comrades, and while away this tedious night. It is hard for all to wait so long, and the babies need a lullaby."

The young men laughed and sang as only German students can sing, making the night musical with blithe drinking songs, tender love-lays, battle-hymns, and Volkslieder sweeter than any songs across the water.

Every heart was cheered and warmed by the magic of the music, the babies fell asleep, strangers grew friendly, fear changed to courage, and the most forlorn felt the romance of that bivouac under the summer sky.

Dawn was reddening the east when a welcome whistle broke up the camp. Every one hurried to the railway, but Helen paused to gather a handful of blue forget-me-nots, saying to Hoffman, who waited with her wraps on his arm,—

"It has been a happy night, in spite of the danger and discomfort. I shall not soon forget it; and take these as a souvenir."

He smiled, standing bare-headed in the chilly wind, for his hat was lost, his coat torn, hair dishevelled, and one hand carelessly bound up in his handkerchief. Helen saw these marks of the night's labors and perils for the first time, and as soon as they were seated desired to see his hand.

"It is nothing,—a scratch, a mere scratch, I give you my word, mademoiselle," he began, but Wilhelm unceremoniously removed the handkerchief, showing a torn and bleeding hand which must have been exquisitely painful.

Helen turned pale, and with a reproachful glance skilfully bound it up again, saying, as she handed a silken scarf to Wilhelm,—

"Make of that a sling, please, and put the poor hand in it. Care must be taken, or harm will come of it."

Hoffman submitted in bashful silence, as if surprised and touched by the young lady's interest. She saw that, and added gratefully,—

"I do not forget that you saved my life, though you seem to have done so. My uncle will thank you better than I can."

"I already have my reward, mademoiselle," he returned, with a respectful inclination and a look she could neither understand nor forget.

III

AMY'S ADVENTURE

The excitement and suspense of the major and Amy can be imagined when news of the accident reached them. Their gratitude and relief were intense when Helen appeared next morning, with the faithful Hoffman still at his post, though no longer able to disguise the fact that he was suffering from his wound.

When the story had been told, Karl was put under the surgeon's care, and all remained at Heidelberg for several days to rest and recover.

On the afternoon of the last day the major and young ladies drove off to the castle for a farewell view. Helen began to sketch the great stone lion's head above the grand terrace, the major smoked and chatted with a party of English artists whom he had met, and Amy, with a little lad for a guide, explored the old castle to her heart's content.

The sun set, and twilight began to fall when Helen put up her pencils, and the major set off to find Amy, who had been appearing and disappearing in every nook and cranny of the half-ruined castle.

Nowhere could he find her, and no voice answered when he called. The other visitors were gone, and the place seemed deserted, except by themselves and the old man who showed the ruins.

Becoming alarmed lest the girl had fallen somewhere, or lost her way among the vaults where the famous Tun lies, the major called out old Hans with his lantern, and searched high and low.

Amy's hat, full of flowers and ferns, was found in the Lady's Walk, as the little terrace is called, but no other trace appeared, and Helen hurried to and fro in great distress, fearing all manner of dangers.

Meanwhile Amy, having explored every other part of the castle, went to take another look at the Tun, the dwarf, and the vaults.

Now little Anderl, her guide, had a great fear of ghosts, and legions were said to haunt the ruins after nightfall, so when Amy rambled on deeper and deeper into the gloom the boy's courage ebbed away with every step; yet he was ashamed to own his fear, seeing that she had none.

Amy wanted to see a certain cell, where a nun was said to have pined to death because she would not listen to the Margraf's love. The legend pleased the romantic girl, and forgetful of waning daylight, gathering damps, and Anderl's reluctant service, she ran on, up steps and down, delighted with little arched doors, rusty chains on the walls, glimpses of sky through shattered roofs, and all manner of mysterious nooks and corners. Coming at last to a narrow cell, with a stone table, and heavy bolts on the old door, she felt sure this was poor Elfrida's prison, and called Anderl to come on with his candle, for the boy had lighted one, for his own comfort rather than hers. Her call was unanswered, and glancing back, she saw the candle placed on the ground, but no Anderl.

"Little coward, he has run away," she said, laughing; and having satisfied her curiosity, turned to retrace her steps,—no easy task to one ignorant of the way, for vault after vault opened on both sides, and no path was discernible. In vain she tried to recall some landmark, the gloom had deepened and nothing was clear. On she hurried, but found no opening, and really frightened, stopped at last, calling the boy in a voice that woke a hundred echoes. But Anderl had fled home, thinking the lady would find her way back, and preferring to lose his kreutzers to seeing a ghost.

Poor Amy's bewilderment and alarm increased with every moment's delay, and hoping to come out somewhere, she ran on till a misstep jostled the candle from her hand and extinguished it.

Left in the dark, her courage deserted her, and she screamed desperately, like a lost child, and was fast getting into a state of frantic terror, when the sound of an approaching step reassured her.

Holding her breath, she heard a quick tread drawing nearer, as if guided by her cries, and, straining her eyes, she caught the outline of a man's figure in the gloom.

A sensation of intense joy rushed over her, and she was about to spring forward, when she remembered that as she could speak no German how could she explain her plight to the stranger, if he understand neither French nor English?

Fear took possession of her at the thought of meeting some rough peasant, or some rollicking student, to whom she could make no intelligible appeal or explanation.

Crouching close against the wall, she stood mute till the figure was very near. She was in the shadow of an angle, and the man paused, as if looking for the person who called for help.

"Who is lost here?" said a clear voice, in German.

Amy shrunk closer to the wall, fearing to speak, for the voice was that of a young man, and a low laugh followed the words, as if the speaker found the situation amusing.

"Mortal, ghost or devil, I'll find it," exclaimed the voice, and stepping forward, a hand groped for and found her.

"Lottchen, is it thou? Little rogue, thou shalt pay dearly for leading me such a chase."

As he spoke he drew the girl toward him, but with a faint cry, a vain effort to escape, Amy's terror reached its climax, and spent with fatigue and excitement, she lost consciousness.

"Who the deuce is it, then? Lottchen never faints on a frolic. Some poor little girl lost in earnest. I must get her out of this gloomy place at once, and find her party afterward."

Lifting the slight figure in his arms, the young man hurried on, and soon came out through a shattered gateway into the shrubbery which surrounds the base of the castle.

Laying her on the grass, he gently chafed her hands, eying the pale, pretty face meantime with the utmost solicitude.

At his first glimpse of it he had started, smiled and made a gesture of pleasure and surprise, then gave himself entirely to the task of recovering the poor girl whom he had frightened out of her senses.

Very soon she looked up with dizzy eyes, and clasping her hands imploringly, cried, in English, like a bewildered child,—

"I am lost! Oh, take me to my uncle."

"I will, the moment you can walk. Upon my soul, I meant to help you when I followed; but as you did not answer, I fancied it was Lottchen, the keeper's little girl. Pardon the fright I've caused you, and let me take you to your friends."

The true English accent of the words, and the hearty tone of sincerity in the apology, reassured Amy at once, and, rising, she said, with a faint smile and a petulant tone,—

"I was very silly, but my guide ran away, my candle went out, I lost the path, and can speak no German; so I was afraid to answer you at first; and then I lost my wits altogether, for it's rather startling to be clutched in the dark, sir."

"Indeed it is. I was very thoughtless, but now let me atone for it. Where is your uncle, Miss Erskine?" asked the stranger, with respectful earnestness.

"You know my name?" cried Amy in her impulsive way.

"I have that happiness," was the answer, with a smile.

"But I don't know *you*, sir;" and she peered at him, trying to see his face in the darkness, for the copse was thick, and twilight had come on rapidly.

"Not yet; I live in hope. Shall we go? Your uncle will be uneasy."

"Where are we?" asked Amy, glad to move on, for the interview was becoming too personal even for her, and the stranger's manner fluttered her, though she enjoyed the romance of the adventure immensely.

"We are in the park which surrounds the castle. You were near the entrance to it from the vaults when you fainted."

"I wish I had kept on a little longer, and not disgraced myself by such a panic."

"Nay, that is a cruel wish, for then I should have lost the happiness of helping you."

They had been walking side by side, but here were forced to pause on reaching a broken flight of steps, for Amy could not see the way before her.

"Let me lead you; it is steep and dark, but better than going a long way round through the dew," he said, offering his hand.

"Must we return by these dreadful vaults?" faltered Amy, shrinking back.

"It is the shortest and safest route, I assure you."

"Are you sure you know the way?"

"Quite sure. I have lived here by the week together. Do you fear to trust me?"

"No; but it is so dark, and everything is so strange to me. Can we get down safely? I see nothing but a black pit."

And Amy still hesitated, with an odd mixture of fear and coquetry.

"I brought you up in safety; shall I take you down again?" asked the stranger, with a smile flickering over his face.

Amy felt rather than saw it, and assuming an air of dignified displeasure, motioned him to proceed, which he did for three steps; then Amy slipped, and gladly caught by the arm extended to save her.

Without a word he took her hand and led her back through the labyrinth she had threaded in her bewilderment. A dim light filled the place, but with unerring steps her guide went on till they emerged into the courtyard.

Major Erskine's voice was audible, giving directions to the keeper, and Helen's figure visible as she groped among the shadows of the ruined chapel for her cousin.

"There are my friends. Now I am safe. Come and let them thank you," cried Amy, in her frank, childlike warmth of manner.

"I want no thanks—forgive me—adieu," and hastily kissing the little hand that had lain so confidingly in his, the stranger was gone.

Amy rushed at once to Helen, and when the lost lamb had been welcomed, chidden, and exulted over, they drove home, listening to the very brief account which Amy gave of her adventure.

"Naughty little gad-about, how could you go and terrify me so, wandering in vaults with mysterious strangers, like the Countess of Rudolstadt. You are as wet and dirty as if you had been digging a well, yet you look as if you liked it," said Helen, as she led Amy into their room at the hotel.

"I do," was the decided answer, as the girl pulled a handkerchief off her head, and began to examine the corners of it. Suddenly she uttered a cry and flew to the light, exclaiming,—

"Nell, Nell, look here! The same letters, 'S. P.', the same coat of arms, the same perfume—it was the baron!"

"What? who? are you out of your mind?" said Helen, examining the large, fine cambric handkerchief, with its delicately stamped initials under the stag's head, and three stars on a heart-shaped shield. "Where did you get it?" she added, as she inhaled the soft odor of violets shaken from its folds.

Amy blushed and answered shyly, "I didn't tell you all that happened before uncle, but now I will. My hat was left behind, and when I recovered my wits after my fright, I found this tied over my head. Oh, Nell, it was very charming there in that romantic old park, and going through the vaults with him, and having my hand kissed at parting. No one ever did that before, and I like it."

Amy glanced at her hand as she spoke, and stood staring at it as if struck dumb, for there on her forefinger shone a ring she had never seen before.

"Look! look! mine is gone, and this in its place! Oh, Nell, what shall I do?" she said, looking half frightened, half pleased.

Helen examined the ring and shook her head, for it was far more valuable than the little pearl one which it replaced. Two tiny hands of finest gold were linked together about a diamond of great brilliancy; and on the inside appeared again the initials, "S. P."

"How did it happen?" she asked, rather sternly.

"Upon my word, I don't know, unless he put it on while I was stupidly fainting. Rude man, to take advantage of me so. But, Nell, it is splendid, and what shall I do about it?"

"Tell uncle, find out the man and send back his things. It really is absurd, the manner in which German boys behave;" and Helen frowned, though she was strongly tempted to laugh at the whole thing.

"He was neither a German nor a boy, but an English gentleman, I'm sure," began Amy, rather offended.

"But 'S. P.' is a baron, you know, unless there are two Richmonds in the field," broke in Helen.

"I forgot that; never mind, it deepens the mystery; and after this performance, I'm prepared for any enormity. It's my fate; I submit," said Amy, tragically, as she waved her pretty hand to and fro, pleased with the flash of the ring.

"Amy, I think on the whole I won't speak to uncle. He is quick to take offence, especially where we are concerned. He doesn't understand foreign ways, and may get into trouble. We will manage it quietly ourselves."

"How, Nell?"

"Karl is discreet; we will merely say we found these things and wish to discover the owner. He may know this 'S. P.,' and, having learned his address, we can send them back. The man will understand; and as we leave to-morrow, we shall be out of the way before he can play any new prank."

"Have in Karl at once, for if I wear this lovely thing long I shall not be able to let it go at all. How dared the creature take such a liberty!" and Amy pulled off the ring with an expression of great scorn.

"Come into the *salon* and see what Karl says to the matter. Let me speak, or you will say too much. One must be prudent before—"

She was going to say "servants," but checked herself, and substituted "strangers," remembering gratefully how much she owed this man.

Hoffman came, looking pale, and with his hand in a sling, but was as gravely devoted as ever, and listened to Helen's brief story with serious attention.

"I will inquire, mademoiselle, and let you know at once. It is easy to find persons if one has a clue. May I see the handkerchief?"

Helen showed it. He glanced at the initials, and laid it down with a slight smile.

"The coat-of-arms is English, mademoiselle."

"Are you sure?"

"Quite so; I understand heraldry."

"But the initials stand for Sigismund Palsdorf, and we know he is a German baron," broke in Amy, forgetting prudence in eagerness.

"If mademoiselle knows the name and title of this gentleman it will not be hard to find him."

"We only fancy it is the same because of the initials. I dare say it is a mistake, and the man is English. Inquire quietly, Hoffman, if you please, as this ring is of value, and I wish to restore it to its owner," said Helen, rather sharply.

"I shall do so, mademoiselle," and with his gentlemanly bow, the courier left the room.

"Bless me, what's that?" cried Amy, a moment afterward, as a ringing laugh echoed through the corridor,—a laugh so full of hearty and infectious merriment that both girls smiled involuntarily, and Amy peeped out to see who the blithe personage might be.

An old gentleman was entering his room near by, and Karl was just about to descend the stairs. Both looked back at the girlish face peeping at them, but both were quite grave, and the peal of laughter remained a mystery, like all the rest of it.

Late in the evening Hoffman returned to report that a party of young Englishmen had visited the castle that afternoon, and had left by the evening train. One of them had been named Samuel Peters, and he, doubtless, was the owner of the ring.

A humorous expression lurked in the courier's eye as he made his report, and heard Amy exclaim, in a tone of disgust and comical despair,—

"Samuel Peters! That spoils all the romance and dims the beauty of the diamond. To think that a Peters should be the hero to whom I owe my safety, and a Samuel should leave me this token of regard!"

"Hush, Amy," whispered Helen. "Thanks, Hoffman; we must wait now for chance to help us."

IV

A POLISH EXILE

"Room for one here, sir," said the guard, as the train stopped at Carlsruhe next day, on its way from Heidelberg to Baden.

The major put down his guide-book, Amy opened her eyes, and Helen removed her shawl from the opposite seat, as a young man, wrapped in a cloak, with a green shade over his eyes, and a general air of feebleness, got in and sank back with a sigh of weariness or pain. Evidently an invalid, for his face was thin and pale, his dark hair cropped short, and the ungloved hand attenuated and delicate as a woman's. A sidelong glance from under the deep shade seemed to satisfy him regarding his neighbors, and drawing his cloak about him with a slight shiver, he leaned into the corner and seemed to forget that he was not alone.

Helen and Amy exchanged glances of compassionate interest, for women always pity invalids, especially if young, comely and of the opposite sex. The major took one look, shrugged his shoulders, and returned to his book.

Presently a hollow cough gave Helen a pretext for discovering the nationality of the new-comer.

"Do the open windows inconvenience you, sir?" she asked, in English.

No answer; the question evidently unintelligible.

She repeated it in French, lightly touching his cloak to arrest his attention.

Instantly a smile broke over the handsome mouth, and in the purest French he assured her that the fresh air was most agreeable, and begged pardon for annoying them with his troublesome cough.

"Not an invalid, I hope, sir?" said the major, in his bluff yet kindly voice.

"They tell me I can have no other fate; that my malady is fatal; but I still hope and fight for my life; it is all I have to give my country now."

A stifled sigh and a sad emphasis on the last word roused the sympathy of the girls, the interest of the major.

He took another survey, and said, with a tone of satisfaction, as he marked the martial carriage of the young man, and caught a fiery glance of the half-hidden eyes, —

"You are a soldier, sir?"

"I was; I am nothing now but an exile, for Poland is in chains."

The words "Poland" and "exile" brought up all the pathetic stories of that unhappy country which the three listeners had ever heard, and won their interest at once.

"You were in the late revolution, perhaps?" asked the major, giving the unhappy outbreak the most respectful name he could use.

"From beginning to end."

"Oh, tell us about it; we felt much sympathy for you, and longed to have you win," cried Amy, with such genuine interest and pity in her tone, it was impossible to resist.

Pressing both hands upon his breast, the young man bent low, with a flush of feeling on his pale cheek, and answered eagerly, —

"Ah, you are kind; it is balm to my sore heart to hear words like these. I thank you, and tell you what you will. It is but little that I do, yet I give my life, and die a long death, instead of a quick, brave one with my comrades."

"You are young to have borne a part in a revolution, sir," said the major, who pricked up his ears like an old war-horse at the sound of battle.

"My friends and myself left the University at Varsovie, as volunteers; we did our part, and now all lie in their graves but three."

"You were wounded, it seems?"

"Many times. Exposure, privation, and sorrow will finish what the Russian bullets began. But it is well. I have no wish to see my country enslaved, and I can no longer help her."

"Let us hope that a happier future waits for you both. Poland loves liberty too well, and has suffered too much for it, to be kept long in captivity."

Helen spoke warmly, and the young man listened with a brightening face.

"It is a kind prophecy; I accept it, and take courage. God knows I need it," he added, low to himself.

"Are you bound for Italy?" said the major, in a most un-English fit of curiosity.

"For Geneva first, Italy later, unless Montreaux is mild enough for me to winter in. I go to satisfy my friends, but doubt if it avails much."

"Where is Montreaux?" asked Amy.

"Near Clarens, where Rousseau wrote his Heloise, and Vevay, where so many English go to enjoy Chillon. The climate is divine for unfortunates like myself, and life more cheap there than in Italy."

Here the train stopped again, and Hoffman came to ask if the ladies desired anything.

At the sound of his voice the young Pole started, looked up, and exclaimed, with the vivacity of a foreigner, in German, —

"By my life, it is Karl! Behold me, old friend, and satisfy me that it is thyself by a handshake."

"Casimer! What wind blows thee hither, my boy, in such sad plight?" replied Hoffman, grasping the slender hand outstretched to him.

"I fly from an enemy for the first time in my life, and, like all cowards, shall be conquered in the end. I wrote thee I was better, but the wound in the breast reopened, and nothing but a miracle will save me. I go to Switzerland; and thou?"

"Where my master commands. I serve this gentleman, now."

"Hard changes for both, but with health thou art king of circumstances, while I?—Ah well, the good God knows best. Karl, go thou and buy me two of those pretty baskets of grapes; I will please myself by giving them to these pitying angels. Speak they German?"

"One, the elder; but they understand not this rattle of ours."

Karl disappeared, and Helen, who *had* understood the rapid dialogue, tried to seem as unconscious as Amy.

"Say a friendly word to me at times; I am so homesick and faint-hearted, my Hoffman. Thanks; they are almost worthy the lips that shall taste them."

Taking the two little osier baskets, laden with yellow and purple clusters, Casimer offered them, with a charming mixture of timidity and grace, to the girls, saying, like a grateful boy,—

"You give me kind words and good hopes; permit that I thank you in this poor way."

"I drink success to Poland," cried Helen, lifting a great, juicy grape to her lips, like a little purple goblet, hoping to hide her confusion under a playful air.

The grapes went round, and healths were drunk with much merriment, for in travelling on the Continent it is impossible for the gruffest, primmest person to long resist the frank courtesy and vivacious chat of foreigners.

The major was unusually social and inquisitive, and while the soldiers fought their battles over again the girls listened and took notes, with feminine wits on the alert to catch any personal revelations which might fall from the interesting stranger. The wrongs and sufferings of Poland were discussed so eloquently that both young ladies were moved to declare the most undying hatred of Russia, Prussia, and Austria, the most intense sympathy for "poor Pologne." All day they travelled together, and as Baden-Baden approached, they naturally fell to talking of the gay place.

"Uncle, I must try my fortune once. I've set my heart upon it, and so has Nell. We want to know how gamblers feel, and to taste the fascination of the game which draws people here from all parts of Europe," said Amy, in her half-pleading, half-imperious way.

"You may risk one napoleon each, as I foolishly promised you should, when I little thought you would ever have an opportunity to remind me of my promise. It's not an amusement for respectable Englishwomen, or men either. You will agree with me there, monsieur?" and the major glanced at the Pole, who replied, with his peculiar smile:—

"Surely, yes. It is great folly and waste of time and money; yet I have known one man who found some good in it, or, rather, brought good out of it. I have a friend who has a mania for giving. His own fortune was spent in helping needy students at the University, and poor professors. This displeased his father, and he refused supplies, except enough for his simple personal wants. Sigismund chafed at this, and being skilful at all games, as a gentleman may be in the way of amusement, he resolved to play with those whose money was wasted on frivolities, and give his winnings to his band of paupers."

"How did it succeed, this odd fancy?" asked Helen, with an interested face, while Amy pinched her arm at the word "Sigismund."

"Excellently. My friend won often, and as his purpose became known it caused no unkind feeling, this unusual success, for fortune seemed to favor his kind object."

"Wrong, nevertheless, to do evil that good may come of it," said the major, morally.

"It may be so; but it is not for me to censure my benefactor. He has done much for my countrymen and myself, and is so truly noble I can see no fault in him."

"What an odd name! Sigismund is German, is it not?" asked Amy, in the most artless tone of interest.

"Yes, mademoiselle, and Palsdorf is a true German; much courage, strength, and intellect, with the gayety and simplicity of a boy. He hates slavery of all kinds, and will be free at all costs. He is a good son, but his father is tyrannical, and asks too much. Sigismund will not submit to sell himself, and so is in disgrace for a time."

"Palsdorf!—was not that the name of the count or baron we heard them talking of at Coblentz?" said Helen to Amy, with a well-feigned air of uncertainty.

"Yes; I heard something of a duel and a broken betrothal, I think. The people seemed to consider the baron a wild young man, so it could not have been your friend, sir," was Amy's demure reply, as she glanced at Helen with mirthful eyes, as if to say, "How our baron haunts us!"

"It is the same, doubtless. Many consider him wild, because he is original, and dares act for himself. As it is well known, I may tell you the truth of the duel and the betrothal, if you care to hear a little romance."

Casimer looked eager to defend his friend, and as the girls were longing to hear the romance, permission was given.

"In Germany, you know, the young people are often betrothed in childhood by the parents, and sometimes never meet till they are grown. Usually all goes well; but not always, for love cannot come at command. Sigismund was plighted, when a boy of fifteen, to his young cousin, and then sent away to the University till of age. On returning, he was to travel a year or two, and then marry. He gladly went away, and with increasing disquiet saw the time draw near when he must keep his troth-plight."

"Hum! loved some one else. Very unfortunate to be sure," murmured the major with a sigh.

"Not so; he only loved his liberty, and pretty Minna was less dear than a life of perfect freedom. He went back at the appointed time, saw his cousin, tried to do his duty and love her; found it impossible, and, discovering that Minna loved another, vowed he would never make her unhappiness as well as his own. The old baron stormed, but the young one was firm, and would not listen to a marriage without love; but pleaded for Minna, wished his rival success, and set out again on his travels."

"And the duel?" asked the major, who took less interest in love than war.

"That was as characteristic as the other act. A son of one high in office at Berlin circulated false reports of the cause of Palsdorf's refusal of the alliance—reports injurious to Minna. Sigismund settled the matter in the most effectual manner, by challenging and wounding the man. But for court influence it would have gone hardly with my friend. The storm, however, has blown over; Minna will be happy with her lover, and Sigismund with his liberty, till he tires of it."

"Is he handsome, this hero of yours?" said Amy, feeling the ring under her glove, for in spite of Helen's advice, she insisted on wearing it, that it might be at hand to return at any moment, should chance again bring the baron in their way.

"A true German of the old type; blond and blue-eyed, tall and strong. My hero in good truth—brave and loyal, tender and true," was the enthusiastic answer.

"I hate fair men," pouted Amy, under her breath, as the major asked some question about hotels.

"Take a new hero, then; nothing can be more romantic than that," whispered Helen, glancing at the pale, dark-haired figure wrapped in the military cloak opposite.

"I will, and leave the baron to you;" said Amy, with a stifled laugh.

"Hush! Here are Baden and Karl," replied Helen, thankful for the interruption.

All was bustle in a moment, and taking leave of them with an air of reluctance, the Pole walked away, leaving Amy looking after him wistfully, quite unconscious that she stood in everybody's way, and that her uncle was beckoning impatiently from the carriage door.

"Poor boy! I wish he had some one to take care of him," she sighed, half aloud.

"Mademoiselle, the major waits;" and Karl came up, hat in hand, just in time to hear her and glance after Casimer, with an odd expression.

V

LUDMILLA

"I wonder what that young man's name was. Did he mention it, Helen?" said the major, pausing in his march up and down the room, as if the question was suggested by the sight of the little baskets, which the girls had kept.

"No, uncle; but you can easily ask Hoffman," replied Helen.

"By the way, Karl, who was the Polish gentleman who came on with us?" asked the major a moment afterward, as the courier came in with newspapers.

"Casimer Teblinski, sir."

"A baron?" asked Amy, who was decidedly a young lady of one idea just then.

"No, mademoiselle, but of a noble family, as the 'ski' denotes, for that is to Polish and Russian names what 'von' is to German and 'de' to French."

"I was rather interested in him. Where did you pick him up, Hoffman?" said the major.

"In Paris, where he was with fellow-exiles."

"He is what he seems, is he?—no impostor, or anything of that sort? One is often deceived, you know."

"On my honor, sir, he is a gentleman, and as brave as he is accomplished and excellent."

"Will he die?" asked Amy, pathetically.

"With care he would recover, I think; but there is no one to nurse him, so the poor lad must take his chance and trust in heaven for help."

"How sad! I wish we were going his way, so that we might do something for him—at least give him the society of his friend."

Helen glanced at Hoffman, feeling that if he were not already engaged by them, he would devote himself to the invalid without any thought of payment.

"Perhaps we are. You want to see the Lake of Geneva, Chillon, and that neighborhood. Why not go now, instead of later?"

"Will you, uncle? That's capital! We need say nothing, but go on and help the poor boy, if we can."

Helen spoke like a matron of forty, and looked as full of maternal kindness as if the Pole were not out of his teens.

The courier bowed, the major laughed behind his paper, and Amy gave a sentimental sigh to the memory of the baron, in whom her interest was failing.

They only caught a glimpse of the Pole that evening at the Kursaal, but next morning they met, and he was invited to join their party for a little expedition.

The major was in fine spirits, and Helen assumed her maternal air toward both invalids, for the sound of that hollow cough always brought a shadow over her face, recalling the brother she had lost.

Amy was particularly merry and charming, and kept the whole party laughing at her comical efforts to learn Polish and teach English as they drove up the mountainside to the old Schloss.

"I'm not equal to mounting all those steps for a view I've seen a dozen times; but pray take care of the child, Nell, or she'll get lost again, as at Heidelberg," said the major, when they had roamed about the lower part of the place; for a cool seat in the courtyard and a glass of beer were more tempting than turrets and prospects to the stout gentleman.

"She shall not be lost; I am her body-guard. It is steep—permit that I lead you, mademoiselle;" Casimer offered his hand to Amy, and they began their winding way. As she took the hand, the girl blushed and half smiled, remembering the vaults and the baron.

"I like this better," she said to herself, as they climbed step by step, often pausing to rest in the embrasures of the loopholes, where the sun glanced in, the balmy wind blew, and vines peeped from without, making a pretty picture of the girl, as she sat with rosy color on her usually pale cheeks, brown curls fluttering about her forehead, laughing lips, and bright eyes full of pleasant changes. Leaning opposite in the narrow stairway, Casimer had time to study the little tableau in many lights, and in spite of the dark glasses, to convey warm glances of admiration, of which, however, the young coquette seemed utterly unconscious.

Helen came leisurely after, and Hoffman followed with a telescope, wishing, as he went, that his countrywomen possessed such dainty feet as those going on before him, for which masculine iniquity he will be pardoned by all who have seen the foot of a German Fraulein.

It was worth the long ascent, that wide-spread landscape basking in the August glow.

Sitting on a fallen block of stone, while Casimer held a sun-umbrella over her, Amy had raptures at her ease; while Helen sketched and asked questions of Hoffman, who stood beside her, watching her progress with interest. Once when, after repeated efforts to catch a curious effect of light and shade, she uttered an impatient little exclamation, Karl made a gesture as if to take the pencil and show her, but seemed to recollect himself and drew back with a hasty, "Pardon, mademoiselle." Helen glanced up and saw the expression of his face, which plainly betrayed that for a moment the gentleman had forgotten he was a courier. She was glad of it, for it was a daily trial to her to order this man about; and following the womanly impulse, she smiled and offered the pencil, saying simply,—

"I felt sure you understood it; please show me."

He did so, and a few masterly strokes gave the sketch what it needed. As he bent near her to do this, Helen stole a glance at the grave, dark face, and suddenly a disturbed look dawned in the eyes fixed on the glossy black locks pushed off the courier's forehead, for he had removed his hat when she spoke to him. He seemed to feel that something was amiss, shot a quick glance at her, returned the pencil and rose erect, with an almost defiant air, yet something of shame in his eye, as his lips moved as if to speak impetuously. But not a word did he utter, for Helen touched her forehead significantly, and said in a low tone,—

"I am an artist; let me recommend Vandyke brown, which is *not* affected by heat."

Hoffman looked over his shoulder at the other pair, but Amy was making an ivy wreath for her hat, and the Pole pulling sprays for the absorbing work. Speaking rapidly, Karl said, with a peculiar blending of merriment, humility, and anxiety in his tone,—

"Mademoiselle, you are quick to discover my disguise; will you also be kind in concealing? I have enemies as well as friends, whom I desire to escape; I would earn my bread unknown; Monsieur le Major keeps my foolish secret; may I hope for equal goodness from yourself?"

"You may, I do not forget that I owe my life to you, nor that you are a gentleman. Trust me, I never will betray you."

"Thanks, thanks! there will come a time when I may confess the truth and be myself, but not yet," and his regretful tone was emphasized by an impatient gesture, as if concealment was irksome.

"Nell, come down to lunch; uncle is signalling as if he'd gone mad. No, monsieur, it is quite impossible; you cannot reach the harebells without risking too much; come away and forget that I wanted them."

Amy led the way, and all went down more quietly than they came up, especially Helen and Hoffman. An excellent lunch waited on one of the tables in front of the old gateway, and having done justice to it, the major made himself comfortable with a cigar, bidding the girls keep near, for they must be off in half an hour. Hoffman went to see to the horses, Casimer strolled away with him, and the young ladies went to gather wild flowers at the foot of the tower.

"Not a harebell here; isn't it provoking, when they grow in tufts up there, where one can't reach them. Mercy, what's that? Run, Nell, the old wall is coming down!"

Both had been grubbing in a damp nook, where ferns and mosses grew luxuriantly; the fall of a bit of stone and a rending sound above made them fly back to the path and look up.

Amy covered her eyes, and Helen grew pale, for part way down the crumbling tower, clinging like a bird to the thick ivy stems, hung Casimer, coolly gathering harebells from the clefts of the wall.

"Hush; don't cry out or speak; it may startle him. Crazy boy! Let us see what he will do," whispered Helen.

"He can't go back, the vines are so torn and weak; and how will he get down the lower wall? for you see the ivy grows up from that ledge, and there is nothing below. How could he do it? I was only joking when I lamented that there were no knights now, ready to leap into a lion's den for a lady's glove," returned Amy, half angry.

In breathless silence they watched the climber till his cap was full of flowers, and taking it between his teeth, he rapidly swung down to the wide ledge, from which there appeared to be no way of escape but a reckless leap of many feet on to the turf below.

The girls stood in the shadow of an old gateway, unperceived, and waited anxiously what should follow.

Lightly folding and fastening the cap together, he dropped it down, and, leaning forward, tried to catch the top of a young birch rustling close by the wall. Twice he missed it; the first time he frowned, but the second he uttered an emphatic, "Deuce take it!"

Helen and Amy looked at each other with a mutual smile and exclamation, —

"He knows some English, then!"

There was time for no more — a violent rustle, a boyish laugh, and down swung the slender tree, with the young man clinging to the top.

As he landed safely, Helen cried, "Bravo!" and Amy rushed out, exclaiming reproachfully, yet admiringly, —

"How could you do it and frighten us so? I shall never express a wish before you again, for if I wanted the moon you'd rashly try to get it, I know."

"*Certainement*, mademoiselle," was the smiling reply, Casimer presented the flowers, as if the exploit was a mere trifle.

"Now I shall go and press them at once in uncle's guide-book. Come and help me, else you will be in mischief again." And Amy led the way to the major with her flowers and their giver.

Helen roamed into one of the ruined courts for a last look at a fountain which pleased her eye. A sort of cloister ran round the court, open on both sides, and standing in one of these arched nooks, she saw Hoffman and a young girl talking animatedly. The girl was pretty, well dressed, and seemed refusing something for which the other pleaded eagerly. His arm was about her, and she leaned affectionately upon him, with a white hand now and then caressing his face, which was full of sparkle and vivacity now. They seemed about to part as Helen looked, for the maiden standing on tiptoe, laughingly offered her blooming cheek, and as Karl kissed it warmly, he said in German, so audibly Helen heard every word,—

"Farewell, my Ludmilla. Keep silent and I shall soon be with you. Embrace the little one, and do not let him forget me."

Both left the place as they spoke, each going a different way, and Helen slowly returned to her party, saying to herself in a troubled tone,—

"'Ludmilla' and 'the little one' are his wife and child, doubtless. I wonder if uncle knows that."

When Hoffman next appeared she could not resist looking at him; but the accustomed gravity was resumed, and nothing remained of the glow and brightness he had worn when with Ludmilla in the cloister.

VI

CHATEAU DE LA TOUR

Helen looked serious and Amy indignant when their uncle joined them, ready to set out by the afternoon train, all having dined and rested after the morning's excursion.

"Well, little girls, what's the matter now?" he asked, paternally, for the excellent man adored his nieces.

"Helen says it's not best to go on with the Pole, and is perfectly nonsensical, uncle," began Amy, petulantly, and not very coherently.

"Better be silly now than sorry by and by. I only suggested that, being interesting, and Amy romantic, she might find this young man too charming, if we see too much of him," said Helen.

"Bless my soul, what an idea!" cried the major. "Why, Nell, he's an invalid, a Catholic, and a foreigner, any one of which objections are enough to settle that matter. Little Amy isn't so foolish as to be in danger of losing her heart to a person so entirely out of the question as this poor lad, is she?"

"Of course not. *You* do me justice, uncle. Nell thinks she may pity and pet any one she likes because she is five years older than I, and entirely forgets that she is a great deal more attractive than a feeble thing like me. I should as soon think of losing my heart to Hoffman as to the Pole, even if he wasn't what he is. One may surely be kind to a dying man, without being accused of coquetry;" and Amy sobbed in the most heart-rending manner.

Helen comforted her by withdrawing all objections, and promising to leave the matter in the major's hands. But she shook her head privately when she saw the ill-disguised eagerness with which her cousin glanced up and down the platform after they were in the train, and she whispered to her uncle, unobserved,—

"Leave future meetings to chance, and don't ask the Pole in, if you can help it."

"Nonsense, my dear. You are as particular as your aunt. The lad amuses me, and you can't deny you like to nurse sick heroes," was all the answer she got, as the major, with true masculine perversity, put his head out of the window and hailed Casimer as he was passing with a bow.

"Here, Teblinski, my good fellow, don't desert us. We've always a spare seat for you, if you haven't pleasanter quarters."

With a flush of pleasure the young man came up, but hesitated to accept the invitation till Helen seconded it with a smile of welcome.

Amy was in an injured mood, and, shrouded in a great blue veil, pensively reclined in her corner as if indifferent to everything about her. But soon the cloud passed, and she emerged in a radiant state of good humor, which lasted unbroken until the journey ended.

For two days they went on together, a very happy party, for the major called in Hoffman to see his friend and describe the places through which they passed. An arrangement very agreeable to all, as Karl was a favorite, and every one missed him when away.

At Lausanne they waited while he crossed the lake to secure rooms at Vevay. On his return he reported that all the hotels and *pensions* were full, but that at La Tour he had secured rooms for a few weeks in a quaint old chateau on the banks of the lake.

"Count Severin is absent in Egypt, and the housekeeper has permission to let the apartments to transient visitors. The suite of rooms I speak of were engaged to a party who are detained by sickness—they are cheap, pleasant, and comfortable. A *salon* and four bed-rooms. I engaged them all, thinking that Teblinski might like a room there till he finds lodgings at Montreaux. We can enter at once, and I am sure the ladies will approve of the picturesque place."

"Well done, Hoffman; off we go without delay, for I really long to rest my old bones in something like a home, after this long trip," said the major, who always kept his little troop in light marching order.

The sail across that loveliest of lakes prepared the new-comers to be charmed with all they saw; and when, entering by the old stone gate, they were led into a large saloon, quaintly furnished and opening into a terrace-garden overhanging the water, with Chillon and the Alps in sight, Amy declared nothing could be more perfect, and Helen's face proved her satisfaction.

An English widow and two quiet old German professors on a vacation were the only inmates besides themselves and the buxom Swiss housekeeper and her maids.

It was late when our party arrived, and there was only time for a hasty survey of their rooms and a stroll in the garden before dinner.

The great chamber, with its shadowy bed, dark mirrors, ghostly wainscot-doors and narrow windows, had not been brightened for a long time by such a charming little apparition as Amy when she shook out her airy muslins, smoothed her curls, and assumed all manner of distracting devices for the captivation of mankind. Even Helen, though not much given to personal vanity, found herself putting flowers in her hair, and studying the effect of bracelets on her handsome arms, as if there was some especial need of looking her best on this occasion.

Both were certainly great ornaments to the drawing-room that evening, as the old professors agreed while they sat blinking at them, like a pair of benign owls. Casimer surprised them by his skill in music, for, though forbidden to sing on account of his weak lungs, he played as if inspired. Amy hovered about him like a moth; the major cultivated the acquaintance of the plump widow; and Helen stood at the window, enjoying the lovely night and music, till something happened which destroyed her pleasure in both.

The window was open, and, leaning from it, she was watching the lake, when the sound of a heavy sigh caught her ear. There was no moon, but through the starlight she saw a man's figure among the shrubs below, sitting with bent head and hidden face in the forlorn attitude of one shut out from the music, light, and gayety that reigned within.

"It is Karl," she thought, and was about to speak, when, as if startled by some sound she did not hear, he rose and vanished in the gloom of the garden.

"Poor man! he thought of his wife and child, perhaps, sitting here alone while all the rest make merry, with no care for him. Uncle must see to this;" and Helen fell into a reverie till Amy came to propose retiring.

"I meant to have seen where all these doors led, but was so busy dressing I had no time, so must leave it for my amusement to-morrow. Uncle says it's a very Radcliffian place. How like an angel that man did play!" chattered Amy, and lulled herself to sleep by humming the last air Casimer had given them.

Helen could not sleep, for the lonely figure in the garden haunted her, and she wearied herself with conjectures about Hoffman and his mystery. Hour after hour rung from the cuckoo-clock in the hall, but still she lay awake, watching the curious shadows in the room, and exciting herself with recalling the tales of German goblins with which the courier had amused them the day before.

"It is close and musty here, with all this old tapestry and stuff about; I'll open the other window," she thought; and, noiselessly slipping from Amy's side, she threw on wrapper and slippers, lighted her candle and tried to unbolt the tall, diamond-paned lattice. It was rusty and would not yield, and, giving it up, she glanced about to see whence air could be admitted. There were four doors in the room, all low and arched, with clumsy locks and heavy handles. One opened into a closet, one into the passage; the third was locked, but the fourth opened easily, and, lifting her light, she peeped into a small octagon room, full of all manner of curiosities. What they were she had no time to see, for her startled eyes were riveted on an object that turned her faint and cold with terror.

A heavy table stood in the middle of the room, and seated at it, with some kind of weapon before him, was a man who looked over his shoulder, with a ghastly face half hidden by hair and beard, and fierce black eyes as full of malignant menace as was the clinched hand holding the pistol. One instant Helen looked, the next flung to the door, bolted it and dropped into a chair, trembling in every limb. The noise did not wake Amy, and a moment's thought showed Helen the wisdom of keeping her in ignorance of this affair. She knew the major was close by, and possessing much courage, she resolved to wait a little before rousing the house.

Hardly had she collected herself, when steps were heard moving softly in the octagon room. Her light had gone out as she closed the door, and sitting close by in the dark, she heard the sound of some one breathing as he listened at the key-hole. Then a careful hand tried the door, so noiselessly that no sleeper would have been awakened; and as if to guard against a second surprise, the unknown person drew two bolts across the door and stole away.

"Safe for a time; but I'll not pass another night under this roof, unless this is satisfactorily cleared up," thought Helen, now feeling more angry than frightened.

The last hour that struck was three, and soon the summer dawn reddened the sky. Dressing herself, Helen sat by Amy, a sleepless guard, till she woke, smiling and rosy as a child. Saying nothing of her last night's alarm, Helen went down to breakfast a little paler than usual, but otherwise unchanged. The major never liked to be disturbed till he had broken his fast, and the moment they rose from the table he exclaimed, —

"Now, girls, come and see the mysteries of Udolpho."

"I'll say nothing, yet," thought Helen, feeling braver by daylight, yet troubled by her secret, for Hoffman might be a traitor, and this charming chateau a den of thieves. Such things had been, and she was in a mood to believe anything.

The upper story was a perfect museum of antique relics, very entertaining to examine. Having finished these, Hoffman, who acted as guide, led them into a little gloomy room containing a straw pallet, a stone table with a loaf and pitcher on it, and, kneeling before a crucifix, where the light from a single slit in the wall fell on him, was the figure of a monk. The waxen mask was life-like, the attitude effective, and the cell excellently arranged. Amy cried out when she first saw it, but a second glance reassured her, and she patted the bald head approvingly, as Karl explained, —

"Count Severin is an antiquarian, and amuses himself with things of this sort. In old times there really was a hermit here, and this is his effigy. Come down these narrow stairs, if you please, and see the rest of the mummery."

Down they went, and the instant Helen looked about her, she burst into a hysterical laugh, for there sat her ruffian, exactly as she saw him, glaring over his shoulder with threatening eyes, and one hand on the pistol. They all looked at her, for she was pale, and her merriment unnatural; so, feeling she had excited curiosity, she gratified it by narrating her night's adventure. Hoffman looked much concerned.

"Pardon, mademoiselle, the door should have been bolted on this side. It usually is, but that room being unused, it was forgotten. I remembered it, and having risen early, crept up to make sure that you did not come upon this ugly thing unexpectedly. But I was too late, it seems; you have suffered, to my sorrow."

"Dear Nell, and that was why I found you so pale and cold and quiet, sitting by me when I woke, guarding me faithfully as you promised you would. How brave and kind you were!"

"Villain! I should much like to fire your own pistols at you for this prank of yours."

And Casimer laughingly filliped the image on its absurdly aquiline nose.

"What in the name of common sense is this goblin here for?" demanded the major, testily.

"There is a legend that once the owner of the chateau amused himself by decoying travellers here, putting them to sleep in that room, and by various devices alluring them thither. Here, one step beyond the threshold of the door, was a trap, down which the unfortunates were precipitated to the dungeon at the bottom of the tower, there to die and be cast into the lake through a water-gate, still to be seen. Severin keeps this flattering likeness of the rascal, as he does the monk above, to amuse visitors by daylight, not at night, mademoiselle."

And Hoffman looked wrathfully at the image, as if he would much enjoy sending it down the trap.

"How ridiculous! I shall not go about this place alone, for fear of lighting upon some horror of this sort. I've had enough; come away into the garden; it's full of roses, and we may have as many as we like."

As she spoke Amy involuntarily put out her hand for Casimer to lead her down the steep stone steps, and he pressed the little hand with a tender look which caused it to be hastily withdrawn.

"Here are your roses. Pretty flower; I know its meaning in English, for it is the same with us. To give a bud to a lady is to confess the beginning of love, a half open one tells of its growth, and a full-blown one is to declare one's passion. Do you have that custom in your land, mademoiselle?"

He had gathered the three as he spoke, and held the bud separately while looking at his companion wistfully.

"No, we are not poetical, like your people, but it is a pretty fancy," and Amy settled her bouquet with an absorbed expression, though inwardly wondering what he would do with his flowers.

He stood silent a moment, with a sudden flush sweeping across his face, then flung all three into the lake with a gesture that made the girl start, and muttered between his teeth.

"No, no: for me it is too late."

She affected not to hear, but making up a second bouquet, she gave it to him, with no touch of coquetry in compassionate eyes or gentle voice.

"Make your room bright with these. When one is ill nothing is so cheering as the sight of flowers."

Meantime the others had descended and gone their separate ways.

As Karl crossed the courtyard a little child ran to meet him with outstretched arms and a shout of satisfaction. He caught it up and carried it away on his shoulder, like one used to caress and be caressed by children.

Helen, waiting at the door of the tower while the major dusted his coat, saw this, and said, suddenly, directing his attention to man and child,—

"He seems fond of little people. I wonder if he has any of his own."

"Hoffman? No, my dear; he's not married; I asked him that when I engaged him."

"And he said he was not?"

"Yes; he's not more than five or six-and-twenty, and fond of a wandering life, so what should he want of a wife and a flock of bantlings?"

"He seems sad and sober sometimes, and I fancied he might have some domestic trouble to harass him. Don't you think there is something peculiar about him?" asked Helen, remembering Hoffman's hint that her uncle knew his wish to travel incognito, and wondering if he would throw any light upon the matter. But the major's face was impenetrable and his answer unsatisfactory.

"Well, I don't know. Every one has some worry or other, and as for being peculiar, all foreigners seem more or less so to us, they are so unreserved and demonstrative. I like Hoffman more and more every day, and shall be sorry when I part with him."

"Ludmilla is his sister, then, or he didn't tell uncle the truth. It is no concern of mine; but I wish I knew," thought Helen anxiously, and then wondered why she should care.

A feeling of distrust had taken possession of her and she determined to be on the watch, for the unsuspicious major would be easily duped, and Helen trusted more to her own quick and keen eye than to his experience. She tried to show nothing of the change in her manner; but Hoffman perceived it, and bore it with a proud patience which often touched her heart, but never altered her purpose.

VII

AT FAULT

Four weeks went by so rapidly that every one refused to believe it when the major stated the fact at the breakfast-table, for all had enjoyed themselves so heartily that they had been unconscious of the lapse of time.

"You are not going away, uncle?" cried Amy, with a panic-stricken look.

"Next week, my dear; we must be off, for we've much to do yet, and I promised mamma to bring you back by the end of October."

"Never mind Paris and the rest of it; this is pleasanter. I'd rather stay here—"

There Amy checked herself and tried to hide her face behind her coffee-cup, for Casimer looked up in a way that made her heart flutter and her cheeks burn.

"Sorry for it, Amy; but go we must, so enjoy your last week with all your might, and come again next year."

"It will never be again what it is now," sighed Amy; and Casimer echoed the words "next year," as if sadly wondering if the present year would not be his last.

Helen rose silently and went into the garden, for of late she had fallen into the way of reading and working in the little pavilion which stood in an angle of the wall, overlooking lake and mountains.

A seat at the opposite end of the walk was Amy's haunt, for she liked the sun, and within a week or two something like constraint had existed between the cousins. Each seemed happier apart, and each was intent on her own affairs. Helen watched over Amy's health, but no longer offered advice or asked confidence. She often looked anxious, and once or twice urged the major to go, as if conscious of some danger.

But the worthy man seemed to have been bewitched as well as the young folks, and was quite happy sitting by the plump, placid widow, or leisurely walking with her to the chapel on the hillside.

All seemed waiting for something to break up the party, and no one had the courage to do it. The major's decision took every one by surprise, and Amy and Casimer looked as if they had fallen from the clouds.

The persistency with which the English lessons had gone on was amazing, for Amy usually tired of everything in a day or two. Now, however, she was a devoted teacher, and her pupil did her great credit by the rapidity with which he caught the language. It looked like pleasant play, sitting among the roses day after day, Amy affecting to embroider while she taught, Casimer marching to and fro on the wide, low wall, below which lay the lake, while he learned his lesson; then standing before her to recite, or lounging on the turf in frequent fits of idleness, both talking and laughing a great deal, and generally forgetting everything but the pleasure of being together. They wrote little notes as exercises—Amy in French, Casimer in English, and each corrected the other's.

All very well for a time; but as the notes increased the corrections decreased, and at last nothing was said of ungrammatical French or comical English, and the little notes were exchanged in silence.

As Amy took her place that day she looked forlorn, and when her pupil came her only welcome was a reproachful—

"You are very late, sir."

"It is fifteen of minutes yet to ten clocks," was Casimer's reply, in his best English.

"Ten o'clock, and leave out 'of' before minutes. How many times must I tell you that?" said Amy, severely, to cover her first mistake.

"Ah, not many times; soon all goes to finish, and I have none person to make this charming English go in my so stupid head."

"What will you do then?"

"I *jeter* myself into the lake."

"Don't be foolish; I'm dull to-day, and want to be cheered up; suicide isn't a pleasant subject."

"Good! See here, then—a little *plaisanterie*—what you call joke. Can you will to see it?" and he laid a little pink cocked-hat note on her lap, looking like a mischievous boy as he did so.

"'Mon Casimer Teblinski;' I see no joke;" and Amy was about to tear it up, when he caught it from destruction, and holding it out of reach, said, laughing wickedly,—

"The 'mon' is one abbreviation of 'monsieur,' but you put no little— how do you say?—period at the end of him; it goes now in English—'*My* Casimer Teblinski,' and that is of the most charming address."

Amy colored, but had her return shot ready.

"Don't exult; that was only an oversight, not a deliberate deception like that you put upon me. It was very wrong and rude, and I shall not forgive it."

"*Mon Dieu!* where have I gone in sinning? I am a *polisson*, as I say each day, but not a villain, I swear to you. Say to me that which I have made of wrong, and I will do penance."

"You told me '*Ma drogha*' was the Polish for 'My pupil,' and let me call you so a long time; I am wiser now," replied Amy, with great dignity.

"Who has said stupidities to you, that you doubt me?" and Casimer assumed an injured look, though his eyes danced with merriment.

"I heard Hoffman singing a Polish song to little Roserl, the burden of which was, '*Ma drogha, Ma drogha*,' and when I asked him to translate it, those two words meant, 'My darling.' How dare you do it, ungrateful creature that you are!"

As Amy spoke, half-confusedly, half-angrily, Casimer went down upon his knees, with folded hands and penitent face, exclaiming, in good English,—

"Be merciful to me a sinner. I was tempted, and I could not resist."

"Get up this instant, and stop laughing. Say your lesson, for this will be your last," was the stern reply, though Amy's face dimpled all over with suppressed merriment.

He rose meekly, but made such sad work with the verb "To love," that his teacher was glad to put an end to it, by proposing to read her French to him. It was "Thaddeus of Warsaw," a musty little translation which she had found in the house, and begun for her own amusement. Casimer read a little, seemed interested, and suggested that they read it together, so that he might correct her accent. Amy agreed, and they were in the heart of the sentimental romance, finding it more interesting than most modern readers, for the girl had an improved Thaddeus before her, and the Pole a fairer, kinder Mary Beaufort.

Dangerous times for both, but therein lay the charm; for, though Amy said to herself each night, "Sick, Catholic, and a foreigner,—it can never be," yet each morning she felt, with increasing force, how blank her day would be without him. And Casimer, honorably restraining every word of love, yet looked volumes, and in spite of the glasses, the girl felt the eloquence of the fine eyes they could not entirely conceal.

To-day, as she read, he listened with his head leaning on his hand, and though she never had read worse, he made no correction, but sat so motionless, she fancied at last that he had actually fallen asleep. Thinking to rouse him, she said, in French,—

"Poor Thaddeus! don't you pity him?—alone, poor, sick, and afraid to own his love."

"No, I hate him, the absurd imbecile, with his fine boots and plumes, and tragedy airs. He was not to be pitied, for he recovered health, he found a fortune, he won his Marie. His sufferings were nothing; there was no fatal blight on him, and he had time and power to conquer his misfortunes, while I—"

Casimer spoke with sudden passion, and pausing abruptly, turned his face away, as if to hide some emotion he was too proud to show.

Amy's heart ached, and her eyes filled, but her voice was sweet and steady, as she said, putting by the book, like one weary of it,—

"Are you suffering to-day? Can we do anything for you? Please let us, if we may."

"You give me all I can receive; no one can help my pain yet; but a time will come when something may be done for me; then I will speak."

And, to her great surprise, he rose and left her, without another word.

She saw him no more till evening; then he looked excited, played stormily, and would sing in defiance of danger. The trouble in Amy's face seemed reflected in Helen's, though not a word had passed between them. She kept her eye on Casimer, with an intentness that worried Amy, and even when he was at the instrument Helen stood near him, as if fascinated, watching the slender hands chase one another up and down the keys with untiring strength and skill.

Suddenly she left the room and did not return. Amy was so nervous by that time, she could restrain herself no longer, and slipping out, found her cousin in their chamber, poring over a glove.

"Oh, Nell, what is it? You are so odd to-night I can't understand you. The music excites me, and I'm miserable, and I want to know what has happened," she said, tearfully.

"I've found him!" whispered Helen, eagerly, holding up the glove with a gesture of triumph.

"Who?" asked Amy, blinded by her tears.

"The baron."

"Where?—when?" cried the girl, amazed.

"Here, and now."

"Don't take my breath away; tell me quick, or I shall get hysterical."

"Casimer is Sigismund Palsdorf, and no more a Pole than I am," was Helen's answer.

Amy dropped in a heap on the floor, not fainting, but so amazed she had neither strength nor breath left. Sitting by her, Helen rapidly went on,—

"I had a feeling as if something was wrong, and began to watch. The feeling grew, but I discovered nothing till to-day. It will make you laugh, it was so unromantic. As I looked over uncle's things when the laundress brought them this afternoon, I found a collar that was not his. It was marked 'S. P.,' and I at once felt a great desire to know who owned it. The woman was waiting for her money, and I asked her. 'Monsieur Pologne,' she said, for his name is too much for her. She took it into his room, and that was the end of it."

"But it may be another name; the initials only a coincidence," faltered Amy, looking frightened.

"No, dear, it isn't; there is more to come. Little Roserl came crying through the hall an hour ago, and I asked what the trouble was. She showed me a prettily-bound prayer-book which she had taken from the Pole's room to play with, and had been ordered by her mother to carry back. I looked into it; no name, but the same coat-of-arms as the glove and the handkerchief. To-night as he played I examined his hands; they are peculiar, and some of the peculiarities have left traces on the glove. I am sure it is he, for on looking back many things confirm the idea. He says he is a *polisson*, a rogue, fond of jokes, and clever at playing them. The Germans are famous for masquerading and practical jokes; this is one, I am sure, and uncle will be terribly angry if he discovers it."

"But why all this concealment?" cried Amy. "Why play jokes on us? You look so worried I know you have not told me all you know or fear."

"I confess I do fear that these men are political plotters as well as exiles. There are many such, and they make tools of rich and ignorant foreigners to further their ends. Uncle is rich, generous, and unsuspicious; and I fear that while apparently serving and enjoying us they are using him."

"Heavens, it may be! and that would account for the change we see in him. I thought he was in love with the widow, but that may be only a cloak to hide darker designs. Karl brought us here, and I dare say it is a den of conspirators!" cried Amy, feeling as if she were getting more of an adventure than she had bargained for.

"Don't be alarmed! I am on the watch, and mean to demand an explanation from uncle, or take you away on my own responsibility, if I can."

Here a maid tapped to say that tea was served.

"We must go down, or some one will suspect trouble. Plead headache to excuse your paleness, and I'll keep people away. We will manage the affair and be off as soon as possible," said Helen, as Amy followed her, too bewildered to answer.

Casimer was not in the room, the major and Mrs. Cumberland were sipping tea side by side, and the professors roaming vaguely about. To leave Amy in peace, Helen engaged them both in a lively chat, and her cousin sat by the window trying to collect her thoughts. Some one was pacing up and down the garden, hatless, in the dew.

Amy forgot everything but the danger of such exposure to her reckless friend. His cloak and hat lay on a chair; she caught them up and glided unperceived from the long window.

"You are so imprudent I fear for you, and bring your things," said a timid voice, as the little white figure approached the tall black one, striding down the path tempestuously.

"You to think of me, forgetful of yourself! Little angel of kindness, why do you take such care of me?" cried Casimer, eagerly taking not only the cloak, but the hands that held it.

"I pitied you because you were ill and lonely. You do not deserve my pity, but I forgive that, and would not see you suffer," was the reproachful answer, as Amy turned away.

But he held her fast, saying earnestly, —

"What have I done? You are angry. Tell me my fault and I will amend."

"You have deceived me."

"How?"

"Will you own the truth?" and in her eagerness to set her fears at rest, Amy forgot Helen.

"I will."

She could not see his face, but his voice was steady and his manner earnest.

"Tell me, then, is not your true name Sigismund Palsdorf?"

He started, but answered instantly, —

"It is not."

"You are not the baron?" cried Amy.

"No; I will swear it if you wish."

"Who, then, are you?"

"Shall I confess?"

"Yes, I entreat you."

"Remember, you command me to speak."

"I do. Who are you?"

"Your lover."

The words were breathed into her ear as softly as ardently, but they startled her so much she could find no reply, and, throwing himself down before her, Casimer poured out his passion with an impetuosity that held her breathless.

"Yes, I love you, and I tell it, vain and dishonorable as it is in one like me. I try to hide it. I say 'it cannot be.' I plan to go away. But you keep me; you are angel-good to me; you take my heart, you care for me, teach me, pity me, and I can only love and die. I know it is folly; I ask nothing; I pray to God to bless you always, and I say, Go, go, before it is too late for you, as now for me!"

"Yes, I must go—it is all wrong. Forgive me. I have been very selfish. Oh, forget me and be happy," faltered Amy, feeling that her only safety was in flight.

"Go! go!" he cried, in a heart-broken tone, yet still kissed and clung to her hands till she tore them away and fled into the house.

Helen missed her soon after she went, but could not follow for several minutes; then went to their chamber and there found Amy drowned in tears, and terribly agitated.

Soon the story was told with sobs and moans, and despairing lamentations fit to touch a heart of stone.

"I do love him—oh, I do; but I didn't know it till he was so unhappy, and now I've done this dreadful harm. He'll die, and I can't help him, see him, or be anything to him. Oh, I've been a wicked, wicked girl, and never can be happy any more."

Angry, perplexed, and conscience-stricken, for what now seemed blind and unwise submission to the major, Helen devoted herself to calming Amy, and when at last the poor, broken-hearted little soul fell asleep in her arms, she pondered half the night upon the still unsolved enigma of the Baron Sigismund.

VIII

MORE MYSTERY

"Uncle, can I speak to you a moment?" said Helen, very gravely, as they left the breakfast-room next morning.

"Not now, my dear, I'm busy," was the hasty reply, as the major shawled Mrs. Cumberland for an early promenade.

Helen knit her brows irefully, for this answer had been given her half a dozen times lately when she asked for an interview. It was evident he wished to avoid all lectures, remonstrances, and explanations; and it was also evident that he was in love with the widow.

"Lovers are worse than lunatics to manage, so it is vain to try to get any help from him," sighed Helen, adding, as her uncle was gallantly leading his stout divinity away into the garden: "Amy has a bad headache, and I shall stay to take care of her, so we can't join your party to Chillon, sir. We have been there once, so you needn't postpone it for us."

"Very well, my dear," and the major walked away, looking much relieved.

As Helen was about to leave the *salon* Casimer appeared. A single glance at her face assured him that she knew all, and instantly assuming a confiding, persuasive air that was irresistible, he said, meekly, —

"Mademoiselle, I do not deserve a word from you, but it desolates me to know that I have grieved the little angel who is too dear to me. For her sake, pardon that I spoke my heart in spite of prudence, and permit me to send her this."

Helen glanced from the flowers he held to his beseeching face, and her own softened. He looked so penitent and anxious, she had not the heart to reproach him.

"I will forgive you and carry your gift to Amy on one condition," she said, gravely.

"Ah, you are kind! Name, then, the condition, I implore you, and I will agree."

"Tell me, then, on your honor as a gentleman, are you not Baron Palsdorf?"

"On my honor as a gentleman, I swear to you I am not."

"Are you, in truth, what you profess to be?"

"I am, in truth, Amy's lover, your devoted servant, and a most unhappy man, with but a little while to live. Believe this and pity me, dearest Mademoiselle Helène."

She did pity him, her eyes betrayed that, and her voice was very kind, as she said,—

"Pardon my doubts. I trust you now, and wish with all my heart that it was possible to make you happy. You know it is not, therefore I am sure you will be wise and generous, and spare Amy further grief by avoiding her for the little time we stay. Promise me this, Casimer."

"I may see her if I am dumb? Do not deny me this. I will not speak, but I must look at my little and dear angel when she is near."

He pleaded so ardently with lips and hands, and eager eyes, that Helen could not deny him, and when he had poured out his thanks she left him, feeling very tender toward the unhappy young lover, whose passion was so hopeless, yet so warm.

Amy was at breakfast in her room, sobbing and sipping, moaning and munching, for, though her grief was great, her appetite was good, and she was in no mood to see anything comical in cracking eggshells while she bewailed her broken heart, or in eating honey in the act of lamenting the bitterness of her fate.

Casimer would have become desperate had he seen her in the little blue wrapper, with her bright hair loose on her shoulders, and her pretty face wet with tears, as she dropped her spoon to seize his flowers,—three dewy roses, one a bud, one half and the other fully blown, making a fragrant record and avowal of the love which she must renounce.

"Oh, my dear boy! how can I give him up, when he is so fond, and I am all he has? Helen, uncle must let me write or go to mamma. She shall decide; I can't; and no one else has a right to part us," sobbed Amy, over her roses.

"Casimer will not marry, dear; he is too generous to ask such a sacrifice," began Helen, but Amy cried indignantly,—

"It is no sacrifice; I'm rich. What do I care for his poverty?"

"His religion!" hinted Helen, anxiously.

"It need not part us; we can believe what we will. He is good; why mind whether he is Catholic or Protestant."

"But a Pole, Amy, so different in tastes, habits, character, and beliefs. It is a great risk to marry a foreigner; races are so unlike."

"I don't care if he is a Tartar, a Calmuck, or any of the other wild tribes; I love him, he loves me, and no one need object if I don't."

"But, dear, the great and sad objection still remains—his health. He just said he had but a little while to live."

Amy's angry eyes grew dim, but she answered, with soft earnestness,—

"So much the more need of me to make that little while happy. Think how much he has suffered and done for others; surely I may do something for him. Oh, Nell, can I let him die alone and in exile, when I have both heart and home to give him?"

Helen could say no more; she kissed and comforted the faithful little soul, feeling all the while such sympathy and tenderness that she wondered at herself, for with this interest in the love of another came a sad sense of loneliness, as if she was denied the sweet experience that every woman longs to know.

Amy never could remain long under a cloud, and seeing Helen's tears, began to cheer both her cousin and herself.

"Hoffman said he might live with care, don't you remember? and Hoffman knows the case better than we. Let us ask him if Casimer is worse. You do it; I can't without betraying myself."

"I will," and Helen felt grateful for any pretext to address a friendly word to Karl, who had looked sad of late, and had been less with them since the major became absorbed in Mrs. Cumberland.

Leaving Amy to compose herself, Helen went away to find Hoffman. It was never difficult, for he seemed to divine her wishes and appear uncalled the moment he was wanted. Hardly had she reached her favorite nook in the garden when he approached with letters, and asked with respectful anxiety, as she glanced at and threw them by with an impatient sigh,—

"Has mademoiselle any orders? Will the ladies drive, sail, or make a little expedition? It is fine, and mademoiselle looks as if the air would refresh her. Pardon that I make the suggestion."

"No, Hoffman, I don't like the air of this place, and intend to leave as soon as possible." And Helen knit her delicate dark brows with an expression of great determination. "Switzerland is the refuge of political exiles, and I hate plots and disguises; I feel oppressed by some mystery, and mean to solve or break away from it at once."

She stopped abruptly, longing to ask his help, yet withheld by a sudden sense of shyness in approaching the subject, though she had decided to speak to Karl of the Pole.

"Can I serve you, mademoiselle? If so, pray command me," he said, eagerly, coming a step nearer.

"You can, and I intend to ask your advice, for there can be nothing amiss in doing so, since you are a friend of Casimer's."

"I am both friend and confidant, mademoiselle," he answered, as if anxious to let her understand that he knew all, without the embarrassment of words. She looked up quickly, relieved, yet troubled.

"He has told you, then?"

"Everything, mademoiselle. Pardon me if this afflicts you; I am his only friend here, and the poor lad sorely needed comfort."

"He did. I am not annoyed; I am glad, for I know you will sustain him. Now I may speak freely, and be equally frank. Please tell me if he is indeed fatally ill?"

"It was thought so some months ago; now I hope. Happiness cures many ills, and since he has loved, he has improved. I always thought care would save him; he is worth it."

Hoffman paused, as if fearful of venturing too far; but Helen seemed to confide freely in him, and said, softly,—

"Ah, if it were only wise to let him be happy. It is so bitter to deny love."

"God knows it is!"

The exclamation broke from Hoffman as if an irrepressible impulse wrung it from him.

Helen started, and for a moment neither spoke. She collected herself soonest, and without turning, said, quietly,—

"I have been troubled by a strong impression that Casimer is not what he seems. Till he denied it on his honor I believed him to be Baron Palsdorf. Did he speak the truth when he said he was not?"

"Yes, mademoiselle."

"Then, Casimer Teblinski is his real name?"

No answer.

She turned sharply, and added,—

"For my cousin's sake, I must know the truth. Several curious coincidences make me strongly suspect that he is passing under an assumed name."

Not a word said Hoffman, but looked on the ground, as motionless and expressionless as a statue.

Helen lost patience, and in order to show how much she had discovered, rapidly told the story of the gloves, ring, handkerchief, prayer-book and collar, omitting all hint of the girlish romance they had woven about these things.

As she ended, Hoffman looked up with a curious expression, in which confusion, amusement, admiration and annoyance seemed to contend.

"Mademoiselle," he said, gravely, "I am about to prove to you that I feel honored by the confidence you place in me. I cannot break my word, but I will confess to you that Casimer does *not* bear his own name."

"I knew it!" said Helen, with a flash of triumph in her eyes. "He *is* the baron, and no Pole. You Germans love masquerades and jokes. This is one, but I must spoil it before it is played out."

"Pardon; mademoiselle is keen, but in this she is mistaken. Casimer is *not* the baron; he did fight for Poland, and his name is known and honored there. Of this I solemnly assure you."

She stood up and looked him straight in the face. He met her eye to eye, and never wavered till her own fell.

She mused a few minutes, entirely forgetful of herself in her eagerness to solve the mystery.

Hoffman stood so near that her dress touched him, and the wind blew her scarf against his hand; and as she thought he watched her while his eyes kindled, his color rose, and once he opened his lips to speak, but she moved at the instant, and exclaimed,—

"I have it!"

"Now for it," he muttered, as if preparing for some new surprise or attack.

"When uncle used to talk about the Polish revolution, there was, I remember a gallant young Pole who did something brave. The name just flashed on me, and it clears up my doubts. Stanislas Prakora—'S. P.'—and Casimer is the man."

Helen spoke with an eager, bright face, as if sure of the truth now; but, to her surprise, Hoffman laughed, a short, irrepressible laugh, full of hearty but brief merriment. He sobered in a breath, and with an entire change of countenance said, in an embarrassed tone,—

"Pardon my rudeness; mademoiselle's acuteness threw me off my guard. I can say nothing till released from my promise; but mademoiselle may rest assured that Casimer Teblinski is as good and brave a man as Stanislas Prakora."

Helen's eyes sparkled, for in this reluctant reply she read confirmation of her suspicion, and thought that Amy would rejoice to learn that her lover was a hero.

"You *are* exiles but, still hope and plot, and never relinquish your heart's desire?"

"Never, mademoiselle!"

"You are in danger?"

"In daily peril of losing all we most love and long for," answered Karl, with such passion that Helen found patriotism a lovely and inspiring thing.

"You have enemies?" she asked, unable to control her interest, and feeling the charm of these confidences.

"Alas! yes," was the mournful reply, as Karl dropped his eyes to hide the curious expression of mirth which he could not banish from them.

"Can you not conquer them, or escape the danger they place you in?"

"We hope to conquer, we cannot escape."

"This accounts for your disguise and Casimer's false name?"

"Yes. We beg that mademoiselle will pardon us the anxiety and perplexity we have caused her, and hope that a time will soon arrive when we may be ourselves. I fear the romantic interest with which the ladies have honored us will be much lessened, but we shall still remain their most humble and devoted servants."

Something in his tone nettled Helen, and she said sharply, —

"All this may be amusing to you, but it spoils my confidence in others to know they wear masks. Is your name also false?"

"I am Karl Hoffman, as surely as the sun shines, mademoiselle. Do not wound me by a doubt," he said, eagerly.

"And nothing more?"

She smiled as she spoke, and glanced at his darkened skin with a shake of the head.

"I dare not answer that."

"No matter; I hate titles, and value people for their own worth, not for their rank."

Helen spoke impulsively, and, as if carried away by her words and manner, Hoffman caught her hand and pressed his lips to it ardently, dropped it, and was gone, as if fearing to trust himself a moment longer.

Helen stood where he left her, thinking, with a shy glance from her hand to the spot where he had stood, —

"It *is* pleasant to have one's hand kissed, as Amy said. Poor Karl, his fate is almost as hard as Casimer's."

Some subtile power seemed to make the four young people shun one another carefully, though all longed to be together. The major appeared to share the secret disquiet that made the rest roam listlessly about, till little Roserl came to invite them to a *fête* in honor of the vintage. All were glad to go, hoping in the novelty and excitement to recover their composure.

The vineyard sloped up from the chateau, and on the hillside was a small plateau of level sward, shadowed by a venerable oak now hung with garlands, while underneath danced the chateau servants with their families, to the music of a pipe played by little Freidel. As the gentlefolk approached, the revel stopped, but the major, who was in an antic mood and disposed to be gracious, bade Freidel play on, and as Mrs. Cumberland refused his hand with a glance at her weeds, the major turned to the Count's buxom housekeeper, and besought her to waltz with him. She assented, and away they went as nimbly as the best. Amy laughed, but stopped to blush, as Casimer came up with an imploring glance, and whispered, —

"Is it possible that I may enjoy one divine waltz with you before I go?"

Amy gave him her hand with a glad assent, and Helen was left alone. Every one was dancing but herself and Hoffman, who stood near by, apparently unconscious of the fact. He glanced covertly at her, and saw that she was beating time with foot and hand, that her eyes shone, her lips smiled. He seemed to take courage at this, for, walking straight up to her, he said, as coolly as if a crown-prince, —

"Mademoiselle, may I have the honor?"

A flash of surprise passed over her face, but there was no anger, pride, or hesitation in her manner, as she leaned toward him with a quiet "Thanks, monsieur."

A look of triumph was in his eyes as he swept her away to dance, as she had never danced before, for a German waltz is full of life and spirit, wonderfully captivating to English girls, and German gentlemen make it a memorable experience when they please. As they circled round the rustic ball-room, Hoffman never took his eyes off Helen's, and, as if fascinated, she looked up at him, half conscious that he was reading her heart as she read his. He said not a word, but his face grew very tender, very beautiful in her sight, as she forgot everything except that he had saved her life and she loved him. When they paused, she was breathless and pale; he also; and seating her he went away to bring her a glass of wine. As her dizzy eyes grew clear, she saw a little case at her feet, and taking it up, opened it. A worn paper, containing some faded forget-me-nots and these words, fell out,—

"Gathered where Helen sat on the night of August 10th."

There was just time to restore its contents to the case, when Hoffman returned, saw it, and looked intensely annoyed as he asked, quickly,—

"Did you read the name on it?"

"I saw only the flowers;" and Helen colored beautifully as she spoke.

"And read *them*?" he asked, with a look she could not meet.

She was spared an answer, for just then a lad came up, saying, as he offered a note,—

"Monsieur Hoffman, madame, at the hotel, sends you this, and begs you to come at once."

As he impatiently opened it, the wind blew the paper into Helen's lap. She restored it, and in the act, her quick eye caught the signature, "Thine ever, Ludmilla."

A slight shadow passed over her face, leaving it very cold and quiet. Hoffman saw the change, and smiled, as if well pleased, but assuming suddenly his usual manner, said deferentially,—

"Will mademoiselle permit me to visit my friend for an hour?—she is expecting me."

"Go, then, we do not need you," was the brief reply, in a careless tone, as if his absence was a thing of no interest to any one.

"Thanks; I shall not be long away;" and giving her a glance that made her turn scarlet with anger at its undisguised admiration, he walked away, humming gayly to himself Goethe's lines,—

> "Maiden's heart and city's wall
> Were made to yield, were made to fall;

When we've held them each their day,
Soldier-like we march away."

IX

"S. P." AND THE BARON

Dinner was over, and the *salon* deserted by all but the two young ladies, who sat apart, apparently absorbed in novels, while each was privately longing for somebody to come, and with the charming inconsistency of the fair sex, planning to fly if certain somebodies did appear.

Steps approached; both buried themselves in their books; both held their breath and felt their hearts flutter as they never had done before at the step of mortal man. The door opened; neither looked up, yet each was conscious of mingled disappointment and relief when the major said, in a grave tone, "Girls, I've something to tell you."

"We know what it is, sir," returned Helen, coolly.

"I beg your pardon, but you don't, my dear, as I will prove in five minutes, if you will give me your attention."

The major looked as if braced up to some momentous undertaking; and planting himself before the two young ladies, dashed bravely into the subject.

"Girls, I've played a bold game, but I've won it, and will take the consequences."

"They will fall heaviest on you, uncle," said Helen, thinking he was about to declare his love for the widow.

The major laughed, shrugged his shoulders, and answered, stoutly, —

"I'll bear them; but you are quite wrong, my dear, in your surmises, as you will soon see. Helen is my ward, and accountable to me alone. Amy's mother gave her into my charge, and won't reproach me for anything that has passed when I explain matters. As to the lads they must take care of themselves."

Suddenly both girls colored, fluttered, and became intensely interested. The major's eyes twinkled as he assumed a perfectly impassive expression, and rapidly delivered himself of the following thunderbolt, —

"Girls, you have been deceived, and the young men you love are impostors."

"I thought so," muttered Helen, grimly.

"Oh, uncle, don't, don't say that!" cried Amy, despairingly.

"It's true, my dears; and the worst of it is, I knew the truth all the time. Now, don't have hysterics, but listen and enjoy the joke as I do. At Coblentz, when you sat in the balcony, two young men overheard Amy sigh for adventures, and Helen advise making a romance out of the gloves one of the lads had dropped. They had seen you by day; both admired you, and being idle, gay young fellows, they resolved to devote their vacation to gratifying your wishes and enjoying themselves. We met at the Fortress; I knew one of them, and liked the other immensely; so when they confided their scheme to me I agreed to help them carry it out, as I had perfect confidence in both, and thought a little adventure or two would do you good."

"Uncle, you were mad," said Helen; and Amy added, tragically,—

"You don't know what trouble has come of it."

"Perhaps I was; that remains to be proved. I do know everything, and fail to see any trouble, so don't cry, little girl," briskly replied the inexplicable major, "Well, we had a merry time planning our prank. One of the lads insisted on playing courier, though I objected. He'd done it before, liked the part, and would have his way. The other couldn't decide, being younger and more in love; so we left him to come into the comedy when he was ready. Karl did capitally, as you will allow; and I am much attached to him, for in all respects he has been true to his word. He began at Coblentz; the other, after doing the mysterious at Heidelberg, appeared as an exile, and made quick work with the prejudices of my well-beloved nieces—hey, Amy?"

"Go on; who are they?" cried both girls, breathlessly.

"Wait a bit; I'm not bound to expose the poor fellows to your scorn and anger. No; if you are going to be high and haughty, to forget their love, refuse to forgive their frolic, and rend their hearts with reproaches, better let them remain unknown."

"No, no; we will forget and forgive, only speak!" was the command of both.

"You promise to be lenient and mild, to let them confess their motives, and to award a gentle penance for their sins?"

"Yes, we promise!"

"Then, come in, my lads, and plead for your lives."

As he spoke the major threw open the door, and two gentlemen entered the room—one, slight and dark, with brilliant black eyes; the other tall and large, with blond hair and beard. Angry, bewildered, and shame-stricken as they were, feminine curiosity overpowered all other feelings for the moment, and the girls sat looking at the culprits with eager eyes, full of instant recognition; for though the disguise was off, and neither had seen them in their true characters but once, they felt no doubt, and involuntarily exclaimed, —

"Karl!"

"Casimer."

"No, young ladies; the courier and exile are defunct, and from their ashes rise Baron Sigismund Palsdorf, my friend, and Sidney Power, my nephew. I give you one hour to settle the matter; then I shall return to bestow my blessing or to banish these scapegraces forever."

And, having fired his last shot, the major prudently retreated, without waiting to see its effect.

It was tremendous, for it carried confusion into the fair enemy's camp; and gave the besiegers a momentary advantage of which they were not slow to avail themselves.

For a moment the four remained mute and motionless: then Amy, like all timid things, took refuge in flight, and Sidney followed her into the garden, glad to see the allies separated. Helen, with the courage of her nature, tried to face and repulse the foe; but love was stronger than pride, maiden shame overcame anger, and, finding it vain to meet and bear down the steady, tender glance of the blue eyes fixed upon her, she drooped her head into her hands and sat before him, like one conquered but too proud to cry "Quarter." Her lover watched her till she hid her face, then drew near, knelt down before her, and said, with an undertone of deep feeling below the mirthful malice of his words, —

"Mademoiselle, pardon me that I am a foolish baron, and dare to offer you the title that you hate. I have served you faithfully for a month, and, presumptuous as it is, I ask to be allowed to serve you all my life. Helen, say you forgive the deceit for love's sake."

"No; you are false and forsworn. How can I believe that anything is true?"

And Helen drew away the hand of which he had taken possession.

"Heart's dearest, you trusted me in spite of my disguise; trust me still, and I will prove that I am neither false nor forsworn. Catechise me, and see if I was not true in spite of all my seeming deception."

"You said your name was Karl Hoffman," began Helen, glad to gain a little time to calm herself before the momentous question came.

"It is; I have many, and my family choose to call me Sigismund," was the laughing answer.

"I'll never call you so; you shall be Karl, the courier, all your life to me," cried Helen, still unable to meet the ardent eyes before her.

"Good; I like that well; for it assures me that all my life I shall be something to you, my heart. What next?"

"When I asked if you were the baron, you denied it."

"Pardon! I simply said my name was Hoffman. You did not ask me point blank if I was the baron; had you done so, I think I should have confessed all, for it was very hard to restrain myself this morning."

"No, not yet; I have more questions;" and Helen warned him away, as it became evident that he no longer considered restraint necessary.

"Who is Ludmilla?" she said, sharply.

"My faith, that is superb!" exclaimed the baron, with a triumphant smile at her betrayal of jealousy. "How if she is a former love?" he asked, with a sly look at her changing face.

"It would cause me no surprise; I am prepared for anything."

"How if she is my dearest sister, for whom I sent, that she might welcome you and bring the greetings of my parents to their new daughter?"

"Is it, indeed, so?"

And Helen's eyes dimmed as the thought of parents, home and love filled her heart with tenderest gratitude, for she had long been an orphan.

"*Leibchen*, it is true; to-morrow you shall see and know how dear you already are to them, for I write often and they wait eagerly to receive you."

Helen felt herself going very fast, and made an effort to harden her heart, less too easy victory should reward this audacious lover.

"I may not go; I also have friends, and in England we are not won in this wild way. I will yet prove you false; it will console me for being so duped if I can call you traitor. You said Casimer had fought in Poland."

"Cruelest of women, he did, but under his own name, Sidney Power."

"Then, he was not the brave Stanislas?—and there is no charming Casimer?"

"Yes, there are both,—his and my friends, in Paris; true Poles, and when we go there you shall see them."

"But his illness was a ruse?"

"No; he was wounded in the war and has been ill since. Not of a fatal malady, I own; his cough misled you, and *he* has no scruples in fabling to any extent. I am not to bear the burden of his sins."

"Then, the romances he told us about your charity, your virtues, and—your love of liberty were false?" said Helen, with a keen glance, for these tales had done much to interest her in the unknown baron.

Sudden color rose to his forehead, and for the first time his eyes fell before hers,—not in shame, but with a modest man's annoyance at hearing himself praised.

"Sidney is enthusiastic in his friendship, and speaks too well for me. The facts are true, but he doubtless glorified the simplest by his way of telling it. Will you forgive my follies, and believe me when I promise to play and duel no more?"

"Yes."

She yielded her hand now, and her eyes were full of happiness, yet she added, wistfully,—

"And the betrothed, your cousin, Minna,—is she, in truth, not dear to you?"

"Very dear, but less so than another; for I could not learn of her in years what I learned in a day when I met you. Helen, this was begun in jest,—it ends in solemn earnest, for I love my liberty, and I have lost it, utterly and forever. Yet I am glad; look in my face and tell me you believe it."

He spoke now as seriously as fervently, and with no shadow on her own, Helen brushed back the blond hair and looked into her lover's face. Truth, tenderness, power, and candor were written there in characters that could not lie; and with her heart upon her lips, she answered, as he drew her close,—

"I do believe, do love you, Sigismund!"

Meanwhile another scene was passing in the garden. Sidney, presuming upon his cousinship, took possession of Amy, bidding her "strike but hear him." Of course she listened with the usual accompaniment of tears and smiles, reproaches and exclamations, varied by cruel exultations and coquettish commands to go away and never dare approach her again.

"*Ma drogha*, listen and be appeased. Years ago you and I played together as babies, and our fond mammas vowed we should one day mate. When I was a youth of fourteen and you a mite of seven I went away to India with my father, and at our parting promised to come back and marry you. Being in a fret because you couldn't go also, you haughtily declined the honor, and when I offered a farewell kiss, struck me with this very little hand. Do you remember it?"

"Not I. Too young for such nonsense."

"I do, and I also remember that in my boyish way I resolved to keep my word sooner or later, and I've done it."

"We shall see, sir," cried Amy, strongly tempted to repeat her part of the childish scene as well as her cousin, but her hand was not free, and he got the kiss without the blow.

"For eleven years we never met. You forgot me entirely, and 'Cousin Sidney' remained an empty name. I was in India till four years ago; since then I've been flying about Germany and fighting in Poland, where I nearly got my quietus."

"My dear boy, were you wounded?"

"Bless you, yes; and very proud of it I am. I'll show you my scars some day; but never mind that now. A little while ago I went to England, seized with a sudden desire to find my wife."

"I admire your patience in waiting; so flattering to me, you know," was the sharp answer.

"It looks like neglect, I confess; but I'd heard reports of your flirtations, and twice of your being engaged, so I kept away till my work was done. Was it true?"

"I never flirt, Sidney, and I was only engaged a little bit once or twice. I didn't like it, and never mean to do so any more."

"I shall see that you don't flirt; but you are very much engaged now, so put on your ring and make no romances about any 'S. P.' but myself."

"I shall wait till you clear your character; I'm not going to care for a deceitful impostor. What made you think of this prank?"

"You did."

"I? How?"

"When in England I saw your picture, though you were many a mile away, and fell in love with it. Your mother told me much about you, and I saw she would not frown upon my suit. I begged her not to tell you I had come, but let me find you and make myself known when I liked. You were in Switzerland, and I went after you. At Coblentz I met Sigismund, and told him my case; he is full of romance, and when we overheard you in the balcony we were glad of the hint. Sigismund was with me when you came, and admired Helen immensely, so he was wild to have a part in the frolic. I let him begin, and followed you unseen to Heidelberg, meaning to personate an artist. Meeting you at the castle, I made a good beginning with the vaults and the ring, and meant to follow it up by acting the baron, you were so bent on finding him, but Sigismund forbade it. Turning over a trunk of things left there the year before, I came upon my old Polish uniform, and decided to be a Thaddeus."

"How well you did it! Wasn't it hard to act all the time?" asked Amy, wonderingly.

"Very hard with Helen, she is so keen, but not a bit so with you, for you are such a confiding soul any one could cheat you. I've betrayed myself a dozen times, and you never saw it. Ah, it was capital fun to play the forlorn exile, study English, and flirt with my cousin."

"It was very base. I should think you'd be devoured with remorse. Aren't you sorry?"

"For one thing. I cropped my head lest you should know me. I was proud of my curls, but I sacrificed them all to you."

"Peacock! Did you think that one glimpse of your black eyes and fine hair would make such an impression that I should recognize you again?"

"I did, and for that reason disfigured my head, put on a mustache, and assumed hideous spectacles. Did you never suspect my disguise, Amy?"

"No. Helen used to say that she felt something was wrong, but I never did till the other night."

"Didn't I do that well? I give you my word it was all done on the spur of the minute. I meant to speak soon, but had not decided how, when you came out so sweetly with that confounded old cloak, of which I'd no more need than an African has of a blanket. Then a scene I'd read in a novel came into my head, and I just repeated it *con amore*. Was I very pathetic and tragical, Amy?"

"I thought so then. It strikes me as ridiculous now, and I can't help feeling sorry that I wasted so much pity on a man who—"

"Loves you with all his heart and soul. Did you cry and grieve over me, dear little tender thing? and do you think now that I am a heartless fellow, bent only on amusing myself at the expense of others? It's not so; and you shall see how true and good and steady I can be when I have any one to love and care for me. I've been alone so long it's new and beautiful to be petted, confided in, and looked up to by an angel like you."

He was in earnest now; she felt it, and her anger melted away like dew before the sun.

"Poor boy! You will go home with us now, and let us take care of you in quiet England. You'll play no more pranks, but go soberly to work and do something that shall make me proud to be your cousin, won't you?"

"If you'll change 'cousin' to 'wife' I'll be and do whatever you please. Amy, when I was a poor, dying, Catholic foreigner you loved me and would have married me in spite of everything. Now that I'm your well, rich, Protestant cousin, who adores you as that Pole never could, you turn cold and cruel. Is it because the romance is gone, or because your love was only a girl's fancy, after all?"

"You deceived me and I can't forget it; but I'll try," was the soft answer to his reproaches.

"Are you disappointed that I'm not a baron?"

"A little bit."

"Shall I be a count? They gave me a title in Poland, a barren honor, but all they had to offer, poor souls, in return for a little blood. Will you be Countess Zytomar and get laughed at for your pains, or plain Mrs. Power, with a good old English name?"

"Neither, thank you; it's only a girlish fancy, which will soon be forgotten. Does the baron love Helen?" asked Amy, abruptly.

"Desperately, and she?"

"I think he will be happy; she is not one to make confidantes, but I know by her tenderness with me, her sadness lately, and something in her way of brightening when he comes, that she thinks much of him and loves Karl Hoffman. How it will be with the baron I cannot say."

"No fear of him; he wins his way everywhere. I wish I were as fortunate;" and the gay young gentleman heaved an artful sigh and coughed the cough that always brought such pity to the girl's soft eyes.

She glanced at him as he leaned pensively on the low wall, looking down into the lake, with the level rays of sunshine on his comely face and figure. Something softer than pity stole into her eye, as she said, anxiously,—

"You are not really ill, Sidney?"

"I have been, and still need care, else I may have a relapse," was the reply of this treacherous youth, whose constitution was as sound as a bell.

Amy clasped her hands, as if in a transport of gratitude, exclaiming, fervently,—

"What a relief it is to know that you are not doomed to—"

She paused with a shiver, as if the word were too hard to utter, and Sidney turned to her with a beaming face, which changed to one of mingled pain and anger, as she added, with a wicked glance,—

"Wear spectacles."

"Amy, you've got no heart!" he cried, in a tone that banished her last doubt of his love and made her whisper tenderly, as she clung to his arm,—

"No, dear; I've given it all to you."

Punctual to the minute, Major Erskine marched into the *salon*, with Mrs. Cumberland on his arm, exclaiming, as he eyed the four young people together again,—

"Now, ladies, is it to be 'Paradise Lost' or 'Regained' for the prisoners at the bar?"

At this point the astonished gentleman found himself taken possession of by four excited individuals, for the girls embraced and kissed him, the young men wrung his hand and thanked him, and all seemed bent on assuring him that they were intensely happy, grateful and affectionate.

From this assault he emerged flushed and breathless, but beaming with satisfaction, and saying paternally,—

"Bless you, my children, bless you. I hoped and worked for this, and to prove how well I practise what I preach, let me present to you—my wife."

As he drew forward the plump widow with a face full of smiles and tears, a second rush was made, and congratulations, salutes, exclamations and embraces were indulged in to every one's satisfaction.

As the excitement subsided the major said, simply,—

"We were married yesterday at Montreaux. Let me hope that you will prove as faithful as I have been, as happy as I am, as blest as I shall be. I loved this lady in my youth, have waited many years, and am rewarded at last, for love never comes too late."

The falter in his cheery voice, the dimness of his eyes, the smile on his lips, and the gesture with which he returned the pressure of the hand upon his arm, told the little romance of the good major's life more eloquently than pages of fine writing, and touched the hearts of those who loved him.

"I have been faithful for eleven years. Give me my reward soon, won't you, dear?" whispered Sidney.

"Don't marry me to-morrow, and if mamma is willing I'll think about it by and by," answered Amy.

"It is beautiful! let us go and do likewise," said Sigismund to his betrothed.

But Helen, anxious to turn the thoughts of all from emotions too deep for words, drew from her pocket a small pearl-colored object, which she gave to Amy with mock solemnity, as she said, turning to lay her hand again in her lover's, —

"Amy, our search is over. *You* may keep the gloves; *I* have the baron."

MY RED CAP

"He who serves well need not fear to ask his wages."

I

IT was under a blue cap that I first saw the honest face of Joe Collins. In the third year of the late war a Maine regiment was passing through Boston, on its way to Washington. The Common was all alive with troops and the spectators who clustered round them to say God-speed, as the brave fellows marched away to meet danger and death for our sakes.

Every one was eager to do something; and, as the men stood at ease, the people mingled freely with them, offering gifts, hearty grips of the hand, and hopeful prophecies of victory in the end. Irresistibly attracted, my boy Tom and I drew near, and soon, becoming excited by the scene, ravaged the fruit-stands in our neighborhood for tokens of our regard, mingling candy and congratulations, peanuts and prayers, apples and applause, in one enthusiastic jumble.

While Tom was off on his third raid, my attention was attracted by a man who stood a little apart, looking as if his thoughts were far away. All the men were fine, stalwart fellows, as Maine men usually are; but this one over-topped his comrades, standing straight and tall as a Norway pine, with a face full of the mingled shrewdness, sobriety, and self-possession of the typical New Englander. I liked the look of him; and, seeing that he seemed solitary, even in a crowd, I offered him my last apple with a word of interest. The keen blue eyes met mine gratefully, and the apple began to vanish in vigorous bites as we talked; for no one thought of ceremony at such a time.

"Where are you from?"

"Woolidge, ma'am."

"Are you glad to go?"

"Wal, there's two sides to that question. I calk'late to do my duty, and do it hearty; but it *is* rough on a feller leavin' his folks, for good, maybe."

There was a sudden huskiness in the man's voice that was not apple-skins, though he tried to make believe that it was. I knew a word about home would comfort him, so I went on with my questions.

"It is very hard. Do you leave a family?"

"My old mother, a sick brother,—and Lucindy."

The last word was uttered in a tone of intense regret, and his brown cheek reddened as he added hastily, to hide some embarrassment,—

"You see, Jim went last year, and got pretty well used up; so I felt as if I'd ought to take my turn now. Mother was a regular old hero about it and I dropped everything, and come off. Lucindy didn't think it was my duty; and that made it awful hard, I tell you."

"Wives are less patriotic than mothers," I began; but he would not hear Lucindy blamed, and said quickly,—

"She ain't my wife yet, but we calk'lated to be married in a month or so; and it was wus for her than for me, women lot so on not being disappointed. I *couldn't* shirk, and here I be. When I git to work, I shall be all right: the first wrench is the tryin' part."

Here he straightened his broad shoulders, and turned his face toward the flags fluttering far in front, as if no backward look should betray the longing of his heart for mother, home, and wife. I liked that little glimpse of character; and when Tom returned with empty hands, reporting that every stall was exhausted, I told him to find out what the man would like best, then run across the street and get it.

"I know without asking. Give us your purse, and I'll make him as happy as a king," said the boy, laughing, as he looked up admiringly at our tall friend, who looked down on him with an elder-brotherly air pleasant to see. While Tom was gone, I found out Joe's name and business, promised to write and tell his mother how finely the regiment went off, and was just expressing a hope that we might meet again, for I too was going to the war as nurse, when the order to "Fall in!" came rolling down the ranks, and the talk was over. Fearing Tom would miss our man in the confusion, I kept my eye on him till the boy came rushing up with a packet of tobacco in one hand and a good supply of cigars in the other. Not a romantic offering, certainly, but a very acceptable one, as Joe's face proved, as we scrambled these treasures into his pockets, all laughing at the flurry, while less fortunate comrades helped us, with an eye to a share of these fragrant luxuries by and by. There was just time for this, a hearty shake of the big hand, and a grateful "Good-by, ma'am;" then the word was given, and they were off. Bent on seeing the last of them, Tom and I took a short cut, and came out on the wide street down which so many troops marched that year; and, mounting some high steps, we watched for our man, as we already called him.

As the inspiring music, the grand tramp, drew near, the old thrill went through the crowd, the old cheer broke out. But it was a different scene now than in the first enthusiastic, hopeful days. Young men and ardent boys filled the ranks then, brave by instinct, burning with loyal zeal, and blissfully unconscious of all that lay before them. Now the blue coats were worn by mature men, some gray, all grave and resolute: husbands and fathers, with the memory of wives and children tugging at their heart-strings; homes left desolate behind them, and before them the grim certainty of danger, hardship, and perhaps the life-long helplessness worse than death. Little of the glamour of romance about the war now: they saw it as it was, a long, hard task; and here were the men to do it well. Even the lookers-on were different now. Once all was wild enthusiasm and glad uproar; now men's lips were set, and women's smileless as they cheered; fewer handkerchiefs whitened the air, for wet eyes needed them; and sudden lulls, almost solemn in their stillness, followed the acclamations of the crowd. All watched with quickened breath and brave souls that living wave, blue below, and bright with a steely glitter above, as it flowed down the street and away to distant battle-fields already stained with precious blood.

"There he is! The outside man, and tallest of the lot. Give him a cheer, auntie: he sees us, and remembers!" cried Tom, nearly tumbling off his perch, as he waved his hat, and pointed out Joe Collins.

Yes, there he was, looking up, with a smile on his brave brown face, my little nosegay in his button-hole, a suspicious bulge in the pocket close by, and doubtless a comfortable quid in his mouth, to cheer the weary march. How like an old friend he looked, though we had only met fifteen minutes ago; how glad we were to be there to smile back at him, and send him on his way feeling that, even in a strange city, there was some one to say, "God bless you, Joe!" We watched the tallest blue cap till it vanished, and then went home in a glow of patriotism, — Tom to long for his turn to come, I to sew vigorously on the gray gown the new nurse burned to wear as soon as possible, and both of us to think and speak often of poor Joe Collins and his Lucindy. All this happened long ago; but it is well to recall those stirring times, — to keep fresh the memory of sacrifices made for us by men like these; to see to it that the debt we owe them is honestly, gladly paid; and, while we decorate the graves of those who died, to remember also those who still live to deserve our grateful care.

II

I never expected to see Joe again; but, six months later, we did meet in a Washington hospital one winter's night. A train of ambulances had left their sad freight at our door, and we were hurrying to get the poor fellows into much-needed beds, after a week of hunger, cold, and unavoidable neglect. All forms of pain were in my ward that night, and all borne with the pathetic patience which was a daily marvel to those who saw it.

Trying to bring order out of chaos, I was rushing up and down the narrow aisle between the rows of rapidly filling beds, and, after brushing several times against a pair of the largest and muddiest boots I ever saw, I paused at last to inquire why they were impeding the passage-way. I found they belonged to a very tall man who seemed to be already asleep or dead, so white and still and utterly worn out he looked as he lay there, without a coat, a great patch on his forehead, and the right arm rudely bundled up. Stooping to cover him, I saw that he was unconscious, and, whipping out my brandy-bottle and salts, soon brought him round, for it was only exhaustion.

"Can you eat?" I asked, as he said, "Thanky, ma'am," after a long draught of water and a dizzy stare.

"Eat! I'm starvin'!" he answered, with such a ravenous glance at a fat nurse who happened to be passing, that I trembled for her, and hastened to take a bowl of soup from her tray.

As I fed him, his gaunt, weather-beaten face had a familiar look; but so many such faces had passed before me that winter, I did not recall this one till the ward-master came to put up the cards with the new-comers' names above their beds. My man seemed absorbed in his food; but I naturally glanced at the card, and there was the name "Joseph Collins" to give me an additional interest in my new patient.

"Why, Joe! is it really you?" I exclaimed, pouring the last spoonful of soup down his throat so hastily that I choked him.

"All that's left of me. Wal, ain't this luck, now?" gasped Joe, as gratefully as if that hospital-cot was a bed of roses.

"What is the matter? A wound in the head and arm?" I asked, feeling sure that no slight affliction had brought Joe there.

"Right arm gone. Shot off as slick as a whistle. I tell you, it's a sing'lar kind of a feelin' to see a piece of your own body go flyin' away, with no prospect of ever coming back again," said Joe, trying to make light of one of the greatest misfortunes a man can suffer.

"That is bad, but it might have been worse. Keep up your spirits, Joe; and we will soon have you fitted out with a new arm almost as good as new."

"I guess it won't do much lumberin', so that trade is done for. I s'pose there's things left-handed fellers can do, and I must learn 'em as soon as possible, since my fightin' days are over," and Joe looked at his one arm with a sigh that was almost a groan, helplessness is such a trial to a manly man,—and he was eminently so.

"What can I do to comfort you most, Joe? I'll send my good Ben to help you to bed, and will be here myself when the surgeon goes his rounds. Is there anything else that would make you more easy?"

"If you could just drop a line to mother to let her know I'm alive, it would be a sight of comfort to both of us. I guess I'm in for a long spell of hospital, and I'd lay easier if I knew mother and Lucindy warn't frettin' about me."

He must have been suffering terribly, but he thought of the women who loved him before himself, and, busy as I was, I snatched a moment to send a few words of hope to the old mother. Then I left him "layin' easy," though the prospect of some months of wearing pain would have daunted most men. If I had needed anything to increase my regard for Joe, it would have been the courage with which he bore a very bad quarter of an hour with the surgeons; for his arm was in a dangerous state, the wound in the head feverish for want of care; and a heavy cold on the lungs suggested pneumonia as an added trial to his list of ills.

"He will have a hard time of it, but I think he will pull through, as he is a temperate fellow, with a splendid constitution," was the doctor's verdict, as he left us for the next man, who was past help, with a bullet through his lungs.

"I don'no as I hanker to live, and be a burden. If Jim was able to do for mother, I feel as if I wouldn't mind steppin' out now I'm so fur along. As he ain't, I s'pose I must brace up, and do the best I can," said Joe, as I wiped the drops from his forehead, and tried to look as if his prospect was a bright one.

"You will have Lucindy to help you, you know; and that will make things easier for all."

"Think so? 'Pears to me I couldn't ask her to take care of three invalids for my sake. She ain't no folks of her own, nor much means, and ought to marry a man who can make things easy for her. Guess I'll have to wait a spell longer before I say anything to Lucindy about marryin' now;" and a look of resolute resignation settled on Joe's haggard face as he gave up his dearest hope.

"I think Lucindy will have something to say, if she is like most women, and you will find the burdens much lighter, for sharing them between you. Don't worry about that, but get well, and go home as soon as you can."

"All right, ma'am;" and Joe proved himself a good soldier by obeying orders, and falling asleep like a tired child, as the first step toward recovery.

For two months I saw Joe daily, and learned to like him very much, he was so honest, genuine, and kind-hearted. So did his mates, for he made friends with them all by sharing such small luxuries as came to him, for he was a favorite; and, better still, he made sunshine in that sad place by the brave patience with which he bore his own troubles, the cheerful consolation he always gave to others. A droll fellow was Joe at times, for under his sobriety lay much humor; and I soon discovered that a visit from him was more efficacious than other cordials in cases of despondency and discontent. Roars of laughter sometimes greeted me as I went into his ward, and Joe's jokes were passed round as eagerly as the water-pitcher.

Yet he had much to try him, not only in the ills that vexed his flesh, but the cares that tried his spirit, and the future that lay before him, full of anxieties and responsibilities which seemed so heavy now when the strong right arm, that had cleared all obstacles away before, was gone. The letters I wrote for him, and those he received, told the little story very plainly; for he read them to me, and found much comfort in talking over his affairs, as most men do when illness makes them dependent on a woman. Jim was evidently sick and selfish. Lucindy, to judge from the photograph cherished so tenderly under Joe's pillow, was a pretty, weak sort of a girl, with little character or courage to help poor Joe with his burdens. The old mother was very like her son, and stood by him "like a hero," as he said, but was evidently failing, and begged him to come home as soon as he was able, that she might see him comfortably settled before she must leave him. Her courage sustained his, and the longing to see her hastened his departure as soon as it was safe to let him go; for Lucindy's letters were always of a dismal sort, and made him anxious to put his shoulder to the wheel.

"She always set consider'ble by me, mother did, bein' the oldest; and I wouldn't miss makin' her last days happy, not if it cost me all the arms and legs I've got," said Joe, as he awkwardly struggled into the big boots an hour after leave to go home was given him.

It was pleasant to see his comrades gather round him with such hearty adieus that his one hand must have tingled; to hear the good wishes and the thanks called after him by pale creatures in their beds; and to find tears in many eyes beside my own when he was gone, and nothing was left of him but the empty cot, the old gray wrapper, and the name upon the wall.

I kept that card among my other relics, and hoped to meet Joe again somewhere in the world. He sent me one or two letters, then I went home; the war ended soon after, time passed, and the little story of my Maine lumberman was laid away with many other experiences which made that part of my life a very memorable one.

III

Some years later, as I looked out of my window one dull November day, the only cheerful thing I saw was the red cap of a messenger who was examining the slate that hung on a wall opposite my hotel. A tall man with gray hair and beard, one arm, and a blue army-coat. I always salute, figuratively at least, when I see that familiar blue, especially if one sleeve of the coat is empty; so I watched the messenger with interest as he trudged away on some new errand, wishing he had a better day and a thicker pair of boots. He was an unusually large, well-made man, and reminded me of a fine building going to ruin before its time; for the broad shoulders were bent, there was a stiffness about the long legs suggestive of wounds or rheumatism, and the curly hair looked as if snow had fallen on it too soon. Sitting at work in my window, I fell into the way of watching my Red Cap, as I called him, with more interest than I did the fat doves on the roof opposite, or the pert sparrows hopping in the mud below. I liked the steady way in which he plodded on through fair weather or foul, as if intent on doing well the one small service he had found to do. I liked his cheerful whistle as he stood waiting for a job under the porch of the public building where his slate hung, watching the luxurious carriages roll by, and the well-to-do gentlemen who daily passed him to their comfortable homes, with a steady, patient sort of face, as if wondering at the inequalities of fortune, yet neither melancholy nor morose over the small share of prosperity which had fallen to his lot.

I often planned to give him a job, that I might see him nearer; but I had few errands, and little Bob, the hall-boy, depended on doing those: so the winter was nearly over before I found out that my Red Cap was an old friend.

A parcel came for me one day, and bidding the man wait for an answer, I sat down to write it, while the messenger stood just inside the door like a sentinel on duty. When I looked up to give my note and directions, I found the man staring at me with a beaming yet bashful face, as he nodded, saying heartily,—

"I mistrusted it was you, ma'am, soon's I see the name on the bundle, and I guess I ain't wrong. It's a number of years sence we met, and you don't remember Joe Collins as well as he does you, I reckon?"

"Why, how you have changed! I've been seeing you every day all winter, and never knew you," I said, shaking hands with my old patient, and very glad to see him.

"Nigh on to twenty years makes consid'able of a change in folks, 'specially if they have a pretty hard row to hoe."

"Sit down and warm yourself while you tell me all about it; there is no hurry for this answer, and I'll pay for your time."

Joe laughed as if that was a good joke, and sat down as if the fire was quite as welcome as the friend.

"How are they all at home?" I asked, as he sat turning his cap round, not quite knowing where to begin.

"I haven't got any home nor any folks neither;" and the melancholy words banished the brightness from his rough face like a cloud. "Mother died soon after I got back. Suddin', but she was ready, and I was there, so she was happy. Jim lived a number of years, and was a sight of care, poor feller; but we managed to rub along, though we had to sell the farm: for I couldn't do much with one arm, and doctor's bills right along stiddy take a heap of money. He was as comfortable as he could be; and, when he was gone, it wasn't no great matter, for there was only me, and I don't mind roughin' it."

"But Lucindy, where was she?" I asked very naturally.

"Oh! she married another man long ago. Couldn't expect her to take me and my misfortins. She's doin' well, I hear, and that's a comfort anyway."

There was a look on Joe's face, a tone in Joe's voice as he spoke, that plainly showed how much he had needed comfort when left to bear his misfortunes all alone. But he made no complaint, uttered no reproach, and loyally excused Lucindy's desertion with a simple sort of dignity that made it impossible to express pity or condemnation.

"How came you here, Joe?" I asked, making a sudden leap from past to present.

"I had to scratch for a livin', and can't do much; so, after tryin' a number of things, I found this. My old wounds pester me a good deal, and rheumatism is bad winters; but, while my legs hold out, I can git on. A man can't set down and starve; so I keep waggin' as long as I can. When I can't do no more, I s'pose there's almshouse and hospital ready for me."

"That is a dismal prospect, Joe. There ought to be a comfortable place for such as you to spend your last days in. I am sure you have earned it."

"Wal, it does seem ruther hard on us when we've give all we had, and give it free and hearty, to be left to knock about in our old age. But there's so many poor folks to be took care of, we don't get much of a chance, for *we* ain't the beggin' sort," said Joe, with a wistful look at the wintry world outside, as if it would be better to lie quiet under the snow, than to drag out his last painful years, friendless and forgotten, in some refuge of the poor.

"Some kind people have been talking of a home for soldiers, and I hope the plan will be carried out. It will take time; but, if it comes to pass, you shall be one of the first men to enter that home, Joe, if I can get you there."

"That sounds mighty cheerin' and comfortable, thanky, ma'am. Idleness is dreadful tryin' to me, and I'd ruther wear out than rust out; so I guess I can weather it a spell longer. But it will be pleasant to look forrard to a snug harbor byme-by. I feel a sight better just hearin' tell about it." He certainly looked so, faint as the hope was; for the melancholy eyes brightened as if they already saw a happier refuge in the future than almshouse, hospital, or grave, and, when he trudged away upon my errand, he went as briskly as if every step took him nearer to the promised home.

After that day it was all up with Bob, for I told my neighbors Joe's story, and we kept him trotting busily, adding little gifts, and taking the sort of interest in him that comforted the lonely fellow, and made him feel that he had not outlived his usefulness. I never looked out when he was at his post that he did not smile back at me; I never passed him in the street that the red cap was not touched with a military flourish; and, when any of us beckoned to him, no twinge of rheumatism was too sharp to keep him from hurrying to do our errands, as if he had Mercury's winged feet.

Now and then he came in for a chat, and always asked how the Soldiers' Home was prospering; expressing his opinion that "Boston was the charitablest city under the sun, and he was sure he and his mates would be took care of somehow."

When we parted in the spring, I told him things looked hopeful, bade him be ready for a good long rest as soon as the hospitable doors were open, and left him nodding cheerfully.

IV

But in the autumn I looked in vain for Joe. The slate was in its old place, and a messenger came and went on his beat; but a strange face was under the red cap, and this man had two arms and one eye. I asked for Collins, but the new-comer had only a vague idea that he was dead; and the same answer was given me at headquarters, though none of the busy people seemed to know when or where he died. So I mourned for Joe, and felt that it was very hard he could not have lived to enjoy the promised refuge; for, relying upon the charity that never fails, the Home was an actual fact now, just beginning its beneficent career. People were waking up to this duty, money was coming in, meetings were being held, and already a few poor fellows were in the refuge, feeling themselves no longer paupers, but invalid soldiers honorably supported by the State they had served. Talking it over one day with a friend, who spent her life working for the Associated Charities, she said, —

"By the way, there is a man boarding with one of my poor women, who ought to be got into the Home, if he will go. I don't know much about him, except that he was in the army, has been very ill with rheumatic fever, and is friendless. I asked Mrs. Flanagin how she managed to keep him, and she said she had help while he was sick, and now he is able to hobble about, he takes care of the children, so she is able to go out to work. He won't go to his own town, because there is nothing for him there but the almshouse, and he dreads a hospital; so struggles along, trying to earn his bread tending babies with his one arm. A sad case, and in your line; I wish you'd look into it."

"That sounds like my Joe, one arm and all. I'll go and see him; I've a weakness for soldiers, sick or well."

I went, and never shall forget the pathetic little tableau I saw as I opened Mrs. Flanagin's dingy door; for she was out, and no one heard my tap. The room was redolent of suds, and in a grove of damp clothes hung on lines sat a man with a crying baby laid across his lap, while he fed three small children standing at his knee with bread and molasses. How he managed with one arm to keep the baby from squirming on to the floor, the plate from upsetting, and to feed the hungry urchins who stood in a row with open mouths, like young birds, was past my comprehension. But he did, trotting baby gently, dealing out sweet morsels patiently, and whistling to himself, as if to beguile his labors cheerfully.

The broad back, the long legs, the faded coat, the low whistle were all familiar; and, dodging a wet sheet, I faced the man to find it was indeed my Joe! A mere shadow of his former self, after months of suffering that had crippled him for life, but brave and patient still; trying to help himself, and slow to ask aid though brought so low.

For an instant I could not speak to him, and, encumbered with baby, dish, spoon, and children, he could only stare at me with a sudden brightening of the altered face that made it full of welcome before a word was uttered.

"They told me you were dead, and I only heard of you by accident, not knowing I should find my old friend alive, but not well, I'm afraid?"

"There ain't much left of me but bones and pain, ma'am. I'm powerful glad to see you all the same. Dust off a chair, Patsey, and let the lady set down. You go in the corner, and take turns lickin' the dish, while I see company," said Joe, disbanding his small troop, and shouldering the baby as if presenting arms in honor of his guest.

"Why didn't you let me know how sick you were? And how came they to think you dead?" I asked, as he festooned the wet linen out of the way, and prepared to enjoy himself as best he could.

"I did send once, when things was at the wust; but you hadn't got back, and then somehow I thought I was goin' to be mustered out for good, and so wouldn't trouble nobody. But my orders ain't come yet, and I am doing the fust thing that come along. It ain't much, but the good soul stood by me, and I ain't ashamed to pay my debts this way, sence I can't do it in no other;" and Joe cradled the chubby baby in his one arm as tenderly as if it had been his own, though little Biddy was not an inviting infant.

"That is very beautiful and right, Joe, and I honor you for it; but you were not meant to tend babies, so sing your last lullabies, and be ready to go to the Home as soon as I can get you there."

"Really, ma'am? I used to lay and kind of dream about it when I couldn't stir without yellin' out; but I never thought it would ever come to happen. I see a piece in the paper describing it, and it sounded dreadful nice. Shouldn't wonder if I found some of my mates there. They were a good lot, and deservin' of all that could be done for 'em," said Joe, trotting the baby briskly, as if the prospect excited him, as well it might, for the change from that damp nursery to the comfortable quarters prepared for him would be like going from Purgatory to Paradise.

"I don't wonder you don't get well living in such a place, Joe. You should have gone home to Woolwich, and let your friends help you," I said, feeling provoked with him for hiding himself.

"No, ma'am!" he answered, with a look I never shall forget, it was so full of mingled patience, pride, and pain. "I haven't a relation in the world but a couple of poor old aunts, and they couldn't do any thing for me. As for asking help of folks I used to know, I couldn't do it; and if you think I'd go to Lucindy, though she is wal off, you don't know Joe Collins. I'd die fust! If she was poor and I rich, I'd do for her like a brother; but I couldn't ask no favors of her, not if I begged my vittles in the street, or starved. I forgive, but I don't forgit in a hurry; and the woman that stood by me when I was down is the woman I believe in, and can take my bread from without shame. Hooray for Biddy Flanagin! God bless her!" and, as if to find a vent for the emotion that filled his eyes with grateful tears, Joe led off the cheer, which the children shrilly echoed, and I joined heartily.

"I shall come for you in a few days; so cuddle the baby and make much of the children before you part. It won't take you long to pack up, will it?" I asked, as we subsided with a general laugh.

"I reckon not as I don't own any clothes but what I set in, except a couple of old shirts and them socks. My hat's stoppin' up the winder, and my old coat is my bed-cover. I'm awful shabby, ma'am, and that's one reason I don't go out more. I can hobble some, but I ain't got used to bein' a scarecrow yet," and Joe glanced from the hose without heels that hung on the line to the ragged suit he wore, with a resigned expression that made me long to rush out and buy up half the contents of Oak Hall on the spot.

Curbing this wild impulse I presently departed with promises of speedy transportation for Joe, and unlimited oranges to assuage the pangs of parting for the young Flanagins, who escorted me to the door, while Joe waved the baby like a triumphal banner till I got round the corner.

There was such a beautiful absence of red tape about the new institution that it only needed a word in the right ear to set things going; and then, with a long pull, a strong pull, and a pull all together, Joe Collins was taken up and safely landed in the Home he so much needed and so well deserved.

A happier man or a more grateful one it would be hard to find, and if a visitor wants an enthusiastic guide about the place, Joe is the one to take, for all is comfort, sunshine, and good-will to him; and he unconsciously shows how great the need of this refuge is, as he hobbles about on his lame feet, pointing out its beauties, conveniences, and delights with his one arm, while his face shines, and his voice quavers a little as he says gratefully,—

"The State don't forget us, you see, and this is a Home wuth havin'. Long life to it!"

[Written in 1867]

WHAT THE BELLS SAW AND SAID

"Bells ring others to church, but go not in themselves."

NO one saw the spirits of the bells up there in the old steeple at midnight on Christmas Eve. Six quaint figures, each wrapped in a shadowy cloak and wearing a bell-shaped cap. All were gray-headed, for they were among the oldest bell-spirits of the city, and "the light of other days" shone in their thoughtful eyes. Silently they sat, looking down on the snow-covered roofs glittering in the moonlight, and the quiet streets deserted by all but the watchmen on their chilly rounds, and such poor souls as wandered shelterless in the winter night. Presently one of the spirits said, in a tone, which, low as it was, filled the belfry with reverberating echoes, —

"Well, brothers, are your reports ready of the year that now lies dying?"

All bowed their heads, and one of the oldest answered in a sonorous voice: —

"My report isn't all I could wish. You know I look down on the commercial part of our city and have fine opportunities for seeing what goes on there. It's my business to watch the business men, and upon my word I'm heartily ashamed of them sometimes. During the war they did nobly, giving their time and money, their sons and selves to the good cause, and I was proud of them. But now too many of them have fallen back into the old ways, and their motto seems to be, 'Every one for himself, and the devil take the hindmost.' Cheating, lying and stealing are hard words, and I don't mean to apply them to *all* who swarm about below there like ants on an ant-hill — *they* have other names for these things, but I'm old-fashioned and use plain words. There's a deal too much dishonesty in the world, and business seems to have become a game of hazard in which luck, not labor, wins the prize. When I was young, men were years making moderate fortunes, and were satisfied with them. They built them on sure foundations, knew how to enjoy them while they lived, and to leave a good name behind them when they died.

"Now it's anything for money; health, happiness, honor, life itself, are flung down on that great gaming-table, and they forget everything else in the excitement of success or the desperation of defeat. Nobody seems satisfied either, for those who win have little time or taste to enjoy their prosperity, and those who lose have little courage or patience to support them in adversity. They don't even fail as they used to. In my day when a merchant found himself embarrassed he didn't ruin others in order to save himself, but honestly confessed the truth, gave up everything, and began again. But now-a-days after all manner of dishonorable shifts there comes a grand crash; many suffer, but by some hocus-pocus the merchant saves enough to retire upon and live comfortably here or abroad. It's very evident that honor and honesty don't mean now what they used to mean in the days of old May, Higginson and Lawrence.

"They preach below here, and very well too sometimes, for I often slide down the rope to peep and listen during service. But, bless you! they don't seem to lay either sermon, psalm or prayer to heart, for while the minister is doing his best, the congregation, tired with the breathless hurry of the week, sleep peacefully, calculate their chances for the morrow, or wonder which of their neighbors will lose or win in the great game. Don't tell me! I've seen them do it, and if I dared I'd have startled every soul of them with a rousing peal. Ah, they don't dream whose eye is on them, they never guess what secrets the telegraph wires tell as the messages fly by, and little know what a report I give to the winds of heaven as I ring out above them morning, noon, and night." And the old spirit shook his head till the tassel on his cap jangled like a little bell.

"There are some, however, whom I love and honor," he said, in a benignant tone, "who honestly earn their bread, who deserve all the success that comes to them, and always keep a warm corner in their noble hearts for those less blest than they. These are the men who serve the city in times of peace, save it in times of war, deserve the highest honors in its gift, and leave behind them a record that keeps their memories green. For such an one we lately tolled a knell, my brothers; and as our united voices pealed over the city, in all grateful hearts, sweeter and more solemn than any chime, rung the words that made him so beloved,—

"'Treat our dead boys tenderly, and send them home to me.'"

He ceased, and all the spirits reverently uncovered their gray heads as a strain of music floated up from the sleeping city and died among the stars.

"Like yours, my report is not satisfactory in all respects," began the second spirit, who wore a very pointed cap and a finely-ornamented cloak. But, though his dress was fresh and youthful, his face was old, and he had nodded several times during his brother's speech. "My greatest affliction during the past year has been the terrible extravagance which prevails. My post, as you know, is at the court end of the city, and I see all the fashionable vices and follies. It is a marvel to me how so many of these immortal creatures, with such opportunities for usefulness, self-improvement and genuine happiness can be content to go round and round in one narrow circle of unprofitable and unsatisfactory pursuits. I do my best to warn them; Sunday after Sunday I chime in their ears the beautiful old hymns that sweetly chide or cheer the hearts that truly listen and believe; Sunday after Sunday I look down on them as they pass in, hoping to see that my words have not fallen upon deaf ears; and Sunday after Sunday they listen to words that should teach them much, yet seem to go by them like the wind. They are told to love their neighbor, yet too many hate him because he possesses more of this world's goods or honors than they; they are told that a rich man cannot enter the kingdom of heaven, yet they go on laying up perishable wealth, and though often warned that moth and rust will corrupt, they fail to believe it till the worm that destroys enters and mars their own chapel of ease. Being a spirit, I see below external splendor and find much poverty of heart and soul under the velvet and the ermine which should cover rich and royal natures. Our city saints walk abroad in threadbare suits, and under quiet bonnets shine the eyes that make sunshine in the shady places. Often as I watch the glittering procession passing to and fro below me, I wonder if, with all our progress, there is to-day as much real piety as in the times when our fathers, poorly clad, with weapon in one hand and Bible in the other, came weary distances to worship in the wilderness with fervent faith unquenched by danger, suffering and solitude.

"Yet in spite of my fault-finding I love my children, as I call them, for all are not butterflies. Many find wealth no temptation to forgetfulness of duty or hardness of heart. Many give freely of their abundance, pity the poor, comfort the afflicted, and make our city loved and honored in other lands as in our own. They have their cares, losses, and heartaches as well as the poor; it isn't all sunshine with them, and they learn, poor souls, that

'Into each life some rain must fall,

Some days must be dark and dreary.'

"But I've hopes of them, and lately they have had a teacher so genial, so gifted, so well-beloved that all who listen to him must be better for the lessons of charity, good-will and cheerfulness which he brings home to them by the magic of tears and smiles. We know him, we love him, we always remember him as the year comes round, and the blithest song our brazen tongues utter is a Christmas carol to the Father of 'The Chimes!'"

As the spirit spoke his voice grew cheery, his old face shone, and in a burst of hearty enthusiasm he flung up his cap and cheered like a boy. So did the others, and as the fairy shout echoed through the belfry a troop of shadowy figures, with faces lovely or grotesque, tragical or gay, sailed by on the wings of the wintry wind and waved their hands to the spirits of the bells.

As the excitement subsided and the spirits reseated themselves, looking ten years younger for that burst, another spoke. A venerable brother in a dingy mantle, with a tuneful voice, and eyes that seemed to have grown sad with looking on much misery.

"He loves the poor, the man we've just hurrahed for, and he makes others love and remember them, bless him!" said the spirit. "I hope he'll touch the hearts of those who listen to him here and beguile them to open their hands to my unhappy children over yonder. If I could set some of the forlorn souls in my parish beside the happier creatures who weep over imaginary woes as they are painted by his eloquent lips, that brilliant scene would be better than any sermon. Day and night I look down on lives as full of sin, self-sacrifice and suffering as any in those famous books. Day and night I try to comfort the poor by my cheery voice, and to make their wants known by proclaiming them with all my might. But people seem to be so intent on business, pleasure or home duties that they have no time to hear and answer my appeal. There's a deal of charity in this good city, and when the people do wake up they work with a will; but I can't help thinking that if some of the money lavished on luxuries was spent on necessaries for the poor, there would be fewer tragedies like that which ended yesterday. It's a short story, easy to tell, though long and hard to live; listen to it.

"Down yonder in the garret of one of the squalid houses at the foot of my tower, a little girl has lived for a year, fighting silently and single-handed a good fight against poverty and sin. I saw her when she first came, a hopeful, cheerful, brave-hearted little soul, alone, yet not afraid. She used to sit all day sewing at her window, and her lamp burnt far into the night, for she was very poor, and all she earned would barely give her food and shelter. I watched her feed the doves, who seemed to be her only friends; she never forgot them, and daily gave them the few crumbs that fell from her meagre table. But there was no kind hand to feed and foster the little human dove, and so she starved.

"For a while she worked bravely, but the poor three dollars a week would not clothe and feed and warm her, though the things her busy fingers made sold for enough to keep her comfortably if she had received it. I saw the pretty color fade from her cheeks; her eyes grew hollow, her voice lost its cheery ring, her step its elasticity, and her face began to wear the haggard, anxious look that made its youth doubly pathetic. Her poor little gowns grew shabby, her shawl so thin she shivered when the pitiless wind smote her, and her feet were almost bare. Rain and snow beat on the patient little figure going to and fro, each morning with hope and courage faintly shining, each evening with the shadow of despair gathering darker round her. It was a hard time for all, desperately hard for her, and in her poverty, sin and pleasure tempted her. She resisted, but as another bitter winter came she feared that in her misery she might yield, for body and soul were weakened now by the long struggle. She knew not where to turn for help; there seemed to be no place for her at any safe and happy fireside; life's hard aspect daunted her, and she turned to death, saying confidingly, 'Take me while I'm innocent and not afraid to go.'

"I saw it all! I saw how she sold everything that would bring money and paid her little debts to the utmost penny; how she set her poor room in order for the last time; how she tenderly bade the doves good-by, and lay down on her bed to die. At nine o'clock last night as my bell rang over the city, I tried to tell what was going on in the garret where the light was dying out so fast. I cried to them with all my strength,—

"'Kind souls, below there! a fellow-creature is perishing for lack of charity! Oh, help her before it is too late! Mothers, with little daughters on your knees, stretch out your hands and take her in! Happy women, in the safe shelter of home, think of her desolation! Rich men, who grind the faces of the poor, remember that this soul will one day be required of you! Dear Lord, let not this little sparrow fall to the ground! Help, Christian men and women, in the name of Him whose birthday blessed the world!'

"Ah me! I rang, and clashed, and cried in vain. The passers-by only said, as they hurried home, laden with Christmas cheer: 'The old bell is merry to-night, as it should be at this blithe season, bless it!'

"As the clocks struck ten, the poor child lay down, saying, as she drank the last bitter draught life could give her, 'It's very cold, but soon I shall not feel it;' and with her quiet eyes fixed on the cross that glimmered in the moonlight above me, she lay waiting for the sleep that needs no lullaby.

"As the clock struck eleven, pain and poverty for her were over. It was bitter cold, but she no longer felt it. She lay serenely sleeping, with tired heart and hands, at rest forever. As the clocks struck twelve, the dear Lord remembered her, and with fatherly hand led her into the home where there is room for all. To-day I rung her knell, and though my heart was heavy, yet my soul was glad; for in spite of all her human woe and weakness, I am sure that little girl will keep a joyful Christmas up in heaven."

In the silence which the spirits for a moment kept, a breath of softer air than any from the snowy world below swept through the steeple and seemed to whisper, "Yes!"

"Avast there! fond as I am of salt water, I don't like this kind," cried the breezy voice of the fourth spirit, who had a tiny ship instead of a tassel on his cap, and who wiped his wet eyes with the sleeve of his rough blue cloak. "It won't take me long to spin my yarn; for things are pretty taut and ship-shape aboard our craft. Captain Taylor is an experienced sailor, and has brought many a ship safely into port in spite of wind and tide, and the devil's own whirlpools and hurricanes. If you want to see earnestness come aboard some Sunday when the Captain's on the quarter-deck, and take an observation. No danger of falling asleep there, no more than there is up aloft, 'when the stormy winds do blow.' Consciences get raked fore and aft, sins are blown clean out of the water, false colors are hauled down and true ones run up to the masthead, and many an immortal soul is warned to steer off in time from the pirates, rocks and quicksands of temptation. He's a regular revolving light, is the Captain,—a beacon always burning and saying plainly, 'Here are life-boats, ready to put off in all weathers and bring the shipwrecked into quiet waters.' He comes but seldom now, being laid up in the home dock, tranquilly waiting till his turn comes to go out with the tide and safely ride at anchor in the great harbor of the Lord. Our crew varies a good deal. Some of 'em have rather rough voyages, and come into port pretty well battered; land-sharks full foul of a good many, and do a deal of damage; but most of 'em carry brave and tender hearts under the blue jackets, for their rough nurse, the sea, manages to keep something of the child alive in the grayest old tar that makes the world his picture-book. We try to supply 'em with life-preservers while at sea, and make 'em feel sure of a hearty welcome when ashore, and I believe the year '67 will sail away into eternity with a satisfactory cargo. Brother North-End made me pipe my eye; so I'll make him laugh to pay for it, by telling a clerical joke I heard the other day. Bell-ows didn't make it, though he might have done so, as he's a connection of ours, and knows how to use his tongue as well as any of us. Speaking of the bells of a certain town, a reverend gentleman affirmed that each bell uttered an appropriate remark so plainly, that the words were audible to all. The Baptist bell cried, briskly, 'Come up and be dipped! come up and be dipped!' The Episcopal bell slowly said, 'Apos-tol-ic suc-cess-ion! apos-tol-ic suc-cess-ion!' The Orthodox bell solemnly pronounced, 'Eternal damnation! eternal damnation!' and the Methodist shouted, invitingly, 'Room for all! room for all!'"

As the spirit imitated the various calls, as only a jovial bell-sprite could, the others gave him a chime of laughter, and vowed they would each adopt some tune-ful summons, which should reach human ears and draw human feet more willingly to church.

"Faith, brother, you've kept your word and got the laugh out of us," cried a stout, sleek spirit, with a kindly face, and a row of little saints round his cap and a rosary at his side. "It's very well we are doing this year; the cathedral is full, the flock increasing, and the true faith holding its own entirely. Ye may shake your heads if you will and fear there'll be trouble, but I doubt it. We've warm hearts of our own, and the best of us don't forget that when we were starving, America—the saints bless the jewel!—sent us bread; when we were dying for lack of work, America opened her arms and took us in, and now helps us to build churches, homes and schools by giving us a share of the riches all men work for and win. It's a generous nation ye are, and a brave one, and we showed our gratitude by fighting for ye in the day of trouble and giving ye our Phil, and many another broth of a boy. The land is wide enough for us both, and while we work and fight and grow together, each may learn something from the other. I'm free to confess that your religion looks a bit cold and hard to me, even here in the good city where each man may ride his own hobby to death, and hoot at his neighbors as much as he will. You seem to keep your piety shut up all the week in your bare, white churches, and only let it out on Sundays, just a trifle musty with disuse. You set your rich, warm and soft to the fore, and leave the poor shivering at the door. You give your people bare walls to look upon, commonplace music to listen to, dull sermons to put them asleep, and then wonder why they stay away, or take no interest when they come.

"We leave our doors open day and night; our lamps are always burning, and we may come into our Father's house at any hour. We let rich and poor kneel together, all being equal there. With us abroad you'll see prince and peasant side by side, school-boy and bishop, market-woman and noble lady, saint and sinner, praying to the Holy Mary, whose motherly arms are open to high and low. We make our churches inviting with immortal music, pictures by the world's great masters, and rites that are splendid symbols of the faith we hold. Call it mummery if ye like, but let me ask you why so many of your sheep stray into our fold? It's because they miss the warmth, the hearty, the maternal tenderness which all souls love and long for, and fail to find in your stern, Puritanical belief. By Saint Peter! I've seen many a lukewarm worshipper, who for years has nodded in your cushioned pews, wake and glow with something akin to genuine piety while kneeling on the stone pavement of one of our cathedrals, with Raphael's angels before his eyes, with strains of magnificent music in his ears, and all about him, in shapes of power or beauty, the saints and martyrs who have saved the world, and whose presence inspires him to follow their divine example. It's not complaining of ye I am, but just reminding ye that men are but children after all, and need more tempting to virtue than they do to vice, which last comes easy to 'em since the Fall. Do your best in your own ways to get the poor souls into bliss, and good luck to ye. But remember, there's room in the Holy Mother Church for all, and when your own priests send ye to the divil, come straight to us and we'll take ye in."

"A truly Catholic welcome, bull and all," said the sixth spirit, who, in spite of his old-fashioned garments, had a youthful face, earnest, fearless eyes, and an energetic voice that woke the echoes with its vigorous tones. "I've a hopeful report, brothers, for the reforms of the day are wheeling into rank and marching on. The war isn't over nor rebeldom conquered yet, but the Old Guard has been 'up and at 'em' through the year. There has been some hard fighting, rivers of ink have flowed, and the Washington dawdlers have signalized themselves by a 'masterly inactivity.' The political campaign has been an anxious one; some of the leaders have deserted; some been mustered out; some have fallen gallantly, and as yet have received no monuments. But at the Grand Review the Cross of the Legion of Honor will surely shine on many a brave breast that won no decoration but its virtue here; for the world's fanatics make heaven's heroes, poets say.

"The flock of Nightingales that flew South during the 'winter of our discontent' are all home again, some here and some in Heaven. But the music of their womanly heroism still lingers in the nation's memory, and makes a tender minor-chord in the battle-hymn of freedom.

"The reform in literature isn't as vigorous as I could wish; but a sharp attack of mental and moral dyspepsia will soon teach our people that French confectionery and the bad pastry of Wood, Braddon, Yates & Co. is not the best diet for the rising generation.

"Speaking of the rising generation reminds me of the schools. They are doing well; they always are, and we are justly proud of them. There may be a slight tendency toward placing too much value upon book-learning; too little upon home culture. Our girls are acknowledged to be uncommonly pretty, witty and wise, but some of us wish they had more health and less excitement, more domestic accomplishments and fewer ologies and isms, and were contented with simple pleasures and the old-fashioned virtues, and not quite so fond of the fast, frivolous life that makes them old so soon. I am fond of our girls and boys. I love to ring for their christenings and